SHIELD
of FAITH

The Power of Religion in the Lives of
LDS Youth and Young Adults

Bruce A. Chadwick
Brent L. Top
Richard J. McClendon

RELIGIOUS STUDIES CENTER
BRIGHAM YOUNG UNIVERSITY

DESERET
BOOK

DESERET
BOOK

Published by the Religious Studies Center, Brigham Young University, Provo, Utah, in cooperation with Deseret Book Company, Salt Lake City, Utah.

http://rsc.byu.edu

Printed in the United States of America by Sheridan Books Inc.

Retail USD $24.99

Cover photo courtesy iStockphoto; cover design by Jacob Frandsen

Library of Congress Cataloging-in-Publication Data

Chadwick, Bruce A.
    Shield of faith : the power of religion in the lives of LDS youth and young adults / Bruce A. Chadwick, Brent L. Top, Richard J. McClendon
        p. cm.
    ISBN 978-0-8425-2761-3 (hard cover : alk. paper)
    1. Mormon youth--Religious life. 2. Young adults--Religious life. I. Top, Brent L. II. McClendon, Richard J. (Richard Jennings), 1962- III. Title.

    BX8643.Y6C43 2010
    .289.3'320835--dc22

                                                        2010010968

The plan designed by the Father contemplates that man and woman, husband and wife, working together, fit each child individually with a shield of faith made to buckle on so firmly that it can neither be pulled off nor penetrated by [Satan's] fiery darts.

It takes the steady strength of a father to hammer out the metal of it and the tender hands of a mother to polish and fit it on. Sometimes one parent is left to do it alone. It is difficult, but it can be done.

In the Church we can teach about the materials from which a shield of faith is made: reverence, courage, chastity, repentance, forgiveness, compassion. In church we can learn how to assemble and fit them together. But the actual making of and fitting on of the shield of faith belongs in the family circle.

—*Boyd K. Packer, "'The Shield of Faith,'" Ensign, May 1995, 8*

CONTENTS

One

DOES RELIGION MATTER?

This book is the result of nearly two decades of research focusing on the influence of religion generally and of the restored gospel of Jesus Christ specifically in the lives of Latter-day Saint (LDS) teenagers and young adults. Some of the groups were enrolled in college, and some were not. Some studies include returned missionaries up to age 40. The initial impetus for our research came from reading the work of sociologists in the 1960s and 1970s who claimed that religion had declined in significance to the point that it was irrelevant in the daily life of Americans. Some social scientists have gone so far as to argue that religion is not only irrelevant but actually harmful.

Such arguments seemed to fly in the face of our own experience, both academic and personal. Although secularism is on the rise in many parts of the world, religion remains an important influence in the lives of many people, including many Latter-day Saints. This seems readily apparent as one observes the practices of faithful Latter-day Saint families. Our challenge, however, was to find out, through scientific studies and analysis of empirical evidence, what role religion actually plays in the lives of LDS teenagers and young adults. There have been relatively few studies on the religiosity of LDS teens and young adults, and these have been largely discounted by social scientists.

In 1977, a study conducted by researchers from Brigham Young University and published in the *Journal for the Scientific Study of Religion* found that LDS teens who were regularly involved in Church activities and who espoused the religious teachings of the Church were less involved in delinquent or deviant behaviors (Albrecht, Chadwick, & Alcorn). Critics of that early work argued that a "real" test of the importance of religion could not be done in Utah or in other LDS strongholds where LDS teens are a large majority of the students in the schools. Because of the large proportion of LDS teens in Utah high schools, critics maintained that religion in Utah is actually a unique social pressure and thus is not a fair test of the influence of personal religious behavior.

This criticism stemmed in a large degree from the mixed results of previous research concerning the relationship between religiosity and delinquency. Some studies showed that teens who belonged to a church and attended services engaged in less delinquent behavior than youth who did not (Hirschi & Stark, 1969; Burkett & White, 1974; Brownfield & Sorenson, 1991; Chadwick & Top, 1993; Free, 1994). On the other hand, many studies found little or no difference in delinquent behavior between churched and unchurched youth (Cochran & Akers, 1989; Cochran, Wood, & Arneklev, 1994; Benda & Corwyn, 1997; Tittle and Welch, 1983; and Baier and Wright, 2001, provide insightful reviews of the inconsistencies found in this research).

From this mixed bag of results, it became clear that additional research was necessary. One of our primary objectives in compiling this book has been to test a theory, now prominent in the sociology of religion, that has become known as the religious ecology theory. This theory alleges that religion only has behavior-affecting power within a religious community with many social restraints. In other words, religion only has power as a result of social contexts, not as a result of personal faith or spirituality. This theory implies that a person does not necessarily live his or her religion because of conviction, but rather because of cultural or social pressures. Such a view seems to diminish the real power of religion. We wanted to know whether or not religion itself has power to affect the lives of teens and young adults or if it is only part of a social culture.

The influence of religion is often so pervasive in the life of a Latter-day Saint that we did not know where to focus our attention; there are so many dimensions that can and should be examined. We decided to focus our research on teens and young adults because this turbulent time of life can presumably provide a rigorous test of the role of religion in everyday life. It seems to be a time of life when a variety of forces other than religion hold great sway. The desire to "fit in," so intense in the lives of this age-group, exposes youth to powerful peer pressures. Many teens are pressured by peers to drink alcohol, to use a variety of recreational drugs, to participate in premarital sex, to cheat on schoolwork, and even to hassle or bully other kids. A number of LDS students validated this view of the high school environment; many wrote on their questionnaires that their parents had no idea of the vulgar language, crude behavior, and pressures to violate the standards of the Church that students face in school every day.

If studies show that religion can counter such pressures and opportunities, then there is evidence that religion is a meaningful force in the lives of young members of the Church. Thus we began our study on how religion impacts the delinquent behaviors of LDS high school students. Over time, our research expanded to also examine the effects of religion on the lives of LDS young adults (ages 18–29). This book reports on our findings from these studies. While there are many important findings that could be examined and discussed, we have limited our focus to the role of religion on LDS teens and young adults.

RELIGION AND DELINQUENCY
AMONG LATTER-DAY SAINT YOUTH

In the first phase of our research, we collected data from LDS high school students living along the East Coast from upstate New York to North Carolina. Each of these students attended a high school where there were few other LDS students. We also collected data from the Pacific Northwest because social scientists have identified this region as the most secular and nonreligious part of the United States (Stark & Bainbridge, 1996); thus this area would provide the most rigorous test of the religious ecology theory. Not only are LDS high school students in Oregon and Washington a minority in their high schools, but the general social climate there appears to be somewhat hostile to religion.

It is interesting to note that we found the same strong link between religion and delinquency in these different regions of the United States as we did in Utah. This is impressive evidence that suggests that personal religious activity—including beliefs, values, and obedience to commandments—is a powerful influence in the lives of LDS teenagers regardless of differing environments or pressures in their lives. These results raised the question of whether or not the gospel has the same impact on teenagers in different cultures and societies. In order to test this notion, we next collected information from LDS high school students in Great Britain, including England, Scotland, and Wales. Great Britain is even more secular than the Pacific Northwest region of the United States. Thus, it provided another opportunity to test the influence of the gospel in a social environment that is hostile to religion.

Finally, we studied LDS high school students in Mexico. Students in both Great Britain and Mexico allowed us the interesting opportunity to ascertain the gospel's influence on LDS youth living in cultures different from those in the United States. Again, we were pleased to discover that in Great Britain and Mexico active LDS youth engaged in much less antisocial or immoral behavior than less-active youth. Each of these different religious cultures showed that higher levels of religiosity resulted in lower levels of delinquent behavior.

RELIGIOSITY

Religious behavior must be defined as involving more than merely being baptized and attending church. Beliefs, values, obedience to commandments, and spiritual feelings are all a part of the mix. Because we expanded our definition of religiosity, our studies suggested a greater relationship between religiosity and reduced delinquency. Earlier studies had defined religiosity merely as affiliation with a denomination and attendance at church services. No wonder the results of early studies were mixed; religiosity is much more complex than that.

In our studies we included seven dimensions of religiosity to assess religion's influence in the lives of LDS youth: (1) public religious behavior, (2) religious beliefs, (3) private religious behavior, (4) spiritual experiences, (5) family religious activities, (6) importance of religion, and (7) feelings of acceptance in church.

Church membership and attendance are public religious behaviors. Both, to a large degree, can be influenced or even controlled by parents who may decide to enroll their children in a local congregation and take them to church. Thus these behaviors do not adequately measure personal religiosity. In our research we included additional behaviors, such as attending seminary, obeying the Word of Wisdom, and sharing testimonies in meetings, since these actions are also good measures of public expressions of religiosity. In addition, we expanded the notion of religiosity to include religious beliefs, private religious behavior, spiritual experiences, family religiosity, and acceptance among other members at church.

Religious beliefs are the foundation upon which a religious orientation is based and thus are a significant component of religiosity. In our studies we looked at a large number of religious beliefs, including traditional Christian beliefs and unique LDS beliefs. For example, we asked the students if they believed that God lives, that Jesus is the Christ, that the Bible is true, that Joseph Smith was a prophet, and that the Book of Mormon is true.

Private religious behaviors, sometimes occurring without parental awareness, are also a very important dimension of religiosity. Private religious behaviors are initiated by the youth rather than by their parents or Church leaders. Personally praying and reading the scriptures are religious behaviors that originate from within the youth and demonstrate that the young person has internalized religious principles. These behaviors are significant evidence of a testimony of the gospel.

Spiritual feelings or experiences are also an important dimension of religion that influences the lives of young people. Those young people who have felt the Spirit's presence in their lives have experienced a powerful personal manifestation of God's existence and love. We asked the youth if they have felt that the Holy Ghost has guided them, if they have felt the Spirit witness the truth of something studied, or if they have felt the peace brought by the Spirit. These are powerful spiritual experiences resulting in the internalization of religiosity.

Social scientists have noted that religion has more impact in a person's life if religion is important to the person, regardless of what the person believes or how he or she behaves. This rather commonsense notion has called attention to the salience of religion for each individual. In order to tap this dimension of religiosity, we asked how important God and religion are to the students and if the students try to keep the commandments.

Obviously parents influence their children's religiosity in a number of ways besides taking them to church. Parents teach their children religious principles, involve them in Christian service, and support them in other religious activities. Therefore, we studied the impact of family religiosity—including holding family home evening, family prayer, and family scripture study—on the behavior of teenagers in LDS families. We also examined whether or not mothers' and fathers' personal righteous living was a positive example that influenced their teenagers' behavior.

Friends, leaders, and teachers in a local ward also impact religious feelings and activity. Acceptance by leaders, advisors, teachers, and friends affect a young person's religious involvement, which in turn impacts other areas of their lives. Thus we included in our study questions regarding feelings of fitting in or feelings of rejection and neglect by other youth, leaders, and the ward in general.

We were also interested in ascertaining if some aspects of religiosity are more important than others in directing youth to keep their feet on the path of gospel righteousness. While all seven aspects of religiosity are related to delinquency, private spiritual experiences were the most powerful influence in avoiding delinquency.

DELINQUENCY

Parents, school officials, church leaders, and political leaders in contemporary society are concerned about delinquency and related antisocial behavior. In recent years, special attention has been given to delinquency in public schools. Cases of school violence have called attention to problems such as bullying and harassment in high schools across the country. The rejection and persecution that some students face have contributed to their harming classmates and teachers. Within the walls of most high schools exists a powerful subculture that fosters drinking, drug use, premarital sex, and putting down and bullying others. High school temptations and pressures may negatively affect LDS youth.

There is also concern that immature teenagers may make youthful mistakes that will have long-term, devastating effects on their lives. Experimenting with drugs may lead to addiction, dropping out of school, or possibly even a life of petty crime to support a drug habit. Premarital sexual behavior may result in unwanted pregnancy, early marriage, or sexually transmitted diseases. Shoplifting, vandalism, and similar activities may result in a criminal record that haunts a young person for years after the fact.

We anticipated that youth who were more active in the Church would have lower rates of delinquency than those who were less active. If religion reduced delinquency among LDS teens, this would be powerful evidence supporting the claim that religion significantly improves the quality of the lives of members of the Church.

Initially, we focused on three widely accepted categories of delinquency. The first category of delinquent activity consists of crimes or offenses against other people, usually fellow teenagers. These include picking on kids at school, getting into fights, pressuring people to engage in sex, making obscene phone calls, and similar acts that harm another person.

The second category of delinquent behaviors is property offenses. These include shoplifting, stealing, and vandalism.

The third is status offenses, sometimes called victimless offenses. These include cheating on tests, truancy, running away from home, underage smoking and drinking, drug use, and involvement in premarital sex. Some of these behaviors are not against the law but violate important LDS standards nonetheless. As the research progressed, we found ourselves conducting detailed analyses of specific delinquent behaviors such as premarital sexual activity, drug use, and victimization by peers.

For example, analyses of data concerning premarital sexual activity revealed that more LDS young women are sexually active than are LDS young men. This finding is contrary to national trends of youth behavior and motivated us to launch a special study focusing on the initiation of sexual activity among LDS young women. We conducted in-depth interviews with 50 young women under the age of 18 living in Utah County who had given birth to a baby out of wedlock. The interview sought information about why LDS young women engage in sexual activity, their response to being pregnant, and how they dealt with issues like the decision to put their baby up for adoption.

Peer Pressure

Peer pressure, especially in high school, is the single most important factor producing antisocial behavior among adolescents (Agnew, 1991; Thornberry, Lizotte, Krohn, Farnworth, & Jang, 1994; Osgood, Wilson, O'Malley, Bachman, & Johnston, 1996; Akers, 1997). Additionally, peers who engage in delinquent behaviors serve as role models—regardless of whether or not they pressure others to participate. Parents are familiar with teens' claim, "Yes, some of my friends do things that are wrong, but they don't pressure me, so hanging out with them is not a danger." Peer pressures and examples can entice youth into unacceptable and unworthy behaviors.

Likewise, positive peer examples exert a different kind of influence—a positive pressure to do what is right and responsible. Thus, we sought to determine whether and to what extent religiosity counters inappropriate peer pressures and helps youth to remain true to gospel principles, Church standards, and parental expectations. We examined the influence of overt peer pressure as well as the more subtle influence of peer example.

Family Characteristics and Processes

Parents and other family members are major influences in the lives of teenagers, even though teens generally seek some independence from family. There is a large body of literature documenting the impact of parenting practices on teen behavior, including delinquency, academic achievement, and self-esteem. Bonds of love between parents and their children as well as setting rules, ascertaining obedience, and administering appropriate punishment all have a powerful influence on teenagers' lives (Baumrind, 1991; Barber & Shagle, 1992; Barnes & Farrell, 1992; Kurdek & Fine, 1994; Steinberg, Fletcher, & Darling, 1994; Barber, 1996; Barber, 1997; Barber, 2001).

To test the influence of religion in real-life situations, we included peer pressure, examples of friends, and a number of family characteristics in our models predicting delinquency, academic achievement, self-esteem, and other behaviors. The effects of religion were assessed in the context of peer pressure, peer examples, family structure, single versus two-parent families, maternal employment, relationship with parents, parental monitoring of behavior, and parents' granting of psychological autonomy, or helping children establish their own choices and values. In all of our studies, religiosity consistently emerged from among the other factors as one of the most significant influences in the lives of LDS teens and young adults.

Academic Achievement

Academic achievement can open doors to a wide range of opportunities that enhance the quality of life. The labor market in the United States continues to change in ways that severely handicap those with limited education. Church leaders recognize this and encourage members, both young and old, to further their education whenever possible.

Because of this, we decided to investigate the influence of religion on academic achievement and aspirations. A high school diploma is often essential to secure even minimum-wage jobs in this country, and a diploma, along with good grades, is usually necessary for admittance to vocational and technical schools or to colleges and universities. We wondered whether those youth who are more active in the Church do better in school and desire more education than those who are less active. If religion has a positive influence on a youth's school performance, it would be of considerable interest to parents, religious leaders, and school officials.

Another reason we focused on education is that most research has found that education fosters secularization and, along with it, a significant decrease in religiosity among college-age and older individuals. It has been found that those who go on to college, and especially to graduate or professional school, often appear to replace their religious faith with science and reason (Berger, 1967; Wilson, 1985; Dobbelaere, 1999). Interestingly, higher education does not always secularize adults. In fact, members of the Church with a higher education are shown to have stronger religious commitment and activity than those with less education (Albrecht & Heaton, 1984; Stott, 1984; Top & Chadwick, 2001; Merrill, Lyon, & Jensen, 2003).

Given this finding concerning adult members of the Church, we wondered whether increased religiosity would likewise strengthen educational ambition and achievement among LDS youth. Thus, we tested the influence of religiosity on LDS students' performance in high school, feelings about education, and intentions to obtain post–high school training.

SELF-ESTEEM

The media makes much of self-esteem and its importance to adolescents. Although some sensational media reporting overemphasizes the significance of self-esteem, feelings of self-worth tied to the realization of being a son or daughter of God are important in the lives of LDS youth. We studied whether or not young men and young women who are committed to the gospel have stronger feelings of self-worth than those who are less committed.

Many findings link high self-esteem to a variety of socially desired behaviors, such as academic achievement, leadership, and marital satisfaction (Andrews, 1984; Chandler, 1985; Ross & Broh, 2000; Sacco & Phares, 2001; Kumashiro, Finkel, & Rusbult, 2002; Murray, Bellavia, Rose, & Griffin, 2003; D'Amico & Cardaci, 2003). On the other hand, low self-esteem has been linked to drug and alcohol abuse, sexual promiscuity, illegitimate births, delinquency, dropping out of high school, and unemployment (Jurich & Andrews, 1984; Chassin & Stager, 1984; Oates & Forrest, 1985; Sutherland & Shepherd, 2002).

Interestingly, some social scientists and therapists argue that religion often creates feelings of guilt in youth because they do not achieve the perfection they think God demands. Such guilt supposedly has an adverse effect on their feelings of self-worth or self-esteem (Gartner, 1983; Moberg, 1983).

Given these findings that link self-esteem to behaviors such as higher academic achievement and lower delinquency, we were anxious to ascertain whether religiosity was related to positive feelings of self-worth among LDS youth, since this would be a very significant finding.

Dating and Marriage

Selecting a mate is one of the most important decisions for an LDS young adult. "The Family: A Proclamation to the World," issued by the First Presidency and Council of the Twelve Apostles, emphasizes the importance of marriage and family. Parents and Church leaders alike are very concerned that LDS youth establish righteous families. Unfortunately, there are a number of trends in American society that are hindering LDS temple marriages. The past three decades have witnessed a steady increase in premarital sex and cohabitation. Along with a dramatic increase in divorce, these trends create doubt in the minds of many youth concerning the necessity and sanctity of marriage.

A recent study of 1,000 coeds attending colleges and universities across this country found that dating has all but disappeared from campuses (Glenn & Marquardt, 2001). Only half of the coeds reported six or more dates during their entire college career. One-third of young women had two or fewer dates during those four years. Instead of dating, college students now "hang out" in mixed groups in a variety of settings, including apartments, dormitory rooms, student centers, pizza parlors, coffee shops, and bars.

Young people who hang out often "hook up" with a member of the opposite sex. Hooking up usually involves drinking and some degree of sexual intimacy. Several research studies have found that over 70% of all college students have sex at least once during the school year (Milanese, 2002). As a consequence of the popularity of hanging out and hooking up, many college students have shifted their focus from seeking marriage to seeking participation in casual sexual relationships. Phrases like "friends with benefits," "sex without strings," and "relationships without rings" are tossed around on campus, and sexual intimacy has evolved into something as casual as a goodnight kiss.

This somewhat startling description of the mate selection process on American campuses motivated us to conduct a study among BYU, BYU–Idaho, and BYU–Hawaii students to ascertain if these trends had invaded Church campuses as well. Interestingly, a non-LDS researcher suggested that, in light of studies about morality on college campuses, parents should steer their children "to religiously affiliated colleges that attract like-minded people" (Kass, 1997). This will help children avoid the hanging-out and hooking-up culture.

We wanted to ascertain whether the BYU campuses' unique dating culture offers the protection that Kass spoke of. In addition, we studied perceptions about marriage, intentions to marry, traits sought in a potential spouse, barriers to marriage, and the point at which an LDS young adult knows that he or she has found the right person to marry.

MISSIONARY SERVICE

Each year, approximately 30,000 LDS young adults, primarily young men, leave their homes to serve missions in various countries throughout the world. For many youth, a mission is a life-altering experience that strengthens testimony and instills lofty horizons. Once these young adults return home from missionary service, many go on to further their education, begin a career, marry, and establish a family.

Missionary service undoubtedly affects many aspects of LDS young adults' lives, including education and career, family life, and involvement in the Church. Missionary work has been a major focus of the Church since the early days of the Restoration. In 1977, President Spencer W. Kimball made it clear that young men in the Church have an obligation to serve a mission. Recently the "bar" permitting missionary service has been raised. Although all young men are encouraged to serve, only the worthy and prepared are allowed this sacred experience. We sought to identify the lasting effects of missionary service in the lives of young adults.

We conducted a study of returned missionaries in order to answer three general questions. The first question is, How are returned missionaries doing in their current spiritual, educational, career, and family pursuits? We looked at the educational attainment, career, family life, and religious activity of men and women who had been back from their missions 2, 5, 10, and 17 years. These major aspects of life provide an insightful portrait of the success of returned missionaries in the various roles of adulthood.

Part of this assessment was to identify similarities and differences between men and women in their lives after a mission. Duke and Johnson (1998) surmise that for LDS returned missionaries in general, "the experiences of men and women are quite different and have a significant impact on the way they feel and worship." Given that young men often define missionary service as an obligation while young women do not, we sought to understand the unique life outcomes for men and women after they return home from a mission.

The second question we set out to answer is, Are missionaries who returned home three decades ago as committed to the gospel as those who have returned more recently? We wanted to ascertain whether the so-called secularization of American society has reduced the faithfulness of returned missionaries (Lechner, 1991; Yamane, 1997). Over 30 years ago, John Madsen (1977) surveyed a large sample of returned missionaries; we compared the religiosity found in the Madsen study to that of the returned missionaries in our study. We anticipated that the religiosity among returned missionaries has at least remained comparable or has perhaps even increased.

Finally, the third question is, What can parents, Church leaders, and the returned missionaries themselves do to ease the adjustment of returning home after a mission? We identified the challenges returned missionaries face; how they cope with these challenges; and what their parents, bishops, elders quorum presidents, Relief Society presidents, and others can do to assist in the adjustment back to life at home. We especially focused on the continued Church activity of the returned missionaries.

While conducting our study of returned missionaries, we were struck by the fact that currently only 30% of LDS young men who live in the United States serve a mission. We became curious about the other 70%. This is a very large proportion of the young men in the Church, and little is known about them. We anticipated that many of the young men who had not served a mission later met an active LDS young woman, married her in the temple, and raised a family in the gospel.

We also collected information about schooling, career development, family life, and Church activity from young men and young women who did not go on missions but were the same age as the returned missionaries we studied. In other words, we examined the activities and accomplishments of young men and women who would have been back from a mission 2, 5, 10, and 17 years, just like their returned-missionary counterparts of the same age.

OVERVIEW

The transition and maturation experiences of LDS teens and young adults we focused on in our 17-year research program included avoiding delinquency; enhancing academic achievement and educational aspirations; strengthening feelings of self-worth; serving a mission at the appropriate age; keeping the commandments; attaining an education; realizing greater self-worth in college; and finally dating, marrying, and establishing an eternal family in a gospel context.

This chapter gives an overview of our research program, including specific descriptions of our various research projects, the different factors we studied, and how we gathered the data. The chapters that follow are in-depth discussions of the various studies and our specific findings. We have organized the book so that each chapter discusses a different aspect of religious influence in the lives of LDS teens and young adults.

Chapter 2 describes the overall religiosity of high school students, college students, and young adults under the age of 40 years. We assess the acceptance of religious beliefs, attendance at church meetings, and other public behaviors; the performance of personal prayer and similar private behaviors; participation in religious experiences such as feeling the Spirit, family home evening, and other family religious practices; and acceptance among fellow Church members. We compare the religiosity of LDS high school students in different regions of the United States, in Great Britain, and in Mexico.

Several chapters examine religiosity's relationship to behaviors that are critical to the maturation of youth into competent adults. LDS youth with high levels of religiosity are compared to those with lower levels. Chapter 3 demonstrates that religiosity may be a deterrent to delinquency. The level of religiosity among LDS high school students, as shown in Chapter 4, is directly related to success in school and youths' educational aspirations and long-term academic achievement. How religiosity enhances feelings of self-worth or self-esteem is demonstrated in Chapter 5. In Chapter 6 we discuss the importance of religiosity to sexual purity. In that chapter we examine those factors that appear to be most directly linked to moral cleanliness in teens.

Latter-day Saint young adults are the primary focus in Chapters 7, 8, and 9. The findings discussed in these chapters are drawn from large samples of young adults throughout the United States and from Brigham Young University students at the three campus sites—Provo, Utah; Laie, Hawaii; and Rexburg, Idaho.

The role of religion in dating and marriage is the focus of Chapter 7. Factors affecting the postponement or avoidance of marriage are examined.

Chapter 8 examines the role of religion in the establishment of families among LDS young adults. We look at the relationships among temple marriage, marital satisfaction, divorce, and the rearing of children. As stated earlier, 70% of the young male members of the Church in the United States do *not* serve missions. As a result of this statistic, we felt it important to also understand the religiosity of that group. Thus, the chapter also reports the religiosity, educational accomplishments, family life, and careers of young adults who did not serve.

Chapter 9 explores the religiosity, educational attainment, family life, and career development of men and women who have served full-time missions for the Church. Information is included about the Church activity, family life, and careers of returned missionaries who have been home for 2 years, 5 years, 10 years, and 17 years.

Considerable media attention has focused on antidepressant prescriptions being exceptionally common in Utah. Many point to the demands of LDS Church membership as the source of deep guilt and associate this guilt with depression in Utahns. Chapter 10 compares rates of depression among members of the Church and the general population. In addition, it explores the relationship between religiosity and mental health. The final chapter summarizes the myriad of findings reported in this book to illustrate the pervasive influence of the gospel on the lives of LDS teens and young adults.

Over the years, our findings from these different studies have been published in a variety of venues. These publications include both scholarly academic journals and works intended for a Latter-day Saint audience (see Appendix C). Many of these previously published articles are not easily accessible to the average reader. In addition, some of the results have never before been published and made available to a general audience. The purpose of this book is to bring all of this research together in a single volume that is accessible and understandable. It is our hope that this work will give a comprehensive view of the role of religion in the lives of Latter-day Saint teens and young adults and help parents, friends, and leaders to better understand what they can do to help young people face the challenges of our modern world.

REFERENCES

Agnew, R. (1991). The interactive effects of peer variables on delinquency. *Criminology, 29*(1), 47–72.

Akers, R. L. (1997). *Social learning and social structure: A general theory of crime and deviance.* Boston: Northeastern University Press.

Albrecht, S. L., Chadwick, B. A., & Alcorn, D. S. (1977). Religiosity and deviance: Application of an attitude-behavior contingent consistency model. *Journal for the Scientific Study of Religion, 16*(3), 263–274.

Albrecht, S. L., & Heaton, T. B. (1984). Secularization, higher education, and religiosity. *Review of Religious Research, 26*(1), 43–58.

Andrews, P. H. (1984). Performance–self-esteem and perceptions of leadership emergence: A comparative study of men and women. *Western Journal of Speech Communications, 48*(1), 1–13.

Baier, C. J., & Wright, B. R. E. (2001). "If you love me, keep my commandments": A meta-analysis of the effects of religion on crime. *Journal of Research in Crime and Delinquency, 38*(1), 3–21.

Barber, B. K. (1996). Parental psychological control: Revisiting a neglected construct. *Child Development, 67*(6), 3296–3319.

Barber, B. K. (1997). Adolescent socialization in context—Connection, regulation, and autonomy in multiple contexts. *Journal of Adolescent Research, 12*(2), 173–177.

Barber, B. K. (Ed.). (2001). *Intrusive parenting: How psychological control affects children and adolescents.* Washington DC: American Psychological Association.

Barber, B. K., & Shagle, S. C. (1992). Adolescent problem behaviors: A social-ecological analysis. *Family Perspective, 26*(4), 493–515.

Barnes, G. M., & Farrell, M. P. (1992). Parental support and control as predictors of adolescent drinking, delinquency, and related problem behaviors. *Journal of Marriage and Family, 54*(4), 763–776.

Baumrind, D. (1991). The influence of parenting style on adolescent competence and substance use. *Journal of Early Adolescence, 11*(1), 56–95.

Benda, B. B., & Corwyn, R. F. (1997). Religion and delinquency: The relationship after considering family and peer influences. *Journal for the Scientific Study of Religion, 36*(1), 81–92.

Berger, P. L. (1967). *The sacred canopy: Elements of a sociological theory of religion.* Garden City, NY: Doubleday.

Brownfield, D., & Sorenson, A. M. (1991). Religion and drug use among adolescents: A social support conceptualization and interpretation. *Deviant Behavior: An Interdisciplinary Journal, 12,* 259–276.

Burkett, S. R., & White, M. (1974). Hellfire and delinquency: Another look. *Journal for the Scientific Study of Religion, 13*(4), 455–462.

Chandler, T. A. (1985). What's negative about positive self-concept? *Clearing House, 58*(5), 225–227.

Chadwick, B. A., & Top, B. L. (1993). Religiosity and delinquency among LDS adolescents. *Journal for the Scientific Study of Religion, 32*(1), 51–67.

Chassin, L., & Stager, S. F. (1984). Determinants of self-esteem among incarcerated delinquents. *Social Psychology Quarterly, 47*(4), 382–390.

Cochran, J. K. & Akers, R. L. (1989). Beyond hellfire: An exploration of the variable effects of religiosity on adolescent marijuana and alcohol use. *Journal of Research in Crime and Delinquency, 26,* 198–225.

Cochran, J. K., Wood, P. B., & Arneklev, B. J. (1994). Is the religiosity-delinquency relationship spurious? A test of arousal and social control theories. *Journal of Research in Crime and Delinquency, 31*(1), 92–123.

D'Amico, A., & Cardaci, M. (2003). Relations among perceived self-efficacy, self-esteem, and school achievement. *Psychological Reports, 92*(3), 745–754.

Dobbelaere, K. (1999). Towards an integrated perspective of the processes related to the descriptive concept of secularization. *Sociology of Religion, 60*(3), 229–248.

Duke, J. T., & Johnson, B. L. (1998). The religiosity of Mormon men and women through the life cycle. In J. T. Duke (Ed.), *Latter-day Saint social life: Social research on the LDS Church and its members* (pp. 315–343). Provo, UT: Religious Studies Center, Brigham Young University.

Free, M. D. (1994). Religiosity, religious conservatism, bonds to school, and juvenile delinquency among three categories of drug users. *Deviant Behavior: An Interdisciplinary Journal, 15*(2), 151–170.

Gartner, J. (1983). Self-esteem tests: A Christian critique. In C. W. Ellison (Ed.), *Your better self: Christianity, psychology, and self-esteem.* New York: HarperCollins.

Glenn, N. L., & Marquardt, E. (2001). *Hooking up, hanging out, and hoping for Mr. Right: College women on dating and mating today.* New York: Institute for American Values.

Hirschi, T., & Stark, R. (1969). Hellfire and delinquency. *Social Problems, 17*(2), 202–213.

Jurich A. P., & Andrews, D. (1984). Self-concepts of rural early adolescent juvenile delinquents. *Journal of Early Adolescence, 4*(1), 41–46.

Kass, L. R. (1997). The end of courtship. *The Public Interest, 26,* 39–63.

Kumashiro, M., Finkel, E. J., & Rusbult, C.E. (2002). Self-respect and pro-relationship behavior in marital relationships. *Journal of Personality, 70*(6), 1009–1049.

Kurdek, L. A., & Fine, M. A. (1994). Family acceptance and family control as predictors of adjustment in young adolescents: Linear, curvilinear, or interactive effects? *Child Development, 65*(4), 1137–1146.

Lechner, F. J. (1991). The case against secularization: A rebuttal. *Social Forces, 69*(4), 1103–1119.

Madsen, J. M. (1977). *Church activity of LDS returned missionaries* (Unpublished doctoral dissertation). Brigham Young University, Provo, UT.

Merrill, R. M., Lyon, J. L., & Jensen, W. J. (2003). Lack of secularizing influence of education on religious activity and parity among Mormons. *Journal for the Scientific Study of Religion, 42*(1), 113–124.

Milanese, M. (2002, May/June). Hooking up, hanging out, making up, moving on. *Stanford Magazine,* 62–65.

Moberg, D. O. (1983). Nature of the social self. In Ellison, *Your better self.*

Murray, S. L., Bellavia, G. M., Rose, P., & Griffin, D. W. (2003). Once hurt, twice hurtful: How perceived regard regulates daily marital interactions. *Journal of Personality and Social Psychology, 84*(1), 126–147.

Oates, R. K., & Forrest, D. (1985). Self-esteem and early background of abusive mothers. *Child Abuse and Neglect, 9*(1), 89–93.

Osgood, D. W., Wilson, J. K., O'Malley, P. M., Bachman, J. G., & Johnston, L. D. (1996). Routine activities and individual deviant behavior. *American Sociological Review, 61*(4), 635–655.

Ross, C. E., & Broh, B. A. (2000). The roles of self-esteem and the sense of personal control in the academic achievement process. *Sociology of Education, 73*(4), 270–284.

Sacco, W. P., and Phares, V. (2001). Partner appraisal and marital satisfaction: The role of self-esteem and depression. *Journal of Marriage and Family, 63*(2), 504–513.

Stark, R., & Bainbridge, W. S. (1996). *Religion, deviance, and social control.* New York: Routledge.

Steinberg, L., Fletcher, A. C., & Darling, N. (1994). Parental monitoring and peer influences on adolescent substance use. *Pediatrics, 93*(6), 1060–1064.

Stott, G. (1984). Effects of college education on the religious involvement of Latter-day Saints. *BYU Studies, 24*(1), 43–52.

Sutherland, I., & Shepherd, J. P. (2002). A personality-based model of adolescent violence. *The British Journal of Criminology, 42*(2), 433–441.

Thornberry, T. P., Lizotte, A. J., Krohn, M. D., Farnworth, M., & Jang, S. J. (1994). Delinquent peers, beliefs, and delinquent behavior: A longitudinal test of interactional theory. *Criminology, 32*(1), 47–83.

Tittle, C. R., and Welch, M. R. (1983). Religiosity and deviance: Toward a contin-
gency theory of constraining effects. *Social Forces, 61*(3), 653–682.

Top, B. L., & Chadwick, B. A. (2001). "Seek learning, even by study and also
by faith": The relationship between personal religiosity and academic achievement among Latter-day Saint high-school students. *Religious Educator, 2*(2),
121–137.

Wilson, B. (1985). Secularization: The inherited model. In P. E. Hammond (Ed.),
The sacred in a secular age. Berkeley: University of California Press.

Yamane, D. (1997). Secularization on trial: In defense of neosecularization paradigm. *Journal for the Scientific Study of Religion, 36*(1), 109–122.

Two

RELIGIOSITY OF LDS
YOUNG PEOPLE

L atter-day Saints are known to be an industrious and hardworking people, particularly when it comes to their spiritual development. This strong "religious work ethic" is what sociologist Rodney Stark (1998) observed to be the key to Mormonism's success in a competitive religious economy. He explained:

> LDS theology maintains that each person is expected to achieve sinlessness. The process may take several million years of posthumous effort, but there is no reason not to get started on the job now. If Christians feel guilt when they sin, Latter-day Saints often seem to feel disappointed and impatient. This seems to be the psychological basis for the very optimistic, "can-do" spirit so many have noticed among Latter-day Saints. (p. 58)

Such a "can-do" attitude is driven by a powerful belief that life is not just about being saved; it is far more profound than that. It's about achieving the highest status of all—godhood. Latter-day Saints see spiritual improvement as a daily pursuit of becoming like their Maker. Elder Dallin H. Oaks (2000) said:

> The Final Judgment is not just an evaluation of a sum total of good and evil acts—what we have *done*. It is an acknowledgement of the final effect of our acts and thoughts—what we have *become*. It is not enough for any-one just to go through the motions. The commandments, ordinances, and covenants of the gospel are not a list of deposits required to be made in some heavenly account. The gospel of Jesus Christ is a plan that shows us how to become what our Heavenly Father desires us to become. (p. 32; emphasis in original)

So how are Latter-day Saints doing at "becoming"? How are they doing in regard to living their religion? In Chapter 1, we discussed several dimensions of religiosity that we examined in our research, including such factors as professed religious beliefs, spiritual feelings and experiences, public and private religious behaviors, social acceptance within a congregation, family religious activities, and future religious plans. We will now look at our findings in each of these categories for both LDS teenagers and LDS college-aged young adults and compare them to national surveys of young people who are not LDS.

RELIGIOSITY OF AMERICAN NON-LDS YOUTH

Not until recently has there been any serious in-depth tracking of the religiosity of adolescents across the United States. However, in 2001 a group of researchers from the University of North Carolina at Chapel Hill began an ambitious project. Their study, known as the National Study of Youth and Religion (NSYR) documents the current state of religiosity among America's youth (Denton & Smith, 2001; Smith & Faris, 2002; Smith & Faris, 2002a; Regnerus, Smith, & Fritsch, 2003; Smith & Kim, 2003; Smith & Kim, 2003a; Smith, Faris, & Denton; 2004).

A review of this work, as well as research conducted by Gallup International Institute, shows first that the majority of U.S. teens are not alienated from religion at all. For example, one Gallup poll found that around 95% of youth across the United States believe in God or a higher power (Gallup & Lindsay, 1999, p. 159); and another poll found that 74% pray on at least an occasional basis (Gallup & Bezilla, 1992). The NSYR found about half of U.S. adolescents attend church at least once a month, with 31% attending once a week or more. Sixty percent feel that religion is either "very important" or "pretty important" (Smith & Faris, 2002, p. 11). In addition, 65% of these youth belong to a family that does something religious at least one day in the week (Smith & Kim, 2003, p. 15). All of this provides support for the claim that religion continues to be a vibrant part of the adolescent culture in the United States.

Second, religion has a powerful positive influence on American teenagers. Youth who have higher rates of religious involvement or beliefs have better physical and emotional health, including better habits of eating, sleeping, and exercising; higher self-esteem, self-adjustment, and pro-social development; and lower distress and thoughts of suicide. Adolescent religiosity is also positively correlated with academic achievement, moral development, and community volunteerism and negatively linked to social delinquency, alcohol, tobacco, and drug use, as well as illicit sexual activity (Regnerus, Smith, & Fritsch, 2003).

Third, the NSYR found that LDS teens, although the sample was relatively small, are consistently higher in their religiosity than youth of other religious affiliations, such as Catholics, Protestants, Jews, other religions, and those who have no religious affiliation (Smith, Faris, & Denton, 2004). This information provides the impetus for us to now turn to our findings on the religiosity of LDS teens and see how they measure up to the current trend of religiosity of teens across the United States.

Religiosity of LDS youth. To compare LDS high school teenagers and LDS college-age young adults with non-LDS students of the same ages, we conducted surveys in various parts of the United States and in two foreign countries. Over a period of years, studies were made of LDS youth living in four places in the United States—Utah County and Castle Dale, Utah, the East Coast, and the Pacific Northwest. We also surveyed LDS teens and young adults in Mexico and Great Britain.

In addition, we studied returned missionaries and unwed mothers in various regions of the United States. We wanted to compare their religiosity and behaviors with other LDS youth and non-LDS youth of the same ages. To learn more about the studies and how they were conducted, see Appendix A.

Religious belief. The first measure of religiosity we assessed was religious belief. Religious belief was measured by seven statements about traditional Christian beliefs, as well as beliefs unique to Latter-day Saint theology. We asked to what degree the teens accepted the following statements: God lives and is real; Jesus Christ is the divine Son of God; Joseph Smith actually saw God the Father and Jesus Christ; the Book of Mormon is the word of God; the Bible is the word of God; the President of the LDS Church is a prophet of God; and God answers prayers. All of the measurement scales can be seen in Appendix B.

As can be seen in Table 1, the vast majority of LDS youth in every geographical region we studied have very strong religious beliefs. Mexico's youth ranked the highest for each specific measure of belief, with 99% of them indicating they "agree" or "strongly agree" that God lives and that Jesus is the Christ, and no lower than 96% of them believe that Joseph Smith saw God and Jesus Christ and that God answers their prayers. Among youth in Great Britain, agreement with these statements, although still relatively high (ranging from 71% to 89%), is the lowest of the six groups.

A belief that God lives and is real is accepted by the majority of LDS teens, regardless of what region of the world we studied. Percentages ranged from an average of 84% in Great Britain to 99% in Mexico. The Pacific Northwest was the highest in the United States, at 97%. Contrasting these figures to what we mentioned earlier, that 95% of the young people across the United States believe in God or a higher being, we see a slightly higher percentage of LDS youth who believe in God compared to their non-LDS U.S. peers. It is encouraging to see such a high number of both LDS and non-LDS youth who say they believe in God.

Belief in Christ as the divine Son of God is clearly the strongest belief measure among LDS teens across all regions. Most regions report percentages in the high 90s. This comes as no surprise, because the central tenet of Latter-day Saint theology, a belief in Jesus Christ, is consistently taught to children at a very young age. Gallup and Lindsay (1999) report that 84% of U.S. adults believe that Jesus is God or the Son of God. This gives us some idea of the high percentage of people, LDS or not, who have a belief in Jesus Christ.

LDS teens are less sure when it comes to knowing whether or not God actually answers their prayers. Regional percentages drop to an average of less than 90% in this category. We suspect that recognizing answers to prayer requires more time and life experience than does attaining a fundamental belief in Christ, especially for teenagers.

Female teenagers generally ranked higher in religious beliefs than their male peers, although girls in Great Britain appear to be an exception. One explanation for this may be related to the fact that Great Britain has a higher rate of converts than the United States, especially among girls. Thirty-two percent of the LDS girls in Great Britain are converts, compared to 23% of the boys. Converts as a whole tend to score lower on measures of religiosity.

Religious feelings and experiences. LDS youth report a moderately high level of agreement when identifying whether they know what it feels like to repent, whether they have felt the Holy Ghost, or whether they have a testimony of the truthfulness of the gospel (see Table 2). Mexico's youth, who rank the

Table 1. Religious Beliefs of LDS Youth, by Percentage

	Utah County		Castle Dale, UT		Pacific Northwest		East Coast		Great Britain		Mexico	
	Males (n = 423)	Females (n = 554)	Males (n = 157)	Females (n = 197)	Males (n = 234)	Females (n = 342)	Males (n = 612)	Females (n = 720)	Males (n = 177)	Females (n = 241)	Males (n = 620)	Females (n = 683)
God lives and is real												
Strongly agree/agree	95	96	94	94	97	97	95	97	86	82	99	99
Mixed feelings	5	3	5	5	3	3	5	3	12	16	1	1
Disagree/strongly disagree	1	1	1	1	0	0	0	0	2	2	0	0
Jesus Christ is the divine Son of God												
Strongly agree/agree	97	98	95	96	97	99	95	98	89	86	99	99
Mixed feelings	3	2	5	3	3	1	4	2	10	12	1	0
Disagree/strongly disagree	0	0	1	1	0	0	1	0	2	3	0	1
Joseph Smith actually saw God the Father and Jesus Christ												
Strongly agree/agree	95	96	91	91	96	95	91	94	75	73	96	96
Mixed feelings	5	4	7	8	4	4	8	6	20	21	4	4
Disagree/strongly disagree	1	0	3	2	0	0	1	1	5	6	0	1
The Book of Mormon is the word of God												
Strongly agree/agree	94	95	94	90	96	95	93	94	80	76	97	97
Mixed feelings	5	5	4	9	4	5	6	5	16	16	2	3
Disagree/strongly disagree	1	0	3	1	0	0	1	1	4	8	1	1

Table 1 (continued)

	Utah County		Castle Dale, UT		Pacific Northwest		East Coast		Great Britain		Mexico	
	Males (n = 423)	Females (n = 554)	Males (n = 157)	Females (n = 197)	Males (n = 234)	Females (n = 342)	Males (n = 612)	Females (n = 720)	Males (n = 177)	Females (n = 241)	Males (n = 620)	Females (n = 683)
The Bible is the word of God												
Strongly agree/agree	92	94	92	91	93	94	93	97	81	79	97	98
Mixed feelings	8	6	6	9	7	6	7	3	15	16	3	2
Disagree/strongly disagree	0	1	2	1	0	0	1	1	5	5	1	1
The President of the LDS Church is a prophet of God												
Strongly agree/agree	96	97	94	94	96	97	95	95	83	75	97	97
Mixed feelings	3	2	4	5	4	3	4	4	12	20	2	2
Disagree/strongly disagree	1	0	3	1	0	0	1	1	5	5	1	1
God answers prayers												
Strongly agree/agree	90	90	91	88	90	92	88	88	73	71	97	96
Mixed feelings	9	9	6	10	10	7	11	11	19	21	2	3
Disagree/strongly disagree	1	1	3	3	0	0	1	1	8	9	1	0

Table 2. *Religious Feelings and Experiences of LDS Youth, by Percentage*

	Utah County		Castle Dale, UT		Pacific Northwest		East Coast		Great Britain		Mexico	
	Males (n = 423)	Females (n = 554)	Males (n = 157)	Females (n = 197)	Males (n = 234)	Females (n = 342)	Males (n = 612)	Females (n = 720)	Males (n = 177)	Females (n = 241)	Males (n = 620)	Females (n = 683)
My relationship with God is an important part of my life												
Strongly agree/agree	81	82	81	82	81	84	78	84	61	65	95	94
Mixed feelings	13	11	16	12	16	13	18	13	25	22	4	3
Disagree/strongly disagree	6	7	3	6	3	3	4	3	14	14	1	3
I have a strong testimony of the truthfulness of the gospel												
Strongly agree/agree	75	81	76	76	77	76	73	75	59	59	87	87
Mixed feelings	20	15	19	18	16	16	21	19	26	18	11	10
Disagree/strongly disagree	6	4	6	6	7	6	6	5	15	23	3	3
I know what it feels like to repent and to be forgiven												
Strongly agree/agree	71	70	70	61	60	65	67	68	56	56	90	88
Mixed feelings	21	23	19	25	28	25	26	24	29	25	7	7
Disagree/strongly disagree	7	7	11	13	12	11	8	9	15	19	3	5

Table 2 (continued)

	Utah County		Castle Dale, UT		Pacific Northwest		East Coast		Great Britain		Mexico	
	Males (n = 423)	Females (n = 554)	Males (n = 157)	Females (n = 197)	Males (n = 234)	Females (n = 342)	Males (n = 612)	Females (n = 720)	Males (n = 177)	Females (n = 241)	Males (n = 620)	Females (n = 683)
I have been guided by the Spirit with some of my problems or decisions												
Strongly agree/agree	75	82	79	73	76	78	74	77	59	62	90	92
Mixed feelings	19	14	14	18	18	17	20	18	27	20	8	6
Disagree/strongly disagree	6	4	7	9	6	4	6	6	15	19	2	3
There have been times in my life when I felt the Holy Ghost												
Strongly agree/agree	86	88	87	82	84	86	81	82	67	72	90	90
Mixed feelings	10	9	9	13	11	11	14	13	22	15	7	5
Disagree/strongly disagree	5	3	4	5	5	3	5	5	12	13	3	5

highest in religious beliefs, appear to have the highest level of religious feelings and experiences. About nine out of ten of the Mexican teens "agree" or "strongly agree" that they have had each of these experiences. Around 75% of the youth in the United States have felt similar feelings. Youth in Great Britain reported the lowest percentages.

Girls report higher levels of religious feelings and experiences than do the boys. Girls in Castle Dale, Utah, are an exception to this, as they are lower than the boys in three out of the five indicators. There does not seem to be any explanation for this, since these girls have higher rates than the boys in their private religious behavior. It is true that their church attendance is lower than the boys', but so are several of the girls in the other regions who, as we said, have higher rates of feelings and experiences than the boys in their respective regions.

Public religious behavior. We found a high level of commitment to public religiosity among LDS youth (see Table 3). About 90% of young people across all regions report attending sacrament meetings "often" or "very often," with the exception of teens in Castle Dale and Great Britain. Around 83% of youth in Castle Dale and 70% in Great Britain reported attending church "often" or "very often." In the U.S., LDS youth in the Pacific Northwest have the highest reported attendance, while youth in Castle Dale have the lowest. With only about 30% of general U.S. teens attending church weekly or more, we can see that LDS youth have a much higher rate than their peers (Denton, Pearce, & Smith, 2008).

Sunday School attendance is relatively low among teens in Castle Dale, with only 65% reporting regular attendance. This lower rate for Sunday School is startling, since we find about 83% of the same teens attending sacrament meeting and around 77% going to priesthood or young women meetings. In other words, between 12% and 17% of Castle Dale youth leave, stay outside, or stay in the halls or foyer during the middle meeting of the three-hour Church block. Contrast this to only about

1 to 10% loss in the other regions of the study. The tradition of skipping Sunday School seems more prevalent among teens in Castle Dale than among teens in the other regions.

Another surprise in our findings is that in most regions, boys attend church meetings more than girls. This is counter to what we normally find in the general population. One explanation may come from the difference in how parents and Church supervisors approach gender when it comes to church truancy. Boys, for example, generally gather in larger groups on Church premises and are more assertively corralled by teachers to get to class. Girls, on the other hand, tend to gather in pairs and may more often leave to change their clothes or adjust their makeup. Teachers or parents may be less assertive with the girls because they see their excuses for leaving as more legitimate.

Although girls have lower church attendance, they are more likely to bear their testimonies than boys are. This makes sense, given that in Western cultures girls are often socialized to share their feelings in public settings, especially in their teenage years.

Besides the law of chastity, the Word of Wisdom is perhaps the second-most emphasized principle to youth in the Church. Our findings show that this emphasis has a positive impact on the youth. We found that in the U.S., 75% to 91% of LDS young people living in the various regions report having never smoked. These percentages drop slightly when it comes to drinking alcohol, with a range of 70% in Castle Dale to 88% (girls) in the Pacific Northwest who have never drunk alcohol. Great Britain, on the other hand, with its more open cultural attitudes towards smoking and drinking, shows that only 30% of LDS boys and 43% of LDS girls have never smoked, and only 36% of the boys and 51% of the girls have completely avoided alcohol.

According to our data, boys in all regions appear more likely to smoke than girls. Results are mixed when it comes to drinking, as rates reported between males and females are generally about the same. Girls in the Pacific Northwest, however,

Table 3. Public Behavior of LDS Youth, by Percentage

	Utah County		Castle Dale, UT		Pacific Northwest		East Coast		Great Britain		Mexico	
	Males (n = 423)	Females (n = 554)	Males (n = 157)	Females (n = 197)	Males (n = 234)	Females (n = 342)	Males (n = 612)	Females (n = 720)	Males (n = 177)	Females (n = 241)	Males (n = 620)	Females (n = 683)
Attend sacrament meeting												
Very often/often	92	91	87	80	98	95	95	95	73	69	95	92
Sometimes	5	4	6	5	1	3	3	3	6	5	4	5
Rarely/never	3	4	7	15	0	2	2	2	20	28	1	3
Attend Sunday School												
Very often/often	86	82	66	65	95	91	95	92	70	65	88	87
Sometimes	7	8	11	16	3	4	3	3	6	6	7	6
Rarely/never	7	10	24	19	2	5	3	4	25	29	5	7
Attend priesthood or young women meeting												
Very often/often	88	88	79	75	98	94	93	93	72	64	85	88
Sometimes	6	5	8	5	1	3	4	4	5	6	9	7
Rarely/never	6	7	13	21	1	4	3	3	24	30	6	5
Give testimony in meeting												
Very often/often	7	13	8	19	11	14	10	19	17	16	34	32
Sometimes	16	24	22	18	19	20	21	26	20	19	24	24
Rarely/never	77	64	70	62	70	66	69	55	63	65	42	44

Table 3 (continued)

	Utah County Males (n = 423)	Utah County Females (n = 554)	Castle Dale, UT Males (n = 157)	Castle Dale, UT Females (n = 197)	Pacific Northwest Males (n = 234)	Pacific Northwest Females (n = 342)	East Coast Males (n = 612)	East Coast Females (n = 720)	Great Britain Males (n = 177)	Great Britain Females (n = 241)	Mexico Males (n = 620)	Mexico Females (n = 683)
Frequency of smoking cigarettes												
Never	90	95	37	22	45	36	79	79	22	18	4	3
Once	4	3	16	52	32	22	5	6	30	27	21	34
2 to 5 times	3	1	47	26	23	41	7	6	49	55	46	43
6 or more times	3	1	0	0	0	0	9	10	0	0	29	20
Frequency of drinking alcohol												
Never	90	92	17	32	30	27	79	75	21	17	5	3
Once	5	4	41	43	55	51	4	4	32	45	20	37
2 to 5 times	3	4	41	24	15	22	9	12	47	39	51	42
6 or more times	3	1	0	0	0	0	9	9	0	0	23	18

do exceed the boys in the number of instances reported for drinking alcohol. It is difficult to say what accounts for this. It may be a cultural phenomenon, or it may just be an anomaly, where the group of girls in our study just happened to be a rowdier sample than the overall population.

Private religious behavior. Table 4 presents several indicators of private religiosity. About seven out of ten LDS youth in the Unites States claim to pray "often" or "very often" each week. When we include those who are in the "sometimes" category, that ratio increases to 85%. As we mentioned earlier, Gallup and Bezilla (1992) report that 74% of adolescents in the United States pray at least on an occasional basis. This comparison shows that LDS teens are about 11% higher in their private prayer practices than their non-LDS peers.

LDS teens in Great Britain and Mexico do not appear to pray as frequently as youth in other regions; only five or six out of ten youth in Great Britain and Mexico report privately praying frequently. More females report praying than males. Utah County ranks the highest in frequency for both males and females.

Anywhere from 41% to 59% of LDS young people from regions in the United States participate in personal scripture study "often" or "very often." Gallup and Lindsay (1999) show that 36% of youth across the United States read the Bible at least weekly. A more recent report from the National Study of Youth and Religion (2004) revealed that only 26% of all teens read the scriptures at least once a week. They found considerable variation between different denominations. Nearly half (48%) of the youth whose families belong to the Church of God in Christ read the Bible this frequently, while only 8% of teens in Episcopalian families regularly read the scriptures. The results are not precisely reflective of those we obtained in the LDS surveys, as we asked the question a little differently, but the results indicate that LDS teens read the scriptures more often than their peers. This general comparison indicates that Latter-day

Table 4. Private Behavior of LDS Youth, by Percentage

	Utah County		Castle Dale, UT		Pacific Northwest		East Coast		Great Britain		Mexico	
	Males (n = 423)	Females (n = 554)	Males (n = 157)	Females (n = 197)	Males (n = 234)	Females (n = 342)	Males (n = 612)	Females (n = 720)	Males (n = 177)	Females (n = 241)	Males (n = 620)	Females (n = 683)
Pray privately												
Very often/often	68	79	60	73	66	73	60	70	45	58	56	65
Sometimes	16	10	20	13	18	13	21	20	25	19	20	17
Rarely/never	16	10	20	15	16	14	19	10	29	23	24	18
Read scriptures on my own												
Very often/often	47	59	50	58	46	58	41	45	33	41	35	39
Sometimes	27	21	20	20	27	22	28	28	28	17	32	30
Rarely/never	27	20	31	21	28	20	31	27	40	42	34	32
Pay full tithing												
Very often/often	73	74	58	52	74	75	74	73	48	45	27	24
Sometimes	11	13	15	15	15	12	12	12	13	16	19	14
Rarely/never	15	13	27	34	11	13	14	15	39	39	54	62
Fast on fast Sunday												
Very often/often	58	61	42	40	59	60	54	56	39	34	29	26
Sometimes	20	18	22	23	18	18	18	20	17	16	26	24
Rarely/never	22	22	36	38	23	22	28	24	44	50	45	50

Saint youth have a higher commitment in this area, albeit their scripture study includes a wider canon, including the Book of Mormon and other LDS scripture as well as the Bible.

As with private prayer, youth in Great Britain and Mexico appear much less likely to study their scriptures as often as those in the United States. Castle Dale boys rank the highest among males, and Utah County girls rank the highest among females. The fact that teens in Utah are higher in both private prayer and scripture study may be attributed to the extensiveness of the state's released-time seminary program. When compared to early morning seminary or home-study, which is more common in outlying regions, released-time seminary has a significantly higher attendance rate and tends to be more effective in promoting private religious behavior.

At first glance, it may be a bit surprising to see that both scripture study and prayer are comparatively low in Mexico, given our previous data showing youth there to have extremely strong religious beliefs and feelings. The religious culture in Mexico, however, with its strong Catholic traditions, fits this outcome, as the Latin culture promotes the ideals of religious belief and faith to a greater extent than the U.S. culture does, thus encouraging religious beliefs, though not necessarily increasing private religious behavior.

Another indicator of private religiosity is the paying of tithing. About 70% of LDS youth in the United States report paying tithing "often" or "very often." Tithing payment among Castle Dale youth drops to a little above 50%, whereas those in Great Britain are just under 50%, and only about one in four teens in Mexico say they pay tithing "often" or "very often." Socioeconomic status of the communities as well as the availability of employment for teenagers in Castle Dale, Great Britain, and Mexico may partially account for lower scores in this category. Lack of family support and a higher percentage of converts may also be factors in this pattern. We found no systematic differences between boys and girls in the payment of tithing.

A little more than half the LDS teens in the United States claim they fast "often" or "very often." Specifically, youth living in Utah County, the Pacific Northwest, and the East Coast fast more often than do those in Mexico and Great Britain. The percentages in these groups range from 26% to 39%.

Overall, Utah County girls rank first in every indicator except for one. This bespeaks something of the apparent unique spiritual strength that is being generated in that area. In saying this, however, we do not minimize the fact that the rates of those in the other regions are also relatively high and are, in most cases, only slightly behind those of Utah County girls.

Family religious behavior. Latter-day Saint parents are responsible to teach and guide their children in the gospel. Elder Russell M. Nelson (1999) counseled, "Happiness at home is most likely to be achieved when practices there are founded upon the teachings of Jesus Christ. Ours is the responsibility to ensure that we have family prayer, scripture study, and family home evening" (pp. 39–40).

As shown in Table 5, family prayer happens more often than not in families of LDS teens in the United States. About one in three LDS youth in the U.S. report having family scripture study at home "often" or "very often." Great Britain and Mexico rank lower, with about one in four reporting family scripture study "often" or "very often."

About 40% of youth across all groups say they hold family home evening at least "often." The lower rate for girls in Great Britain may in part be attributed to the higher rate of female converts in the region. Also, it is possible that family home evening rates from Mexico are lower than they should be; some of the Mexican data was collected from youth who lived at a boarding school. Their reporting of family religious activities may be skewed, since they were not living at home at the time.

Religious social acceptance. How much acceptance a young person feels within his or her peer group at church is very important for self-worth and participation in church activities.

Table 5. Family Religious Behavior of LDS Youth, by Percentage

	Utah County		Castle Dale, UT		Pacific Northwest		East Coast		Great Britain		Mexico	
	Males (n = 423)	Females (n = 554)	Males (n = 157)	Females (n = 197)	Males (n = 234)	Females (n = 342)	Males (n = 612)	Females (n = 720)	Males (n = 177)	Females (n = 241)	Males (n = 620)	Females (n = 683)
Family has family prayer												
Very often/often	65	58	57	42	71	58	57	54	51	37	42	37
Sometimes	14	12	15	12	9	15	15	14	15	17	18	15
Rarely/never	22	31	28	46	20	28	28	32	35	47	40	49
Family reads scriptures together												
Very often/often	38	32	38	28	34	26	28	25	29	20	25	20
Sometimes	21	17	12	14	17	21	19	16	23	17	19	17
Rarely/never	42	51	50	58	49	54	52	59	48	63	57	62
Family holds family home evening												
Very often/often	45	40	41	30	51	42	47	41	41	29	39	33
Sometimes	21	21	17	21	13	18	18	19	22	13	18	16
Rarely/never	34	39	43	49	36	40	36	40	37	58	43	52

We asked three questions that measured this issue (see Table 6). About two-thirds of LDS teens agree that they feel liked by their ward members. About one-third agree that they sometimes feel like an outsider at church. Fewer girls than boys appear to feel accepted in church, although Mexico is an exception to this pattern. Economic status may play a prominent part in how much attention girls place on being accepted at church. For example, teens who have more wealth may think that acceptance by their peers is based on what type of clothes they can afford to wear. Girls in the lower economic regions may be less inclined to feel like an outsider at church because of these reasons. There are, no doubt, other reasons why girls (and boys) do not feel accepted at church.

Religious plans. The final indicator we analyzed among teens was the religious plans they have for the future. From Table 7, we see that around 75% of the boys agree that they plan on serving a mission. Boys in Great Britain are much lower, with only 55% reporting plans to serve a mission. More than half of the girls in Mexico and slightly less than half in Utah county agree that they want to serve a mission. The vast majority of all youth have plans to marry in the temple and to stay active in the Church. Again, teens in Great Britain generally appear less committed to these plans than those in the other regions.

RELIGIOSITY AMONG LDS YOUNG ADULTS

Religiosity among adults in the United States continues to remain strong, despite numerous predictions by social scientists and theorists over past decades that religion would decline as modernization and scientific enlightenment flourished. In their recent book *Surveying the Religious Landscape*, Gallup and Lindsay (1999) show that the vast majority of Americans continue to believe in God or a higher power, most are members of a church and pray daily, nearly half read the Bible weekly, and two out of five attend church on a weekly basis. These figures, of course, represent adults of all

Table 6. Acceptance of LDS Youth in Church Settings, by Percentage

	Utah County		Castle Dale, UT		Pacific Northwest		East Coast		Great Britain		Mexico	
	Males (n = 423)	Females (n = 554)	Males (n = 157)	Females (n = 197)	Males (n = 234)	Females (n = 342)	Males (n = 612)	Females (n = 720)	Males (n = 177)	Females (n = 241)	Males (n = 620)	Females (n = 683)
I seem to fit in very well with the people in my ward												
Strongly agree/agree	61	58	68	47	70	58	63	63	59	49	85	77
Mixed feelings	17	23	14	28	15	22	24	26	22	22	9	13
Disagree/strongly disagree	22	19	18	25	14	20	13	11	19	29	7	10
I am well liked by members of my ward												
Strongly agree/agree	66	65	62	51	80	69	74	77	68	60	77	71
Mixed feelings	23	26	31	32	16	24	21	20	22	25	17	19
Disagree/strongly disagree	10	9	7	17	5	7	6	4	11	15	7	10
I sometimes feel like an outsider in the Church												
Strongly agree/agree	25	31	35	37	24	32	27	32	38	47	36	33
Mixed feelings	15	17	17	21	18	21	16	19	17	18	12	14
Disagree/strongly disagree	60	52	48	42	59	47	57	49	45	36	52	53

Table 7. *Religious Plans of LDS Youth, by Percentage*

	Utah County		Castle Dale, UT		Pacific Northwest		East Coast		Great Britain		Mexico	
	Males (n = 423)	Females (n = 554)	Males (n = 157)	Females (n = 197)	Males (n = 234)	Females (n = 342)	Males (n = 612)	Females (n = 720)	Males (n = 177)	Females (n = 241)	Males (n = 620)	Females (n = 683)
I plan to serve a mission												
Strongly agree/agree	76	46	77	21	82	37	75	29	55	18	89	56
Mixed feelings	13	40	16	47	14	45	18	51	23	39	10	30
Disagree/strongly disagree	3	14	8	32	4	18	7	20	22	43	2	15
I plan to marry in the temple												
Strongly agree/agree	91	92	87	82	92	91	88	88	63	61	93	93
Mixed feelings	7	6	11	15	8	8	10	9	23	21	6	5
Disagree/strongly disagree	2	1	3	4	1	1	3	3	14	18	2	2
I plan to be active in the Church												
Strongly agree/agree	92	93	82	85	94	92	90	89	68	62	95	95
Mixed feelings	7	7	13	11	5	7	8	9	20	23	4	4
Disagree/strongly disagree	2	1	5	5	2	2	2	2	12	15	1	1

ages across the United States. But what about young adults specifically?

A 2001 Gallup Poll shows that U.S. young adults are moderately strong in religiosity but are lower in almost every measure compared to older adults. For example, church attendance for those ages 18 to 29 is about 15% lower (32%) than the national average of all ages combined. Only 47% of these young adults feel that religion is "very important," compared to 60% of those ages 50 to 64. About 60% of 18- to 29-year-olds say they are members of a church. This is lower than the older age groups, including 50- to 64-year-olds and 65- to 74-year-olds, who are at 72% and 70%, respectively. A very high percentage (96%) of those aged 18 to 29 believe in God or a universal spirit. This is around the same level as the older age groups (Gallup, 2002).

With these national figures in mind, we now turn to our research on the religiosity of Latter-day Saint young adults. Generally we find that young adults in the Church, whether attending BYU or not, are much higher in their religiosity than their non-LDS peers of similar age across the United States. Religiosity levels for students attending BYU are particularly high, and we recognize this may represent something of a selection bias, since BYU's honor code requires students attending the university to maintain strict religious standards. Nonetheless, additional analysis from our second young adult study (the returned-missionary/non-returned-missionary study) substantiates that high religiosity is not specific to attendance at an LDS college, but that LDS young adults, no matter where they are, generally hold relatively strong religious values and convictions. Let's take a look at these outcomes more specifically.

Religious belief. The religiosity of college-aged LDS young adults is extremely high. Table 8 shows several religious belief measures of those who attend BYU in Provo, Idaho, or Hawaii. There is practically no variance in any of these measures, with no less than 96% of students who either "agree" or "strongly

Table 8. Religious Beliefs of LDS BYU Students, by Percentage

	BYU		BYU–Idaho		BYU–Hawaii	
	Males (n = 495)	Females (n = 576)	Males (n = 436)	Females (n = 751)	Males (n = 298)	Females (n = 521)
God lives and is real						
Strongly agree/agree	100	99	100	100	99	100
Mixed feelings	0	1	0	0	1	0
Disagree/strongly disagree	0	0	0	0	0	0
Jesus Christ is the divine Son of God						
Strongly agree/agree	99	99	100	100	99	100
Mixed feelings	1	1	0	0	1	0
Disagree/strongly disagree	0	0	0	0	0	0
Joseph Smith saw God and Jesus Christ						
Strongly agree/agree	98	98	100	100	96	98
Mixed feelings	1	1	1	0	3	2
Disagree/strongly disagree	0	0	0	0	1	0
The Book of Mormon is the word of God						
Strongly agree/agree	98	99	100	100	97	99
Mixed feelings	1	1	1	0	2	1
Disagree/strongly disagree	0	0	0	0	1	0
The Bible is the word of God						
Strongly agree/agree	98	98	99	100	96	98
Mixed feelings	1	2	1	0	3	2
Disagree/strongly disagree	0	0	0	0	1	0
The President of the Church is a prophet						
Strongly agree/agree	99	99	100	100	98	100
Mixed feelings	1	1	1	0	1	0
Disagree/strongly disagree	0	0	0	0	1	0

agree" that God lives, Jesus Christ is the Son of God, Joseph Smith saw God, the Book of Mormon is true, the Bible is the word of God, and the President of the Church is a prophet. As mentioned earlier, the Gallup poll found around 96% of young adults across the United States of similar age (ages 18 to 29) believe in a God or a universal spirit. This provides some idea that LDS and non-LDS young adults alike are extremely high in their belief in God.

Table 9. Religious Feelings of LDS BYU Students, by Percentage

	BYU		BYU–Idaho		BYU–Hawaii	
	Males (*n* = 495)	Females (*n* = 576)	Males (*n* = 436)	Females (*n* = 751)	Males (*n* = 298)	Females (*n* = 521)
My relationship with God is important						
Strongly agree/agree	96	98	97	98	93	96
Mixed feelings	2	1	3	2	5	3
Disagree/strongly disagree	2	1	1	0	2	1
I have a strong testimony						
Strongly agree/agree	96	98	97	98	93	95
Mixed feelings	2	1	2	2	4	4
Disagree/strongly disagree	1	1	1	1	3	1
I have felt repentance						
Strongly agree/agree	94	92	93	93	90	92
Mixed feelings	5	7	5	7	8	7
Disagree/strongly disagree	1	1	2	1	2	1
I have been guided by the Spirit						
Strongly agree/agree	96	97	95	97	93	96
Mixed feelings	3	3	5	3	5	4
Disagree/strongly disagree	1	1	0	0	2	0
I have felt the Holy Ghost						
Strongly agree/agree	98	99	98	99	98	98
Mixed feelings	2	1	1	1	2	2
Disagree/strongly disagree	1	1	1	0	0	1

Religious feeling and experiences. Religious feelings of BYU students (Table 9) are also relatively strong, indicating a high level of agreement across all measures. Ninety-three to 98% say that their relationship with God is important and that they have a strong testimony (of the Church).

Between 93% and 99% of the LDS men and women from these schools said they have felt the Holy Ghost or have been guided by the Spirit in their lives. Knowing what it feels like to repent and be forgiven ranked as the lowest of the five indicators, ranging from 90% of the men at BYU–Hawaii to 94% of the men at BYU in Provo.

Public religious behavior. Table 10 shows that most LDS students on the Provo, Rexburg, and Laie campuses attend sacrament meeting almost every week. Women appear slightly more likely than men to attend. With student wards established on campus for both single and married students, Church attendance is easily facilitated.

One of the requirements of the honor code at BYU campuses is to keep the Word of Wisdom. There seems to be very little problem with students holding to this requirement, as 92% to 98% of the student body claim to obey the Word of Wisdom completely. Around half of the students claim they bear their testimonies at least sometimes at Church. The other half rarely or never share their testimonies. About one in five say they bear their testimony "very often" or "often." Men at Rexburg and Laie appear slightly more likely to bear their testimonies than the women, but the reverse is true at the Provo campus.

Private religious behavior. Private religious behavior at BYU campuses is relatively high, although students at BYU–Hawaii have lower levels in all of the indicators when compared to the other two institutions (see Table 11). Aside from the men at BYU–Hawaii, over 90% of students report praying at least a few times a week, and anywhere from 68% to 86% report studying their scriptures several times a week. Students at the Provo campus show higher rates of these two practices than

Table 10. Religious Feelings of LDS BYU Students, by Percentage

	BYU		BYU–Idaho		BYU–Hawaii	
	Males (n = 495)	Females (n = 576)	Males (n = 436)	Females (n = 751)	Males (n = 298)	Females (n = 521)
I attend sacrament meeting						
Almost every week/2 or 3 times a month	99	99	98	99	96	98
Once a month	1	0	1	0	2	1
A few times a semester/never	1	1	1	1	2	1
I attend Sunday School						
Almost every week/2 or 3 times a month	96	98	96	98	93	96
Once a month	2	1	2	1	4	2
A few times a semester/never	2	1	2	2	4	3
I attend priesthood or Relief Society						
Almost every week/2 or 3 times a month	96	98	96	98	92	96
Once a month	3	2	2	1	3	1
A few times a semester/never	1	1	2	2	5	3
I obey the Word of Wisdom						
Yes—completely	98	98	97	98	92	95
Most of the time	2	2	2	2	6	5
No	1	0	1	0	2	0
I bear my testimony in sacrament meeting						
Very often/often	17	20	21	19	19	19
Sometimes	35	36	35	35	34	31
Rarely/never	48	45	44	47	47	50

students in Rexburg or Laie. This may be a result of the difference in concentration of returned missionaries between the Provo campus and the other two schools. The Gallup Poll (Winseman, 2002) shows that about 65% of Americans say they "agree" or "strongly agree" that they spend time in worship or prayer every day. There are no numbers from Gallup specifically for young adults.

Table 11. Private Behavior of LDS BYU Students, by Percentage

	BYU		BYU–Idaho		BYU–Hawaii	
	Males (*n* = 495)	Females (*n* = 576)	Males (*n* = 436)	Females (*n* = 751)	Males (*n* = 298)	Females (*n* = 521)
I pray privately						
Every day/a few times a week	94	96	92	96	83	90
About once a week/about once a month	5	4	5	6	12	7
Less than once a month/not at all	1	1	2	1	5	3
I read scriptrues privately						
Every day/a few times a week	82	86	77	82	69	68
About once a week/about once a month	14	12	19	14	29	25
Less than once a month/not at all	4	2	4	2	11	7
I fast on fast Sunday						
Very often/often	75	84	71	80	56	67
Sometimes	15	9	15	11	22	17
Rarely/never	11	7	14	9	22	16
Payment of tithing						
Full-tithe payer	96	96	96	96	90	88
Partial-tithe payer	3	3	3	3	6	9
Non-tithe payer	1	1	2	2	4	2

The reported percentage of full-tithe payers at the Provo and Rexburg campuses are exactly the same, at 96%. Lower rates are found at BYU–Hawaii, but these are still relatively high. A high frequency of fasting on fast Sunday is found among about seven in ten of the LDS students. Students at BYU in Provo have a higher rate in this category, followed by students at BYU–Idaho and then BYU–Hawaii.

Religious social acceptance and plans. Like LDS teens, LDS young adults also find social acceptance by others important. Campus wards are a unique place for students to enjoy social interaction. Most students say they get along with members of their ward, and about three-fourths of them see themselves as well liked in their ward (see Table 12). We found about one in six students say they feel like an outsider at church. About

Table 12. Feelings of Acceptance in Church, by Percentage

	BYU		BYU–Idaho		BYU–Hawaii	
	Males (*n* = 495)	Females (*n* = 576)	Males (*n* = 436)	Females (*n* = 751)	Males (*n* = 298)	Females (*n* = 521)
I feel like an outsider						
Strongly agree/agree	18	13	13	12	28	17
Mixed feelings	11	16	17	13	16	20
Disagree/strongly disagree	71	72	70	75	56	66
I get along with ward members						
Strongly agree/agree	63	66	69	71	64	61
Mixed feelings	27	24	24	22	23	29
Disagree/strongly disagree	10	10	7	7	13	10
I am well liked by members of my ward						
Strongly agree/agree	77	78	81	77	70	71
Mixed feelings	20	21	17	22	26	25
Disagree/strongly disagree	3	1	2	1	5	4

Table 13. Religious Plans of LDS BYU Students, by Percentage

	BYU		BYU–Idaho		BYU–Hawaii	
	Males (*n* = 495)	Females (*n* = 576)	Males (*n* = 436)	Females (*n* = 751)	Males (*n* = 298)	Females (*n* = 521)
I plan to marry in the temple						
Strongly agree/agree	98	98	99	99	92	92
Mixed feelings	2	1	1	1	4	6
Disagree/strongly disagree	0	1	0	1	3	3
I plan to stay active all my life						
Strongly agree/agree	97	98	99	99	90	94
Mixed feelings	2	1	1	1	6	4
Disagree/strongly disagree	1	1	0	0	4	2

one in four BYU–Hawaii men identify themselves as an outsider at church.

Given a lifetime of strong socialization surrounding temple worship and Church activity, it is not surprising that we found a solid commitment by almost all LDS students on BYU campuses to marry in the temple and stay active in the Church throughout their lives (see Table 13). Ninety-seven to 99% of the LDS students at Provo and Rexburg plan to marry in the temple and to stay active in the Church all their lives. Although still relatively high, the percentage of students at BYU–Hawaii was lower in these areas when compared to those at the other two campuses.

RELIGIOSITY OF LDS RETURNED MISSIONARIES

In addition to data from LDS college students attending Church universities, data from our studies of returned missionaries and those who did not serve missions help us assess young adult religiosity in the Church. As we look at outcomes, our primary focus is not to highlight the differences between returned missionaries and non-returned missionaries, since these differences are probably linked to factors that occur much earlier than the mission field. Instead, we look to provide further information and corroborate what has already been discovered: That religiosity among LDS young adults remains relatively high, regardless of post–high school activity.

Religious feelings and experiences. As can be seen in Table 14, the vast majority of returned missionaries, both men and women, claim that their relationship with God is important to them and that the Holy Ghost is an important part of their lives. Around one in five indicate having felt spiritual experiences on a weekly basis. Returned missionaries in their 20s appear more likely to have stronger feelings about their relationship with God than those who are older. However, there is a difference in this pattern between men and women. Women report their lowest religiosity in their 40s, whereas men report their lowest religiosity in their 30s. Across all but one of the indicators, women score higher than men in their religious feelings and experiences.

As for those who did not serve a mission, about three-fourths of the men say they feel strongly about their relationship

Table 14. Religious Feelings and Experiences of LDS Young Adults, by Percentage

	Returned Missionaries (Age)						Non-Returned Missionaries (Age)					
	Males			Females			Males			Females		
	20	30	40	20	30	40	20	30	40	20	30	40
	(n = 1007)	(n = 594)	(n = 466)	(n = 644)	(n = 520)	(n = 369)	(n = 198)	(n = 95)	(n = 87)	(n = 307)	(n = 171)	(n = 142)
My relationship with God is an important part of my life												
Exactly/very much	96	94	94	99	98	98	73	73	80	92	96	96
Somewhat	3	5	5	1	2	2	20	19	14	7	4	4
Not very much/not at all	1	1	1	0	0	1	7	8	6	1	0	1
The Holy Ghost is an important part of my life												
Exactly/very much	84	77	80	95	92	90	51	51	62	82	82	89
Somewhat	12	15	17	4	7	7	25	27	18	12	14	5
Not very much/not at all	4	7	3	1	1	3	25	23	20	6	4	6
I know what it feels like to repent and to be forgiven												
Exactly/very much	83	76	79	86	81	78	54	60	60	72	69	79
Somewhat	14	17	18	13	18	16	17	22	25	17	23	12
Not very much/not at all	3	7	3	1	1	6	30	18	15	11	8	9

Table 14 (continued)

	Returned Missionaries (Age)						Non-Returned Missionaries (Age)					
	Males			Females			Males			Females		
	20	30	40	20	30	40	20	30	40	20	30	40
	(n = 1007)	(n = 594)	(n = 466)	(n = 644)	(n = 520)	(n = 369)	(n = 198)	(n = 95)	(n = 87)	(n = 307)	(n = 171)	(n = 142)
I have been guided by the Spirit with some of my problems or decisions												
Exactly/very much	77	73	77	93	89	87	42	51	61	75	77	84
Somewhat	19	20	20	6	9	11	29	28	26	16	19	10
Not very much/not at all	4	7	4	1	2	2	29	20	13	8	4	5
I have felt the Spirit of God in sacrament meeting												
Exactly/very much	84	77	82	91	85	86	54	58	65	81	83	84
Somewhat	11	16	14	7	12	10	16	19	11	12	10	10
Not very much/not at all	5	7	5	2	3	4	30	23	25	7	5	6

Table 15. *Public Behavior of LDS Young Adults, by Percentage*

	Returned Missionaries (Age)						Non-Returned Missionaries (Age)					
	Males			Females			Males			Females		
	20	30	40	20	30	40	20	30	40	20	30	40
	(n=1007)	(n=594)	(n=466)	(n=644)	(n=520)	(n=369)	(n=198)	(n=95)	(n=87)	(n=307)	(n=171)	(n=142)
Attend sacrament meeting												
Almost every week/2 or 3 times a month	95	93	95	98	95	94	47	62	60	76	84	86
Once a month	2	2	2	1	1	1	6	38	3	4	1	1
Every other month/a few times a year/never	3	5	4	1	4	5	47	0	37	20	15	14
Attend Sunday School												
Almost every week/2 or 3 times a month	91	87	91	96	91	91	44	58	52	68	77	83
Once a month	4	5	3	2	2	1	6	1	5	5	4	1
Every other month/a few times a year/never	5	9	7	2	6	8	50	41	43	27	19	16
I obey the Word of Wisdom												
Yes—completely	96	93	95	98	97	97	53	66	64	81	84	86
Most of the time	2	4	4	1	2	1	14	11	16	12	10	7
No	2	3	2	1	1	2	34	23	20	7	6	7
Priesthood status												
High priest	1	11	32	NA	NA	NA	1	2	13	NA	NA	NA
Elder	99	89	68	NA	NA	NA	52	68	64	NA	NA	NA
Aaronic priesthood office	0	0	0	NA	NA	NA	28	20	14	NA	NA	NA
No priesthood	1	1	0	NA	NA	NA	19	10	8	NA	NA	NA

with God, yet only around half claim that the Holy Ghost is an important part of their lives. The older the men are, the more they appear to increase in their religious feelings and experiences. Women who did not serve full-time missions show relatively high ratings for religious feelings and experiences, although generally not as high as the returned-missionary women.

Public religious behavior. The vast majority of returned missionaries attend sacrament meeting on a weekly basis (see Table 15). About 94% of males attend sacrament meeting at least two to three times a month, with about 96% of females in the same category. Sunday School attendance is around 90% for males who served full-time missions and 93% for females who served full-time missions. As for Word of Wisdom observance, around 95% of the returned-missionary males indicate that they keep it completely, while 97% of females in that category do the same. Priesthood status among the returned-missionary males in their 40s shows that 32% are high priests and 68% are elders.

Public religious behavior for returned-missionary males in their 20s starts at an extremely high rate, which then makes a slight decrease as they move into their 30s. It then appears to shift back up in their 40s. Returned-missionary females in their 30s and 40s have a modest drop in their public religious behavior as compared to those in their 20s. The numbers for keeping the Word of Wisdom showed little variation across these age groups for both men and women.

Public religiosity among non-returned missionaries is much lower when compared to returned missionaries. Of LDS males in their 20s who have not served full-time missions, under half attend sacrament meeting two or three times a month or more. Females in this category report higher rates, with around 76% reporting attending two to three times a month or more. This percentage is substantially higher than the 32% of Americans aged 18 to 29 who claim they attended church in the last seven days (Gallup, 2002).

Among non-returned missionaries, Sunday School rates are slightly lower than that of sacrament meeting attendance. About three out of five males in this category say they obey the Word of Wisdom completely. More than 80% of the females claim the same. As for the priesthood status among non-returned-missionary males in their 40s, 13% are ordained high priests, 64% are elders, 14% hold the Aaronic Priesthood, and 8% do not hold the priesthood.

The pattern across the three age-groups indicates that women increase in their public religious behavior as they get older. Non-returned-missionary males appear especially low in public religiosity in their 20s, but report an increase in these indicators among those in their 30s and 40s.

Private religious behavior. Table 16 shows the rate of private religious behavior among both samples. Private prayer continues to be significantly practiced among returned missionaries throughout their lives. About nine out of ten of those in their 20s pray at least several times a week. This rate drops as they get into their 30s, but begins to pick up again in their 40s.

This pattern is different for non-returned missionaries. For the women, private prayer actually appears to increase for every decade of age. For the males, only about 34% pray several times a week while they are in their 20s, as compared to 70% of the females. For males this rate increases by almost 50% as they move into their 30s and holds near that rate once they are in their 40s.

When it comes to scripture study, around 40% of males who served full-time missions read their scriptures several times a week. This rate is slightly higher for the females in the same category. Those in their 20s who have served full-time missions appear to maintain higher rates than those who are older. About one out of five males who did not serve a mission make a consistent habit of studying the scriptures several times a week and about one out of every three of the females in this category do the same. A remarkable difference from the returned-missionary sample, older non-returned missionaries

Table 16. *Private Behavior of LDS Young Adults, by Percentage*

	Returned Missionaries (Age)						Non-Returned Missionaries (Age)					
	Males			Females			Males			Females		
	20	30	40	20	30	40	20	30	40	20	30	40
	(n = 1007)	(n = 594)	(n = 466)	(n = 644)	(n = 520)	(n = 369)	(n = 198)	(n = 95)	(n = 87)	(n = 307)	(n = 171)	(n = 142)
I pray privately												
Every day/a few times a week	91	70	75	88	79	85	34	55	52	70	79	82
About once a week/2 to 3 times a month/about once a month	4	20	16	10	17	12	28	23	24	21	17	14
Less than once a month/not at all	5	11	9	2	5	3	39	21	23	10	4	4
I read scriptures on my own												
Every day/a few times a week	48	32	43	63	49	49	19	20	29	36	31	51
About once a week/2 to 3 times a month/about once a month	39	46	39	31	36	35	29	35	34	36	40	31
Less than once a month/not at all	13	22	18	6	16	16	53	45	37	28	29	18
Payment of Tithing												
Full-tithe payer	89	83	88	94	90	94	35	46	54	66	71	77
Partial-tithe payer	6	10	6	4	5	1	6	16	8	10	13	9
Non-tithe payer	5	7	7	2	5	5	47	38	38	25	16	15
Temple recommend												
Yes	91	87	91	96	91	91	44	58	52	68	77	83
No	4	5	3	2	2	1	6	1	5	5	4	1

Table 17. Family Religious Behavior among Married LDS Young Adults, by Percentage

	Returned Missionaries (Age)						Non-Returned Missionaries (Age)					
	Males			Females			Males			Females		
	20	30	40	20	30	40	20	30	40	20	30	40
	(n = 639)	(n = 539)	(n = 443)	(n = 388)	(n = 407)	(n = 300)	(n = 116)	(n = 75)	(n = 70)	(n = 247)	(n = 153)	(n = 129)
Family prayer												
Every day/a few times a week	76	72	75	81	79	77	39	48	41	63	62	62
About once a week/2 to 3 times a month/about once a month	14	16	16	14	13	14	24	23	19	15	20	13
Less than once a month/not at all	7	12	10	4	8	9	37	29	41	22	17	24
Family scripture study												
Every day/a few times a week	40	29	41	45	46	48	19	20	13	33	32	35
About once a week/2 to 3 times a month/about once a month	35	38	25	36	28	31	32	29	32	27	34	32
Less than once a month/not at all	23	33	24	17	26	20	49	51	55	40	33	33
Family home evening												
Full-tithe payer	44	57	68	52	67	72	30	32	27	44	54	54
Partial-tithe payer	15	17	13	14	11	11	10	17	15	16	15	13
Non-tithe payer	38	25	19	31	22	17	60	51	57	40	31	33

appear much more likely to read their scriptures consistently than those who are younger.

The payment of tithing and temple recommend status appear at high levels among returned-missionaries. For males who did not serve missions, about half pay a full tithe. About half also hold a current temple recommend. The overall rate appears to increase with age. This is also true for the non-returned-missionary females, but the females' rates are consistently higher than the males'.

Family religious behavior. Family religious behavior is also different between men and women and returned missionaries and non-returned missionaries (see Table 17). About three-fourths of those who served missions report holding family prayer more than once a week. No significant differences appear across each age-group. About 40% of non-returned-missionary males hold family prayer several times a week. This is also true of around 60% of females in the same category. The overall rate generally increases as they move into their 30s and then drops once they enter their 40s.

Family scripture study rates are lower than family prayer. Between 45% and 48% of returned-missionary females report holding family scripture study more than once a week. Returned-missionary males are next, with just above one-third reporting the same. One-third of non-returned-missionary females report this, and only about 17% of the non-returned-missionary men have family scripture study several times a week.

More than half of returned missionaries hold regular family home evening. The overall rate increases with age. For females who did not serve a full-time mission, the rate is about 50%. About 30% of males in this category have regular home evening activities with their families.

Religious marriage status. We included in our study two categories that we predict will measure the religious status of one's marriage (see Table 18). An overwhelming 98% of returned missionaries who are married have a spouse who is

Table 18. *Religious Marriage Status among Married LDS Adults, by Percentage*

	Returned Missionaries (Age)						Non-Returned Missionaries (Age)					
	Males			Females			Males			Females		
	20	30	40	20	30	40	20	30	40	20	30	40
	(n = 656)	(n = 540)	(n = 444)	(n = 393)	(n = 490)	(n = 307)	(n = 117)	(n = 75)	(n = 70)	(n = 250)	(n = 155)	(n = 131)
Spouse is a member of the LDS Church												
Yes	99	99	99	99	98	95	81	87	83	90	92	94
No	1	2	1	1	2	5	18	13	17	10	8	6
Type of wedding ceremony												
Temple sealing	93	87	90	96	89	86	32	25	26	63	70	60
Civil ceremony	3	4	5	2	5	8	41	35	33	26	20	19
Civil ceremony followed by temple sealing	4	9	6	2	6	7	27	40	41	11	10	21

LDS. The vast majority of these men and women also married in the temple.

The story is different for non-returned missionaries. While the large majority of females (92%) have a spouse who is LDS, only about 80% have been sealed in an LDS temple. Around 83% of the males in this category have an LDS spouse, and about two-thirds of these have temple sealings. A significant number of these temple marriages came as a temple sealing after being civilly married. This statistic indicates the probable impact that family members, friends, and Church leaders have on motivating these men in furthering their religious commitment.

CONCLUSION

Many members of The Church of Jesus Christ of Latter-day Saints take their religion seriously. Findings from our study show that most LDS teens, like many of their peers across the United States, do not feel alienated from religion at all. Almost all of them believe in God and Jesus Christ. The vast majority say they feel a close relationship with God and have been guided by the Spirit in their decisions. Youth in Mexico appear to be the strongest in their religious beliefs and feelings, while teens in Great Britain report more struggles. Very few LDS teens miss their Church meetings. Most stay away from tobacco and alcohol, although the majority of youth in Great Britain report having used these substances at least once.

About two out of every three LDS youth say that they pray "often" or "very often," and a little less than half of them read their scriptures at the same rate. Youth in the United States generally have higher rates of private prayer and scripture study than teens outside the country. Utah County teens report the highest rates in the United States for these two religious practices. The majority of the families of LDS youth appear to hold family prayer quite regularly. Only around three in ten families have consistent family scripture study, and the rate of those who hold regular family home evening is about four in ten.

The majority of LDS teens feel they are accepted at church, although about one-third say they often do not. Girls in Castle Dale and in Great Britain report having the hardest time feeling like they fit in well with their Church peers.

The vast majority of LDS male teens are planning to serve a mission, although only about half the boys in Great Britain report having such a goal. Almost nine out of ten LDS teens have plans to marry in the temple and slightly more report planning to be active in the Church the rest of their lives. Again, youth in Great Britain are the exception to this pattern.

Our findings on the religiosity of LDS young adults of college age, particularly those who either attend BYU or serve missions, are extremely impressive. Non-returned missionaries appear much less inclined toward religiosity, however. For example, no LDS student we polled at Church colleges disagreed that he or she believed in God, and almost all of them, including returned missionaries, claim they have felt the Spirit in their lives.

Church attendance, private prayer, observance of the Word of Wisdom, and the payment of tithing are all relatively high among young adults who attend BYU as well as among those who served a mission. Rates among non-returned missionaries tend to be much lower in each of these categories. This same pattern occurs for family religious behavior as well, with returned-missionary males' families holding family prayer, scripture study, and family home evening nearly twice as much as non-returned-missionary males' families, and returned-missionary females' families report about 20% higher statistics in these family religiosity indicators than non-returned-missionary females' families.

When it comes to marriage, almost every married, returned-missionary young adult has an LDS spouse and a temple sealing. About 84% of the married males and 92% of the married females who did not serve a full-time mission have an LDS spouse. About 70% of people in this category have a temple sealing.

With this descriptive data in mind, we now turn to see how religiosity influences various aspects of Latter-day Saint lives. We will start by assessing religion's impact on delinquency and antisocial behavior among LDS teens.

REFERENCES

Denton, M. L., Pearce, L. D., & Smith, C. (2008). *Religion and spirituality on the path through adolescence*. Research report from the National Study of Youth and Religion (8). Retrieved from http://www.youthandreligion.org/publications/docs/w2_pub_report_final.pdf.

Denton, M. L., & Smith, C. (2001). *Methodological issues and challenges in the study of American youth and religion*. Research report from the National Study of Youth and Religion. Retrieved from http://www.youthandreligion.org/publications/docs/methods.pdf

Gallup, G. H., Jr. (2002, June 4). *The religiosity cycle*. The Gallup Organization. Retrieved from http://www.gallup.com/poll/6124/religiosity-cycle.aspx

Gallup, G. H., & Bezilla, R. (1992). *The religious life of young Americans: A compendium of surveys on the spiritual beliefs and practices of teenagers and young adults*. Princeton, NJ: George H. Gallup International Institution.

Gallup, G., Jr., & Lindsay, D. M. (1999). *Surveying the religious landscape: Trends in U.S. beliefs*. Harrisburg, PA: Morehouse Publishing.

National Study of Youth and Religion (NSYR). (2004). *Few U.S. Protestant teens regularly read the Bible*. Retrieved from http://www.youthandreligion.org/news/2004-0623.html

Nelson, R. M. (1999, May). Our sacred duty to honor women. *Ensign, 29*(5), 38–40.

Oaks, D. H. (2000, November). The challenge to become. *Ensign, 30*(11), 32–34.

Regnerus, M., Smith, C., & Fritsch, M. (2003). *Religion in the lives of American adolescents: A review of the literature*. Research report from the National Study of Youth and Religion (3). Retrieved from http://www.youthandreligion.org/publications/docs/litreview.pdf

Smith, C., & Faris, R. (2002). *Religion and American adolescent delinquency, risk behaviors and constructive social activities*. Research report from the National Study of Youth and Religion (1). Retrieved from http://www.youthandreligion.org/publications/docs/RiskReport1.pdf

Smith, C., & Faris, R. (2002a). *Religion and the life attitudes and self-images of American adolescents.* Research report from the National Study of Youth and Religion (2). Retrieved from http://www.youthandreligion.org/publications/docs/Attitudes.pdf

Smith, C., Faris, R., & Denton, M. L. (2004). *Are American youth alienated from organized religion?* Research report from the National Study of Youth and Religion (6). Retrieved from http://www.youthandreligion.org/publications/docs/Alienation.pdf

Smith, C., & Kim, P. (2003). *Family religious involvement and the quality of family relationships for early adolescents.* Research report from the National Study of Youth and Religion (4). Retrieved from http://www.youthandreligion.org/publications/docs/family-report.pdf

Smith, C., & Kim, P. (2003a). *Family religious involvement and the quality of parental relationships for families with early adolescents.* Research report from the National Study of Youth and Religion (5). Retrieved from http://www.youthandreligion.org/publications/docs/family-report2.pdf

Stark, R. (1998). The basis of Mormon success: A theoretical application. In J. T. Duke (Ed.), *Latter-day Saint social life: Social research on the LDS Church and its members* (pp. 29–70). Provo, UT: Religious Studies Center, Brigham Young University.

Winseman, A. L. (2002). "I spend time in worship or prayer every day." The Gallup Organization. Retrieved from http://www.gallup.com/poll/6127/Spend-Time-Worship-Prayer-Every-Day.aspx

Three

DELINQUENCY

One of the initial objectives of our research was to explore the relationship between religiosity and delinquency in the hope of demonstrating the influence of religion on the lives of members of the Church. We wanted to know if higher levels of religiosity resulted in lower levels of delinquency among LDS high school students. We selected delinquency as a test of religion's influence because adolescence is a stressful time when youth, who are establishing their own identities and gaining independence from their parents, commonly participate in delinquent behaviors.

Acceptance among peers becomes paramount during this time, and teens will do almost anything to fit in. Adolescence can thus be a dangerous time when young people may engage in risky behavior, lose their faith, and drift away from the Church. The presence (or absence) of such behaviors provides an excellent test of the influence of religion on everyday life. We examined the effects of religion on delinquency within the context of peer influences, family characteristics, school experiences, and personality by testing the multivariate model shown

Figure 1. Conceptual Model with Religiosity, Peer Influence, Personality Traits, and Family Characteristics Predicting Adolescent Delinquency

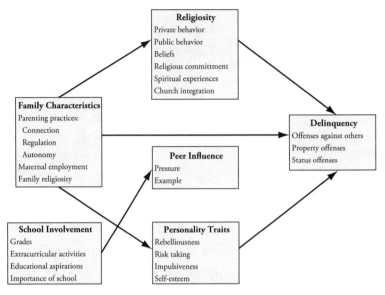

in Figure 1. This kind of testing assessed the statistical significance of religiosity on delinquency while competing with peer, family, school, and personality factors in real-life situations.

The relationship between religiosity and delinquency, sometimes called the "hell-fire and damnation hypothesis," was formulated by Hirschi and Stark in the early 1960s. They argued that religiosity fosters conformity to moral and legal standards that prohibit delinquent behavior. The hypothesis was frequently tested following Hirschi and Stark's early work (see Cochran & Akers, 1989). However, support for a link between religion and delinquency has been limited (Albrecht, Chadwick, & Alcorn, 1977; Brownfield & Sorenson, 1991; Chadwick & Top, 1993; Free, 1994). Given the lack of research support, the hell-fire hypothesis has been largely discarded.

Chadwick and Top (1993) argued that using church membership and attendance as measures of religiosity contributed to the lack of support. They assert that these measures alone fail to tap the essence of personal religiosity and feelings of spirituality that are related to level of delinquency. Using additional measures of religiosity, they found among a sample of 1,700 LDS adolescents living along the East Coast that private religious behavior, including personal prayer and scripture reading, demonstrated a significant inverse relationship to delinquency, while public religious behavior (attendance) did not. Litchfield et al. (1997), studying a sample of LDS youth, similarly found that various dimensions of religiosity affect delinquency differently.

Some researchers argue that the link between religiosity and decreased delinquency disappears when other factors such as peer influences, personality traits, school experiences, and family characteristics are included in the model (Cochran, Wood, & Arneklev, 1994; Benda & Corwyn, 1997). Benda and Corwyn (1997) studied 724 high school students living in the Midwest. Neither church attendance, time in prayer, Bible study, nor financial contributions were related to delinquency in the presence of these other factors. However, they did find that talking about religion and trying to convert others was negatively related to adolescent crime even after controlling for the other factors. Thus we included in our model seven dimensions of religiosity: public behavior, beliefs, private behavior, importance of religion, spiritual experiences, family religious behavior, and feelings of social acceptance into their congregations. This allowed the various dimensions of religiosity to compete with peer, family, school, and personal traits to explain delinquency.

Peer Influences and Delinquency

Many studies of delinquency have clearly demonstrated that peers are the single most powerful predictor of delinquency (Agnew, 1991; Warr & Stafford, 1991; Thornberry et al., 1994). For example, Agnew (1991) tested the influence of attachment to peers, time spent with peers, and the extent of friends' delinquency on delinquent behavior. He analyzed interview data collected in 1979 (Elliot, Huizinga, & Ageton, 1985) and found that all three peer factors strongly predicted delinquency.

McBride, Joe, and Simpson (1991) tested a model predicting drug and alcohol use among a sample of 175 Hispanic youth who participated in a drug abuse prevention program. Peer pressure was a significant contributor to alcohol use among young men, but not among young women. Male teens who had a strong need to be liked by their friends more often joined them in drinking than those with a lower need for acceptance. In addition, McBride and his associates found that peer example was a significant contributor to delinquency. Other research has confirmed that watching friends participate in delinquent activities, even in the absence of overt pressure, significantly predicts youths' delinquent behavior (Thornberry et al., 1994; Dishion, Andrews, & Crosby, 1995). Akers (1998) reviewed the major studies of delinquency and concluded that "the best single predictor of the onset, continuance, or desistance of delinquency is differential association with law-violating or norm-violating peers" (p. 164).

In order to clearly demonstrate the influence of religion on delinquency in the real world, we included both peer pressure and peer example in the model. Thus, religion has to compete with peer influences to predict delinquency.

FAMILY CHARACTERISTICS AND DELINQUENCY

Family structure, maternal employment, family conflict, and parenting practices have all been identified as being related to delinquency. Teens raised in single-parent families have higher rates of delinquency because they are generally more weakly connected to their fathers, and this weak attachment fails to inhibit delinquency. Wells and Rankin (1991) performed an analysis of 50 studies investigating the impact of single-parent family structure on delinquency and concluded that such youth are significantly more delinquent than those living in two-parent families. The strongest relationship was found between family structure and status offenses—mainly truancy and running away.

Because divorce is usually a consequence of family conflict to which adolescents are witnesses, if not participants, several researchers have sought to determine whether divorce or conflict has the strongest relationship to delinquency. Findings indicate that family conflict, especially parent-child conflict, is more important than divorce in predicting delinquency (LeFlore, 1988; Wells & Rankin, 1991; Brody & Forehand, 1993).

Although the effects of maternal employment on younger children have been widely studied, its effects on adolescents have been largely ignored. Orthner (1990) reviewed previous research and found little support linking working mothers to delinquent teenagers. He cautioned, however, that existing research is somewhat inadequate and that care should be exercised in rejecting a relationship between maternal employment and delinquency.

A study by Hillman, Sawilowsky, and Becker (1993) supports the tentative conclusion that working mothers are not associated with delinquency among children. They studied the drinking and drug use of 389 high school students in three midwestern metropolitan areas. For teens who used alcohol and drugs, there were no significant differences between those whose mothers did not work and those whose mothers worked full-time or part-time.

Parenting practices, such as support and control, have been found in a large body of research related to delinquency (Rollins & Thomas, 1979; Steinberg, 1987; Baumrind, 1991; Lamborn, Mounts, Steinberg, & Dornbusch, 1991; Kurdek & Fine, 1994).

Family connection is the interpersonal relationship and emotional ties between parents and children. Teens' attachment to parents enhances parental control over their teens, and thus reduces delinquency. Barber (1997) theorized that connection with parents and siblings also provides adolescents with essential social skills and a sense of security, both of which facilitate positive peer relationships and, in turn, contribute to limited involvement in delinquent activities. Studies have found that youth who were raised in warm and supportive family environments report lower incidence of deviance, alcohol and drug use, and school misconduct (Johnson & Pandina, 1991; Barnes & Farrell, 1992; Kurdek & Fine, 1994). For example, Kurdek and Fine (1994) surveyed over 1,100 fifth- through seventh-grade students attending two schools in a midwestern city. Family acceptance was negatively related to failing grades, drug use, threats against others, fighting, and arguments with teachers.

Parental regulation involves parents setting rules for their children, monitoring their activities, and administering appropriate discipline. Youth who experience limited parental regulation do not develop internal conventional commitments and are more likely to participate in delinquent activities because of unchecked hedonistic impulses. Barber (1996) argues that inadequate regulation leads to a lack of self-discipline, which leaves youth susceptible to delinquency and negative social influences.

Several studies have confirmed the significance of parental regulation in deterring delinquency (McCord, 1979; Patterson & Stouthamer-Loeber, 1984; Barber & Shagle, 1992). Patterson and Stouthamer-Loeber (1984) concluded from their study:

> Initially it [parental regulation] may determine which youths become engaged in the delinquency process. Second, it may determine which youths become recidivists. Youths characterized as recidivists were from families in which the monitoring process was even more disrupted than for those only peripherally engaged. The fact that the findings held for both the official records and for self-reported delinquency scores leads one to emphasize the potential importance of this variable. (p. 1305)

Psychological autonomy is defined as parents encouraging, rather than intruding upon, their adolescent children's development of an individual identity, sense of efficacy, and feelings of self-worth. Parents who refuse to listen to, or quickly dismiss, their teenagers' ideas, opinions, and feelings limit their children's sense of self and the inner control necessary to resist delinquent impulses. Importantly, the use of psychological control techniques, such as guilt induction or love withdrawal, have been found to be associated with low psychological autonomy. Recent research has shown that a lack of psychological autonomy predicted delinquency (Barber, 1996; Barber, Thomas, & Proskauer, 1997).

In order to more fully understand the relationship between religion and delinquency, we added several family characteristics and processes to the model. The family traits included are family structure, maternal employment, family conflict, family connectedness, parental regulation, and the granting of psychological autonomy.

THE FAMILY'S INDIRECT EFFECTS ON DELINQUENCY

In 1998, Judith Rich Harris summarized the large body of research linking family characteristics to adolescent behaviors, including delinquency, and concluded that parents are largely irrelevant. She came to the conclusion that parents have little influence on the kind of young adults into which their teenage children evolve, because most of the research connecting family factors to teenagers' behavior has found few direct associations. What Harris failed to recognize is that family characteristics often have an indirect effect on their teenage children's behavior. In the case of delinquency, parents influence the choice of friends, the ability to withstand peer pressures, and religiosity—all of which reduce delinquency.

Bahr, Marcos, and Maughan (1995) assessed the association between connection to parents, grades, time spent on homework, educational expectations, and drinking alcohol with a very large sample of 27,000 high school students living in Utah. They found a strong relationship between family connectedness and educational commitment, which in turn was related to lower rates of alcohol use. Connection was also moderately associated with a reduced number of drug-using friends, which was also linked to less drinking. These findings indicate that while family connectedness only weakly affected alcohol use directly, it had a strong indirect effect through educational commitment and peers.

Bahr, Maughan, Marcos, and Li (1998) tested a similar model predicting drug use among 13,250 high school students also living in Utah. They found that maternal and paternal connectedness with teenagers, parental regulation, and family conflict had weak direct relationships with drug use. On the other hand, maternal connectedness had a strong indirect effect on drug participation through a lower association with friends who used drugs. These findings suggest that since parents are not in the high school or at teen parties, their influence is not as direct as peers who are active participants at the parties. But parents do influence the selection of friends, ability to resist peer pressure, religiosity, moral values, school achievement, and other factors, which in turn reduce delinquency.

Based on these findings, we placed family characteristics in the model so that we could assess the direct effects as well as the indirect effects of the family on delinquency through peers, religiosity, personality traits, and school experiences (see Figure 1).

Personality Traits and Delinquency

Personality traits are conceptualized as an indication of a youth's commitment to conformity (Hirschi, 1969). Limited research has identified two clusters of personality traits, namely self-esteem and rebelliousness, which appear to be related to delinquency. Low self-esteem has frequently been associated with higher levels of delinquency (Rosenberg & Rosenberg, 1978; Rosenberg, Schooler, & Schoenback, 1989; Evans, Levy,

Sullenberger, & Yvas, 1991). Rosenberg, Schooler, and Schoen-back (1989) investigated whether the relationship between self-esteem and delinquency was reciprocal. They concluded that self-esteem has a stronger causal relationship to delinquency than delinquency has to lower self-esteem.

A related concept, locus of control, is the feelings one has about what causes the events in one's life. A high internal locus of control—that is, the perception that one has personal control over the events in one's life—has been linked to lower delinquency (Ollendick, Elliott, & Matson, 1980). On the other hand, Gerstein and Briggs (1993) found that violent delinquents had higher internal locus of control, that is, they were more willing to admit their faults and weaknesses than were nonviolent youth, who more often believed they had experienced some bad luck. This study suggests that the relationship between locus of control and delinquency may differ by the type of offense committed.

Finally, research has shown rebelliousness and other closely related personality traits such as impulsiveness and risk taking to be positively correlated with delinquency (Smith & Fogg, 1979; Krueger et al., 1994; Rowe & Flannery, 1994; Wood, Cochran, Pfefferbaum, & Arneklev, 1995). Wood et al. (1995) studied questionnaires from 1,179 ninth- through twelfth-grade students in Oklahoma to ascertain the relationship between sensation seeking and impulsiveness and substance use. They found that youth with sensation-seeking and impulsiveness traits had higher rates of drug use.

Although the contribution of various personality traits to predicting delinquency is limited, we included self-esteem, locus of control, rebelliousness, impulsiveness, and risk taking in the model in order to better understand religiosity's strength in predicting delinquency.

SCHOOL INVOLVEMENT AND DELINQUENCY

Attachments to teachers, positive school experiences, involvement in school and extracurricular activities, and future educational aspirations decrease the likelihood of delinquency (Johnson, 1979). However, tests of the relationship between school experiences and delinquency have produced mixed results. For example, Finn, Stott, and Zarichny (1988) discovered in their sample of delinquents processed by the juvenile courts that substantial proportions of delinquents were two or more years behind in reading, received barely passing or failing grades, had been held back a grade, and had been formally suspended at least once. On the other hand, Tygart (1992) failed to find a significant correlation between grades and self-reported delinquency. Furthermore, some researchers have proposed that any relationship between dropping out of high school and delinquency may be caused by other factors, such as socioeconomic status and academic interest (Tygart, 1992; Jarjoura, 1993).

School involvement and educational aspirations are theoretically important factors that may predict delinquent activity. We added grades, the importance of school, participation in extracurricular activities, and educational aspirations as significant school experiences to make the test of religiosity's impact even more rigorous.

MEASUREMENT OF VARIABLES

Delinquency. In limited research, LDS youth have been found to exhibit relatively low levels of delinquency, especially status offenses, compared to adolescents across the nation. For example, only 23% of LDS young men and 20% of LDS young women in a national sample reported having ever imbibed alcoholic beverages, compared to 81% and 80% respectively in a national sample (Johnston, Bachman, & O'Malley, 1995).

Another study (Chadwick & Top, 1993) reported that only 12% of young men and 17% of the young women among the LDS youth were sexually experienced, compared to 55% of similar-age young men and 50% of young women respectively in a national sample (Centers for Disease Control and Prevention, 1995). Thus, asking the youth in our study how often they had committed each offense during the past year or two years would have produced little reported delinquency.

Consequently, we measured delinquency using forty items that asked if the youth had ever engaged in specific delinquent activities, and if so, how often they had ever done each offense. The questions used to measure all of the variables in this analysis are presented in Appendix B. We assessed three dimensions of delinquency in the questionnaire.

- *Offenses against others* were determined by twelve items involving verbal and physical attacks on peers, school officials, and parents.
- *Property offenses* were assessed by eleven items focusing on activities such as shoplifting, theft, and vandalism.
- *Status offenses* were measured by fifteen items that focused on alcohol and drug use and truancy, as well as premarital sexual behavior. These are mainly activities that are legal for adults but are illegal for youth because of their minor status.

We also included activities that are not only legal, but are widely accepted in general society. For example, premarital sex was included as a status offense because it violates the spiritually important principle of chastity. We summed the number of different delinquent activities a young person had participated in as the measure of delinquency.

Religiosity. Religious beliefs were measured by ten questions examining traditional Christian beliefs such as "Jesus Christ is the divine Son of God," as well as unique LDS doctrine such as "The Book of Mormon is the word of God." Four questions about frequency of attendance at sacrament, Sunday School, and priesthood/young women meetings, and participation in Church-sponsored socials gauged public religious behavior.

Private religious behavior was assessed by four questions asking the frequency of personal prayer, scripture reading, fasting, and paying tithing. Five response categories for the frequency of public and private religious behavior ranged from "never" to "very often." Three items probed the youths' history of spiritual experiences. One example is, "I have been guided by the Spirit with some of my problems or decisions."

Eight items assessed youths' feelings about the importance of religion in their lives. Examples are, "My relationship with God is an important part of my life," and "During the past year, I have really tried to live the standards of the Church."

Family religiosity combined the frequency with which the student's family held family prayer, read the scriptures together, and engaged in family home evening.

Three items measured perceptions of social acceptance, which involved adolescents' feelings of fitting in with fellow Church members and leaders. Response categories for the belief and attitudinal items ranged on a five-point scale from "strongly disagree" to "strongly agree."

Peer influences. We measured two dimensions of peer influences. Peer pressure was determined by asking the LDS youth if their friends had ever tried to get them to do 27 of the 40 deviant activities on the survey. The number of items was reduced since peer pressure did not seem relevant for some activities, such as being arrested. The response categories were "yes" or "no." The number of "yes" replies was summed to provide a measure of peer pressure.

Peer example was measured by asking how many of the respondents' friends had ever engaged in the 40 delinquent activities. The response categories were "none," "some," "most," or "all." The proportion of friends who had engaged in the activities was summed to provide a measure of peer example.

In addition, the youth were asked how many of their friends were LDS. Response categories included "none," "a few," "about half," "most," and "all." We anticipated that youth with a higher proportion of LDS peers would experience less negative peer pressure, especially for activities against LDS standards, such as using tobacco, drinking alcohol, or having premarital sex.

Family influences. Family structure was measured by a single item that asked with whom the youth lived. Six response categories included "mother and father," "mother and stepfather," "father and stepmother," "mother alone," "father alone," and "other." Responses were grouped into single- and two-parent families.

Perceived family conflict was assessed by three questions concerning whether the adolescents' parents nagged and complained about each other, often argued, and yelled and screamed at each other when the youth were around. Possible responses included "not true," "somewhat true," and "true."

Maternal employment was measured by asking the youth if their mothers were employed. Response categories included "no," "yes, part-time," and "yes, full-time."

The teenagers' feelings of family connection were assessed using ten items originally developed by Schaefer (1965) and later tested by Barber, Olsen, and Shagle (1994). The items asked separately whether a specific activity described the respondent's mother and father. A sample item is: "My mother (father) is a person who makes me feel better after talking over my worries with her (him)." The response categories were "not like her (him)," "somewhat like her (him)," and "a lot like her (him)."

Parental regulation was determined using five items which assessed the degree to which parents monitor their adolescents' activities (Dornbusch, Ritter, Leiderman, Roberts, & Fraleigh, 1987; Steinberg, Fletcher, & Darling, 1994). The five monitoring questions asked separately if their mother and father really know who the teens' friends are, where they go at night, how they spend their money, what they do with their free time, and where they are most afternoons after school. The response categories included "doesn't know," "knows a little," and "knows a lot."

Psychological autonomy was also measured by ten questions developed by Schaefer (1965) and recently used by Barber, Olsen, and Shagle (1994). A sample item is: "My mother (father) will avoid looking at me when I have disappointed her (him)." The response categories were the same three used for family connection.

Self-esteem and personality traits were measured using two standard scales. First, 10 items from the Rosenberg (1965) self-esteem scale were included in addition to eight items from the Nowicki and Strickland (1973) locus of control scale. The five response categories ranged from "strongly disagree" to "strongly agree." Eight items, five of which were adapted from Smith and Fogg (1979), gauged rebellious tendencies in the youth. A sample item is, "I like to shock or 'freak out' my parents or other adults just for the fun of it." We also asked about three risk-taking items, two of which were taken from Bachman, Johnston, and O'Malley (1993). An example is, "I get a real kick out of doing things that are a little dangerous." Impulsiveness was measured by three items adapted from the California Psychological Inventory (Gough, 1965). A sample item is, "I often act on the spur of the moment without stopping to think."

School involvement. Four dimensions of school experiences were included in the model. The youth were asked what grades they received in school. Eight response categories ranged from "mostly As" to "Ds and Fs." The importance of school was assessed by a single item which asked how important the student felt it was to receive good grades in school. Four response categories ranged from "not important" to "extremely important."

The youth were asked which extracurricular activities, including sports, music, student government, student newspaper/yearbook, and various academic and vocational clubs, they were involved in. They checked as many activities as applied. These were summed to provide a cumulative measure of participation in extracurricular activities.

Educational aspirations were also measured by a single question which asked the youth's educational expectations. Six possible responses ranged from, "I don't expect to finish high school," to "I expect to get an advanced degree after graduation from college."

DELINQUENCY RESULTS

The percentages of LDS young men and young women who have ever committed any of the 12 offenses against others are presented in Table 1 (males) and Table 2 (females). It is informative to examine how many LDS youth have participated in activities ranging from making telephone threats to defying school teachers. Three major trends concerning LDS teens injuring others emerge from the two tables.

The first trend is that LDS youth behave pretty much the same, regardless of where they live. There are a couple of exceptions, but overall the similarity is amazing. The young men living in Great Britain reported somewhat less fighting than did their American and Mexican peers. They were significantly less likely to have made threatening telephone calls or to have picked on other kids. Church leaders in Great Britain advised us to delete the question about participation in gang fights because they were convinced British youth were not involved in gangs. Given the level of gang fighting among the other groups, we wish we had asked this question of youth in Great Britain anyway, to verify the absence of a gang scene. Although the British youth were a little less frequently involved in picking on other kids, the overall similarity among the LDS young people in the six different regions of the world is remarkable.

The second general trend is that the young women are nearly as involved in attacking others as are the young men. They reported less real physical abuse, such as beating someone

Table 1. Male LDS High School Students Who Committed
Offenses against Others, by Percentage

Delinquent Activity	Utah County (n = 460)	Castle Dale, UT (n = 168)	East Coast (n = 636)	Pacific Northwest (n = 251)	Great Britain (n = 193)	Mexico (n = 764)
Made telephone threats	27	31	21	32	7	20
Picked on other kids	41	48	53	52	29	42
Picked fights with other kids	23	25	25	26	22	29
Beat up other kids	19	24	25	25	19	23
Took money by force	4	8	2	6	3	8
Hurt a kid so he or she needed a doctor	9	13	8	10	11	9
Used a weapon against other kids	5	7	6	6	6	5
Was in a gang fight	6	9	8	6	—	18
Cursed at a parent	21	23	19	19	21	17
Pushed, shoved, hit a parent	9	10	10	12	11	7
Defied a teacher/leader at church	16	18	20	12	23	12
Defied a teacher/officer at school	27	30	37	34	34	21

Table 2. Female LDS High School Students Who Committed
Offenses against Others, by Percentage

Delinquent Activity	Utah County (n = 460)	Castle Dale, UT (n = 168)	East Coast (n = 636)	Pacific Northwest (n = 251)	Great Britain (n = 193)	Mexico (n = 764)
Made telephone threats	27	31	24	27	11	18
Picked on other kids	31	31	43	34	30	32
Picked fights with other kids	10	16	12	11	19	16
Beat up other kids	5	7	8	6	12	9
Took money by force	1	2	2	1	2	3
Hurt a kid so he or she needed a doctor	2	2	3	1	5	3
Used a weapon against other kids	1	2	2	1	4	2
Was in a gang fight	2	5	2	3	—	10
Cursed at a parent	20	27	21	20	26	18
Pushed, shoved, hit a parent	8	11	14	10	8	6
Defied a teacher/leader at church	12	12	18	10	16	7
Defied a teacher/officer at school	18	21	27	22	26	14

up, using a weapon, or inflicting serious wounds that require
a doctor. On the other hand, as many young women as young
men made telephone threats, cursed or swore at their parents,
defied a teacher at church, or defied a teacher at school. Recently,
school officials have noted that young women are becoming
more violent, as evidenced by vicious fighting between girls.
This trend is not unique to LDS youth but seems to be a national
phenomenon that may be fueled in part by women's libera-
tion and movement into the workforce. Both of these social
movements have resulted in women becoming more like men
and emulating men's assertive or aggressive behavior. Movies,
television, and video games probably also have an influence on
female aggression.

The third trend to emerge from the data is the confronta-
tional culture that has emerged in high schools. It is obvious why
bullying has become such a crisis in the public schools around
the world. About half of the young men and about one-third
of the young women acknowledged that they have "picked on
the other kids, or made fun of them." It seems that one way
high school students seek acceptance in the school community,
or perhaps in a specific clique, is to demonstrate their superiority
by belittling and putting down others. The putting down of others involves harassment in the halls and classrooms and ridicule
of looks, dress, or academic performance.

The devastating consequences of being victimized by high
school bullying have been well documented in the highly publi-
cized cases where frustrated and angry students have responded
with violent outbursts. The widely discussed assault on students and faculty at Columbine High School was mounted by
two outcast students seeking revenge for the harassment they
had suffered. All too frequently we read in the paper or see on
television examples of students who have become so angry at
the daily ridicule they suffered that they sought violent retalia-
tion against their fellow students.

Unfortunately, the abuse does not always stop with harassment and ridicule, but occasionally escalates into picking fights and beating up other kids. It is disturbing that 10% of the LDS young men and 7% of the young women admit, or perhaps brag, that they have physically hurt someone so seriously that they required medical attention from a doctor. It is disturbing that over 5% of the boys and about 2% of the girls claim they have used a weapon like a gun, knife, or club in their attacks on other students.

Finally, LDS youth are not immune to the allure of gang membership. Over 5% of the boys have actually been in a gang fight, as have 2% or 3% of the girls. The youth in Mexico are significantly more immersed in gangs, where 18% of the boys and 10% of the girls have participated in a gang fight.

It is equally disturbing to note that over 20% of both young men and young women have cursed or sworn at their parents, and that about 10% have hit, shoved, or pushed their moms or dads. The defiance of authority figures is also evident in the number of youth who have confronted a teacher or advisor at church. Nearly a third have had serious conflict with a teacher, principal, or other school official. Although society accepts some rebellion from adolescents, this level of conflict with authority figures bodes problems for some of these youth in the future. Such behaviors are likely to continue with spouses, employers, coworkers, neighbors, and eventually the police and courts.

The data in these two tables suggest there is considerable need for LDS youth to resist the temptation to enhance their own standing in the high school scene at the expense of others. The cutting comments, the refusals to associate with, the snide remarks, and the petty harassment have devastating consequences for both the perpetrator and the victim. The more serious violence is an even greater cause for concern.

In addition, the frequency of conflict with parents, Church leaders, and teachers is worrisome. Parents, Church leaders, school officials, police and courts, and the community in general need to combat this "macho," "me first," or "I am number one" mentality among high school students. It is hoped that LDS students can rise to the challenge and become more kind and caring in their association with other students.

Tables 3 and 4 report the percentages of youth who have participated in offenses against property. These include shoplifting, stealing, and trespassing on or vandalizing others' property. As with offenses against other people, LDS youth living in the different geographical and cultural areas had very similar rates of stealing or damaging the property of others. The youth in Great Britain and in Mexico reported less involvement in these types of activities. LDS young women are somewhat less involved in property offenses than are young men. The differences are not large but not surprising. Fewer young women reported stealing and damaging property than did young men.

Shoplifting is a serious problem among teenagers. About a third of the LDS boys and a fourth of the girls have shoplifted at least once. Stealing from someone's locker, purse, or desk has occurred much less frequently. About 10% of the boys have taken a car without permission. It is suspected that most "borrowed" the car of a relative to take on a joy ride rather than stealing a car to destroy or sell. A sizable number of young men, and quite a few young women, have vandalized others' property. Given their heavy immersion in high school culture, it is not surprising that a substantial number of youth have vandalized school property.

The results for status offenses are presented in Tables 5 and 6. As mentioned earlier, status offenses are activities that are illegal because of the youthful age of the offender. Such offenses include activities that are often not against the law for adults, such as drinking and smoking. In addition, we included actions that are legal even for youth, but which are considered by many in American society to be deviant. Viewing pornography, petting, and sexual intercourse under most circumstances are not illegal and are actually acceptable to many in society,

Table 3. Male LDS High School Students Who Committed Property Offenses, by Percentage

Delinquent Activity	Utah County (n = 460)	Castle Dale, UT (n = 168)	East Coast (n = 636)	Pacific Northwest (n = 251)	Great Britain (n = 193)	Mexico (n = 764)
Shoplifted	36	39	34	39	22	24
Stole something from a purse, desk, or locker	18	21	13	17	10	12
Stole something worth less than $5	33	41	37	40	25	23
Stole something worth $5 to $50	19	20	19	22	15	13
Stole something worth $50 or more	6	10	6	6	6	4
Took a car without permission	12	18	8	10	5	7
Broke into a building	13	13	16	11	8	12
Went into someone's property	51	51	54	51	34	16
Damaged someone's property	29	24	26	29	11	18
Damaged school property	20	32	15	20	14	22
Threw things like rocks, bottles, or eggs at cars or buildings	40	36	42	40	34	28

Table 4. *Female LDS High School Students Who Committed Property Offenses, by Percentage*

Delinquent Activity	Utah County (n = 460)	Castle Dale, UT (n = 168)	East Coast (n = 636)	Pacific Northwest (n = 251)	Great Britain (n = 193)	Mexico (n = 764)
Shoplifted	19	23	20	22	29	14
Stole something from a purse, desk, or locker	11	13	11	12	9	9
Stole something worth less than $5	19	23	23	21	24	13
Stole something worth $5 to $50	10	14	10	12	12	8
Stole something worth $50 or more	4	5	2	4	3	2
Took a car without permission	12	13	7	8	2	3
Broke into a building	6	11	4	5	2	6
Went into someone's property	37	34	35	34	18	8
Damaged someone's property	13	7	12	11	11	9
Damaged school property	10	11	9	9	13	15
Threw things like rocks, bottles, or eggs at cars or buildings	17	24	18	14	17	16

but because these behaviors violate important gospel principles, we included them as status offenses.

Cheating on high school tests or exams is one inappropriate behavior for which LDS students match their nonmember peers. National studies have reported that 70 to 75% of students admit they cheat on tests and the completion of homework. LDS youth justify this dishonest behavior with justifications like "Everyone is doing it," and "I will be disadvantaged in grades and admittance to college if I don't cheat." It is interesting to note that the LDS students living in Great Britain have significantly lower rates of cheating—17% for the young men and 25% for the young women. It is suspected that a different student culture, as well as stricter school monitoring of examinations, is responsible for this difference. Cheating is a national problem in the United States, and parents, Church leaders, and school officials should increase their efforts to teach youth that such behavior is dishonest.

The frequency of committing the various status offenses is similar between the young people living in the six geographical areas. There are some minor variations, but in general, LDS teenagers appear to behave the same, regardless of where they live. Although the differences are small, the Utah County young women generally had the lowest frequency of committing the 15 status offenses.

Contrary to expectations, young women report almost as much involvement in status offenses as do young men. One surprising finding was that a greater percentage of LDS young women revealed they were sexually active than did LDS young men. This is contrary to the national trend of young men initiating sexual activity at a younger age and being more active than young women. We explore the reasons for this difference in Chapter 6.

Although the level of status offense delinquency is much lower among LDS high school students than among their national peers, too many of the youth in the Church are

Table 5. *Male LDS High School Students Who Committed Status Offenses, by Percentage*

Delinquent Activity	Utah County (n = 460)	Castle Dale, UT (n = 168)	East Coast (n = 636)	Pacific Northwest (n = 251)	Great Britain (n = 193)	Mexico (n = 764)
Cheated on a test	69	70	66	72	17	74
Skipped school without an excuse	52	39	45	41	43	36
Was suspended from school	13	24	20	19	24	17
Ran away from home	13	12	12	10	14	11
Smoked cigarettes	17	26	25	18	31	25
Drank alcohol	16	31	24	13	37	22
Used marijuana	8	19	7	8	17	4
Used cocaine	2	5	2	2	3	3
Used other drugs	5	7	3	4	5	2
Got drunk or high	8	27	12	8	24	8
Read pornography	37	45	47	48	37	38
Watched pornography	39	44	43	46	41	38
Engaged in heavy petting	19	32	29	23	27	34
Had sexual intercourse	6	13	8	6	17	19
Forced someone to have sex	6	9	5	6	2	2

Table 6. Female LDS High School Students Who Committed
Status Offenses, by Percentage

Delinquent Activity	Utah County (n = 460)	Castle Dale, UT (n = 168)	East Coast (n = 636)	Pacific Northwest (n = 251)	Great Britain (n = 193)	Mexico (n = 764)
Cheated on a test	65	77	73	74	25	79
Skipped school without an excuse	46	30	42	48	40	34
Was suspended from school	5	10	6	7	8	13
Ran away from home	12	16	13	13	14	11
Smoked cigarettes	9	22	24	19	42	24
Drank alcohol	13	29	27	19	49	22
Used marijuana	4	12	5	9	15	3
Used cocaine	0.5	5	0.9	0.6	4	2
Used other drugs	2	5	3	3	7	2
Got drunk or high	7	18	13	11	28	6
Read pornography	11	14	20	15	14	13
Watched pornography	16	23	27	21	26	15
Engaged in heavy petting	19	32	33	29	34	22
Had sexual intercourse	5	16	12	6	19	7
Forced someone to have sex	4	8	5	3	6	2

experimenting with risky behaviors like drinking, using drugs, and having premarital sex; these behaviors can have long-term consequences as teens become addicted to alcohol, drugs, or sex.

The measure of delinquency we have examined so far in this chapter is the number of different delinquent activities in which a youth has engaged. In order to ascertain whether LDS youth have only experimented with an inappropriate act or whether they are frequent offenders, we calculated how often those who had participated had committed the specific act. For example, we separated out those youth who had smoked marijuana and then calculated the average of how many times they reported they had done so. In other words, we ascertained whether LDS youth who reported they had smoked marijuana had only tried it once or twice, or whether they regularly used it.

The results for offenses against others are presented in Tables 7 and 8. It should be pointed out that so few LDS teens had committed some of the acts that the averages are meaningless. For example, only one British young man had taken money by force, and only five young men in Castle Dale, Utah, had used a weapon against other youth. In such cases, the averages should be disregarded.

Fighting, including picking on other kids, picking fights, and beating up other kids, was engaged in by substantial numbers of both young men and women. The frequency of doing so was fairly high for LDS youth in most of the six geographical regions. The young people in Great Britain exhibited a tendency to defy both Church and school authorities. The answer to the question of whether or not LDS youth only experiment with delinquency or are regularly involved in it seems to be a little of both. For some offenses against others, the involvement is rather low, indicating experimentation. But some of the behaviors, such as fighting, reveal that LDS youth are regular participants.

Table 7. *Average Number of Times Male LDS High School Students Committed Offenses against Others**

Delinquent Activity	Utah County		Castle Dale, UT		East Coast		Pacific Northwest		Great Britain		Mexico	
	n	Mean	n	Mean	n	Mean	n	Mean	n	Mean	n	Mean
Made telephone threats	121	3.1	21	5.3	130	5.7	55	5.7	9	14.9	106	5.7
Picked on other kids	177	4.9	33	8.5	309	12.2	68	9.0	40	15.5	174	6.8
Picked fights with other kids	103	2.7	22	3.1	158	7.0	45	2.9	27	4.8	154	4.5
Beat up other kids	85	3.0	26	2.9	156	6.3	46	2.2	20	4.7	129	4.8
Took money by force	18	2.3	7	2.4	15	4.4	5	5.6	1	2.0	38	4.2
Hurt a kid so he or she needed a doctor	38	1.9	10	2.4	52	4.9	15	1.9	14	1.3	52	2.2
Used a weapon against other kids	22	2.2	5	3.2	36	5.3	7	1.4	7	2.0	18	2.2
Was in a gang fight	27	2.0	7	3.0	49	5.1	6	1.7	—	—	92	3.6
Cursed at a parent	93	5.2	25	4.5	118	7.8	32	3.8	26	8.6	73	6.4
Pushed, shoved, hit a parent	38	1.8	7	1.7	62	5.4	20	2.3	14	3.1	35	2.6
Defied a teacher/leader at church	71	1.9	15	2.5	124	7.3	18	4.9	31	12.2	56	2.6
Defied a teacher/officer at school	120	3.2	24	5.2	223	7.7	53	4.8	44	12.3	112	2.5

*Average was calculated only for those youth who had engaged in the specific action.

Table 8. *Average Number of Times Female LDS High School Students Committed Various Offenses against Others**

Delinquent Activity	Utah County n	Mean	Castle Dale, UT n	Mean	East Coast n	Mean	Pacific Northwest n	Mean	Great Britain n	Mean	Mexico n	Mean
Made telephone threats	154	3.6	32	5.3	175	6.9	65	3.6	25	6.2	114	3.8
Picked on other kids	177	3.6	34	5.6	316	11.7	57	6.1	59	7.6	179	6.5
Picked fights with other kids	56	2.7	21	2.9	91	5.0	26	2.7	45	3.7	96	3.3
Beat up other kids	30	1.4	9	3.2	63	5.0	17	1.8	28	7.2	56	2.6
Took money by force	7	1.3	1	1.0	13	3.4	3	1.3	4	1.5	9	6.4
Hurt a kid so he or she needed a doctor	9	1.3	2	3.5	23	2.5	3	1.7	11	3.5	14	1.9
Used a weapon against other kids	7	1.1	3	4.7	15	2.7	5	1.0	8	2.1	5	3.0
Was in a gang fight	12	2.3	5	1.6	16	5.6	8	2.5	—	—	52	2.3
Cursed at a parent	116	3.3	34	4.1	156	8.1	57	2.8	56	8.8	92	5.1
Pushed, shoved, hit a parent	45	2.6	11	1.6	102	4.5	30	3.5	16	2.0	37	3.3
Defied a teacher/leader at church	66	2.4	15	2.7	132	5.4	26	3.5	32	10.6	42	2.5
Defied a teacher/officer at school	101	2.2	31	6.4	197	7.0	61	2.3	52	9.3	86	2.9

*Average was calculated only for those youth who had engaged in the specific action.

Table 9. Average Number of Times Male LDS High School Students Committed Property Offenses[*]

Delinquent Activity	Utah County		Castle Dale, UT		East Coast		Pacific Northwest		Great Britain		Mexico	
	n	Mean	n	Mean	n	Mean	n	Mean	n	Mean	n	Mean
Shoplifted	148	3.7	40	5.1	212	6.9	75	4.1	35	6.3	144	3.9
Stole something from a purse, desk, or locker	78	3.7	20	3.0	79	7.0	29	2.8	14	8.8	69	3.1
Stole something worth less than $5	146	4.0	38	6.6	230	7.2	77	2.9	36	7.1	129	4.7
Stole something worth $5 to $50	86	3.8	20	6.5	118	6.1	40	3.5	19	6.7	76	3.3
Stole something worth $50 or more	28	2.8	10	1.7	40	4.9	8	2.4	5	5.0	15	1.9
Took a car without permission	54	2.7	17	4.9	52	4.9	17	2.2	5	2.0	34	5.7
Broke into a building	59	2.1	14	2.0	97	4.3	19	1.6	10	4.2	70	3.6
Went into someone's property	224	3.0	47	5.4	334	8.8	93	4.1	48	5.2	96	2.9
Damaged someone's property	129	2.7	20	5.3	162	6.8	50	3.5	15	7.6	96	3.7
Damaged school property	89	2.6	29	5.1	107	6.0	32	3.2	18	5.6	128	4.9
Threw things like rocks, bottles, or eggs at cars or buildings	173	4.7	36	4.9	261	7.1	70	4.5	40	7.0	155	5.2

[*]Average was calculated only for those youth who had engaged in the specific action.

Table 10. Average Number of Times Female LDS High School Students Committed Property Offenses*

	Utah County		Castle Dale, UT		East Coast		Pacific Northwest		Great Britain		Mexico	
	n	Mean	n	Mean	n	Mean	n	Mean	n	Mean	n	Mean
Shoplifted	108	2.8	34	4.5	150	5.0	62	5.3	67	5.7	101	3.9
Stole something from a purse, desk, or locker	62	2.4	17	3.5	85	2.7	30	3.0	18	5.0	58	4.4
Stole something worth less than $5	113	2.4	35	3.6	168	4.8	54	3.5	53	3.8	86	3.7
Stole something worth $5 to $50	58	2.1	15	5.4	73	5.7	28	8.4	24	6.1	45	3.6
Stole something worth $50 or more	21	1.8	5	7.4	13	1.3	9	1.6	6	13.0	13	1.2
Took a car without permission	67	2.2	20	2.5	42	3.1	23	1.8	6	12.0	13	3.0
Broke into a building	35	1.6	11	3.1	33	1.7	15	1.4	6	1.2	35	2.6
Went into someone's property	213	2.4	49	3.9	258	5.6	97	2.8	33	5.5	50	2.2
Damaged someone's property	76	2.5	10	4.0	91	4.3	30	4.6	25	5.4	54	3.3
Damaged school property	55	2.1	15	2.6	69	5.7	25	3.3	26	7.0	91	2.8
Threw things like rocks, bottles, or eggs at cars or buildings	98	2.6	29	.9	132	5.6	42	2.6	36	7.9	99	3.2

*Average was calculated only for those youth who had engaged in the specific action.

Table 11. *Average Number of Times Male LDS High School Students Committed Status Offenses**

	Utah County		Castle Dale, UT		East Coast		Pacific Northwest		Great Britain		Mexico	
	n	Mean	n	Mean	n	Mean	n	Mean	n	Mean	n	Mean
Cheated on a test	305	3.7	69	8.1	435	10.3	113	4.7	28	5.8	400	6.5
Skipped school without an excuse	224	6.2	38	6.3	277	7.0	76	6.0	58	8.7	189	5.8
Was suspended from school	59	2.6	28	4.6	123	3.1	35	2.0	22	3.3	132	2.6
Ran away from home	57	2.4	10	2.3	75	2.6	17	2.4	14	3.0	57	3.6
Smoked cigarettes	68	3.1	17	8.0	146	9.0	33	5.1	38	10.3	134	6.9
Drank alcohol	65	3.2	28	7.6	145	9.2	22	6.8	44	9.8	126	6.0
Used marijuana	28	3.8	17	10.9	41	7.9	12	6.8	20	9.8	12	5.4
Used cocaine	9	5.4	4	8.0	10	3.6	1	6.0	3	9.7	7	7.9
Used other drugs	20	5.0	3	1.3	18	12.5	3	3.3	5	9.2	6	3.2
Got drunk or high	31	2.4	18	7.7	71	10.2	11	12.2	26	9.7	33	3.1
Read pornography	164	4.1	35	6.5	293	6.9	90	5.3	51	7.7	213	4.9
Watched pornography	173	3.5	34	8.8	266	6.2	84	4.8	56	7.6	200	5.5
Engaged in heavy petting	82	4.7	26	6.9	184	7.3	41	2.9	32	10.3	158	5.4
Had sexual intercourse	28	6.1	7	4.6	46	7.9	8	1.3	22	14.0	46	3.6
Forced someone to have sex	27	1.3	5	2.4	33	4.7	8	3.5	2	1.5	21	3.5

*Average was calculated only for those youth who had engaged in the specific action.

Table 12. *Average Number of Times Female LDS High School Students Committed Status Offenses*[*]

	Utah County		Castle Dale, UT		East Coast		Pacific Northwest		Great Britain		Mexico	
	n	Mean	n	Mean	n	Mean	n	Mean	n	Mean	n	Mean
Cheated on a test	378	2.8	100	4.4	543	8.7	184	4.2	57	4.6	485	5.6
Skipped school without an excuse	262	5.5	38	4.4	310	6.8	129	7.7	80	6.7	204	4.2
Was suspended from school	30	1.8	16	1.8	45	2.5	19	1.4	18	2.2	78	2.4
Ran away from home	67	1.6	24	1.6	94	1.6	34	2.6	28	1.9	63	2.0
Smoked cigarettes	51	4.2	24	7.0	171	11.0	35	4.2	69	10.3	136	5.2
Drank alcohol	73	2.6	38	6.7	198	7.9	50	6.0	85	8.3	126	3.9
Used marijuana	23	5.4	13	7.2	36	10.0	20	7.4	31	10.0	8	4.9
Used cocaine	3	1.3	5	2.4	7	5.3	1	1.0	6	5.3	7	4.1
Used other drugs	13	1.9	4	9.3	224	8.2	7	3.6	13	5.9	7	2.3
Got drunk or high	36	3.1	20	8.3	93	9.2	23	6.5	51	9.2	30	4.2
Read pornography	64	2.3	18	3.9	149	5.1	44	2.4	24	4.8	84	3.0
Watched pornography	93	2.5	28	3.5	202	4.0	57	2.9	49	6.3	106	3.23
Engaged in heavy petting	110	3.2	31	6.1	241	8.6	70	8.0	54	11.8	132	3.2
Had sexual intercourse	31	3.4	20	8.1	91	8.8	21	17.7	35	11.0	32	2.7
Forced someone to have sex	24	2.0	8	3.8	34	3.5	6	3.7	4	1.3	9	3.4

[*]Average was calculated only for those youth who had engaged in the specific action.

The average number of times property offenses occurred is shown in Tables 9 and 10. Overall, there is more experimentation with property offenses and less regular involvement as compared to offenses against other people. Both the young men and young women reported repeating shoplifting, petty theft, trespassing, and school vandalism most often. The general trend is that LDS youth who have been involved in property offenses have done so rather infrequently.

Some status offenses, such as smoking, drinking, and using drugs, can be addictive, and thus we would expect to see more frequent use among those who have started participating in these activities. Such is the case (see Tables 11 and 12). Those young people who have sampled alcohol and drugs have engaged in such behavior fairly frequently. This pattern appeared among both the young men and young women. Also, the British young men and the young women in the Pacific Northwest who initiated sexual behavior became fairly promiscuous. The sexually active young women in the Pacific Northwest had engaged in sexual intercourse an average of nearly 18 times.

These six tables contain good news and bad news. The good news is that for many of the delinquent activities, the LDS high school students in our studies had tried them, but few had continued them. This was especially true for property offenses. The not-so-good news is that LDS teens who become embroiled in fighting at school tend to persist in their aggressive activities. The bad news is that those LDS teens who try drinking, drugs, and sex keep returning to participate in them. This is not surprising given the addictive nature of these substances and behaviors.

Previous research has suggested that LDS youth tend to have lower rates of delinquency than their non-LDS peers. We tested this assertion, which is based on rather limited research, by comparing the delinquency of the high school seniors in our sample to a large national sample of high school seniors

(Johnston, Bachman, & O'Malley, 1995). Each year nearly 20,000 high school seniors across the nation are surveyed about their intentions for their future following high school. The survey also asks detailed questions about alcohol and drug use and a few questions about other delinquent behaviors.

In order to make our data comparable to that of the national survey, we first selected out only the seniors among the LDS students. Unfortunately, this greatly reduced our sample size in some of the geographic locations. Second, we located questions from the national sample that asked if the youth had *ever* committed the activity. There was a limited number of such questions, and thus we had to include questions that asked whether or not the act had been committed during the previous twelve months. These latter questions underreport the extent of delinquency among the national sample as compared to the LDS samples. Finally, many of the questions were not worded exactly the same, so the responses may not be exactly comparable. Although these differences suggest that some caution should be exercised in interpreting the comparisons, the overall trends should be apparent.

Comparisons between the national sample and LDS seniors on five offenses against others are shown in Tables 13 and 14. It is a little surprising that just as many male LDS seniors have engaged in fighting behavior as young men in the national sample. Slightly fewer LDS young women have been this involved in violent acts against fellow students. A significantly lower proportion of LDS young men and young women reported having been in a gang fight. The only LDS group to come close to the national norm of gang fighting was the Mexican LDS young men, and they probably should not be compared to a U.S. national average.

A major difference between LDS and non-LDS youth is that LDS seniors report only a fraction of the conflict with parents that their peers in the national sample did. Even in verbal conflict, the LDS youth reported arguing only a fourth

Table 13. *Comparison between U.S. Average and Male LDS High School Seniors Who Committed Offenses against Others, by Percentage*

	U.S. (n = 1,294)	Utah County (n = 82)	Castle Dale, UT (n = 44)	East Coast (n = 116)	Pacific Northwest (n = 56)	Great Britain (n = 62)	Mexico (n = 179)
Was in a serious fight at school[1]	22	20	19	27	29	22	25
Hurt a kid so he or she needed a doctor[2]	11	10	12	8	14	14	13
Used a weapon against other kids[3]	8	4	2	4	9	5	4
Was in a gang fight[4]	29	9	5	9	8	—	22
Pushed, shoved, hit a parent[5]	84	9	5	11	14	5	6

Table 14. *Comparison between U.S. Average and Female LDS High School Seniors Who Committed Offenses against Others, by Percentage*

	U.S. (n = 1,321)	Utah County (n = 108)	Castle Dale, UT (n = 54)	East Coast (n = 139)	Pacific Northwest (n = 92)	Great Britain (n = 63)	Mexico (n = 182)
Was in a serious fight at school[1]	13	6	4	6	8	7	9
Hurt a kid so he or she needed a doctor[2]	5	0	2	4	2	5	2
Used a weapon against other kids[3]	1	2	0	4	4	0	1
Was in a gang fight[4]	15	1	6	2	1	—	8
Pushed, shoved, hit a parent[5]	92	7	6	14	10	5	4

1. **LDS** youth were asked: "Have you ever physically beat up other kids?" **National** youth were asked: ""During the last twelve months, how often have you gotten into a serious fight in school or at work?"
2. **LDS**: "Have you ever hurt someone badly enough that they had to go to a doctor?" **National**: "During the last twelve months, how often have you hurt someone badly enough to need bandages or a doctor?"
3. **LDS**: "Have you ever threatened or attacked someone with a knife, gun, or other weapon?" **National**: "During the last twelve months, how often have you used a knife, gun, or some other thing (like a club) to get something from a person?"
4. **LDS**: "Have you ever been in a gang fight?" **National**: "During the last twelve months, how often have you taken part in a fight where a group of your friends were against another group?"
5. **LDS**: "Have you ever cursed or sworn at one of your parents? Or pushed, shoved, or hit one of your parents?" **National**: "During the last twelve months, how often have you argued or had a fight with either of your parents?"

as often as youth in the national sample. This indicates that LDS youth are similar to their national peers in their behavior towards their peers in school, but that they have much more peaceful and supportive relationships with their parents.

The comparisons for six property offenses are presented in Tables 15 and 16. As can be seen, LDS seniors, both men and women, have been as active in shoplifting and stealing as the national sample. The only differences are that the national sample of high school seniors engaged in more breaking into buildings, while more LDS seniors reported vandalizing school property. We cannot think of any reasons explaining these two differences and suspect they are just random fluctuations. So our belief that fewer LDS youth engage in property offenses turned out to be entirely incorrect. Again, we should point out the difference between ever having committed the offense and having committed it during the past twelve months.

Not surprisingly, large differences appear in the comparisons for status offenses (see Tables 17 and 18). Society at large, and most churches, encourage youth to avoid drugs and to be careful with the use of alcohol. On the other hand, LDS youth are schooled in the Word of Wisdom, and for most youth it becomes a behavioral guide that keeps them away from drinking and drug use. Previous research relating religion to delinquency has discovered that church affiliation and attendance are more strongly related to status offenses than to other types of delinquency. The differences between the national sample of seniors and the LDS youth for smoking, drinking, using marijuana, and trying cocaine are rather impressive. Also, we noted earlier the substantially lower rate of premarital sex among LDS youth as compared to their peers.

We had anticipated that fewer LDS youth had been involved in delinquent activities than their peers. Such was certainly the case for status offenses like smoking and drinking. Also, LDS young people indicated they had much less conflict with their parents. But we discovered that LDS youth are just

Table 15. *Comparison between U.S. Average and Male LDS High School Seniors Who Committed Property Offenses, by Percentage*

	U.S. (n = 1,294)	Utah County (n = 82)	Castle Dale, UT (n = 44)	East Coast (n = 116)	Pacific Northwest (n = 56)	Great Britain (n = 62)	Mexico (n = 179)
Shoplifted[1]	38	44	36	45	24	24	22
Stole something worth less than $50[2]	40	31	18	24	13	13	12
Stole something worth $50 or more[3]	13	11	8	4	10	10	5
Took a car without permission[4]	12	18	10	14	8	8	7
Broke into a building[5]	34	16	15	8	11	11	11
Vandalized school property[6]	12	29	14	24	21	21	21

Table 16. *Comparison between U.S. Average and Female LDS High School Seniors Who Committed Offenses against Others, by Percentage*

	U.S. (n = 1,321)	Utah County (n = 108)	Castle Dale, UT (n = 54)	East Coast (n = 139)	Pacific Northwest (n = 92)	Great Britain (n = 63)	Mexico (n = 182)
Shoplifted[1]	23	22	19	22	18	33	15
Stole something worth less than $50[2]	24	12	10	10	10	10	7
Stole something worth $50 or more[3]	4	3	2	1	4	0	3
Took a car without permission[4]	2	10	6	4	5	0	3
Broke into a building[5]	17	7	4	2	2	0	5
Vandalized school property[6]	7	6	4	8	4	7	12

1. **LDS** youth were asked: "Have you ever taken something from a store without paying for it?" **National** youth were asked: "During the last twelve months, how often have you taken something from a store without paying for it?"
2. **LDS**: "Have you ever stolen anything worth less than $50?" **National**: "During the last twelve months, how often have you taken something not belonging to you?"
3. **LDS**: "Have you ever stolen anything worth more than $50?" **National**: "During the last twelve months, how often have you taken something worth over $50?"
4. **LDS**: "Have you ever taken a car without the owner's permission?" **National**: "During the last twelve months, how often have you taken a car that did not belong to someone in your family without permission of the owner?"
5. **LDS**: "Have you ever broken into a building, car, house, etc.?" **National**: "During the last twelve months, how often have you gone into some building or house when you weren't supposed to be there?"
6. **LDS**: "Have you ever purposely damaged or destroyed things at school?" **National**: "During the last twelve months, how often have you damaged school property on purpose?"

Table 17. *Comparison between U.S. Average and Male LDS High School Seniors Who Committed Status Offenses, by Percentage*

	Nation (n = 1,294)	Utah County (n = 82)	Castle Dale, UT (n = 44)	East Coast (n = 116)	Pacific Northwest (n = 56)	Great Britain (n = 62)	Mexico (n = 179)
Smoked cigarettes[1]	64	28	23	22	26	22	25
Drank alcohol[2]	87	28	34	23	16	33	25
Used marijuana[3]	39	18	21	9	10	14	4
Used cocaine[4]	8	5	2	2	4	5	3
Got drunk or high[5]	76	19	27	18	12	22	7

Table 18. *Comparison between U.S. Average and Female LDS High School Seniors Who Committed Status Offenses, by Percentage*

	Nation (n = 1,321)	Utah County (n = 108)	Castle Dale, UT (n = 54)	East Coast (n = 139)	Pacific Northwest (n = 92)	Great Britain (n = 63)	Mexico (n = 182)
Smoked cigarettes[1]	60	9	20	24	5	45	22
Drank alcohol[2]	87	16	29	25	20	57	22
Used marijuana[3]	31	7	10	9	5	20	2
Used cocaine[4]	5	0	4	2	0	20	1
Got drunk or high[5]	69	9	20	15	13	32	6

1. **LDS** youth were asked: "Have you ever smoked cigarettes?" **National** youth were asked: "Have you ever smoked cigarettes?"
2. **LDS**: "Have you ever drunk alcoholic beverages (beer, wine, liquor)?" **National**: "Have you ever had any beer, wine coolers, or liquor to drink?"
3. **LDS**: "Have you ever used marijuana (grass or pot)?" **National**: "On how many occasions (if any) have you used marijuana (grass, pot) or hashish (hash, hash oil) in your lifetime?"
4. **LDS**: "Have you ever used cocaine (crack or coke)?" **National**: "On how many occasions (if any) have you used cocaine (sometimes called coke, crack rock) in your lifetime?"
5. **LDS**: "Have you ever been drunk or high on drugs?" **National**: "On the occasions that you drink alcoholic beverages, how often do you drink enough to feel pretty high?"

as frequently involved as their peers in fighting at school and in almost all types of property offenses such as shoplifting and petty theft. In hindsight, we wish we had used questions that ask about the frequency of delinquent activities during the last twelve months. This analysis suggests an interesting question: If parents and Church leaders increase their focus on refraining from fighting, shoplifting, and stealing, will fewer LDS youth become involved in these delinquent activities?

RELIGION AND DELINQUENCY

Tables 19 and 20 contain the bivariate (involving two variables) correlations between the six dimensions of religiosity and delinquency for LDS young men and young women. These correlations do not describe a social reality where many forces influence whether a teen engages in a delinquent action. Rather, they identify the relationship of each of the dimensions of religiosity to delinquency if all other things were equal.

It is impressive that every dimension of religiosity except one is significantly related to delinquency for both men and women in all six geographic regions. It is obvious that the most influential aspect of religion in the lives of young people is their commitment to it. Private religious behavior, especially personal prayer, strongly contributes to reducing delinquency. Having spiritual experiences, such as feeling the Holy Ghost guide a decision, give assurance of a path followed, or confirm a truth accepted are also important.

Public religious behaviors, which are defined in this study as attendance at various church meetings, also make a contribution to a testimony and to lower delinquency. Family religious behaviors were also significant predictors of delinquency. The one nonsignificant relationship between a dimension of religion and delinquency was the association between family religious behavior and delinquency among young men in Utah County. Even though the relationship is not significant for this one set of teens, overall the results suggest that parents

Table 19. *Bivariate Correlations for Male LDS High School Students between the Six Measures of Religiosity and Delinquency, by Geographic Region*

	Utah County (n = 411)	Castle Dale, UT (n = 156)	East Coast (n = 619)	Pacific Northwest (n = 227)	Great Britain (n = 152)	Mexico (n = 587)
Religious beliefs	-.314	-.223	-.289	-.206	-.356	.143
Public religious behavior	-.432	-.354	-.248	-.271	-.396	-.184
Private religious behavior	-.503	-.299	-.386	-.339	-.408	-.272
Spiritual experience	-.289	-.314	-.267	-.239	-.311	-.234
Religious commitment	-.461	-.419	-.497	-.369	-.458	-.323
Family religiosity	*	-.206	-.162	-.204	-.204	-.113
Acceptance in church	-.353	-.268	-.259	-.330	-.330	-.246

*Not statistically significant.

Table 20. *Bivariate Correlations for Female LDS High School Students between the Six Measures of Religiosity and Delinquency, by Geographic Region*

	Utah County (n = 543)	Castle Dale, UT (n = 198)	East Coast (n = 738)	Pacific Northwest (n = 343)	Great Britain (n = 219)	Mexico (n = 635)
Religious beliefs	-.342	-.442	-.351	-.301	-.501	-.201
Public religious behavior	-.498	-.407	-.316	-.298	-.411	-.144
Private religious behavior	-.516	-.541	-.449	-.440	-.488	-.246
Spiritual experience	-.352	-.448	-.297	-.247	-.403	-.215
Religious commitment	-.550	-.596	-.527	-.537	-.543	-.388
Family religiosity	-.245	-.298	-.194	-.178	-.367	-.159
Acceptance in church	-.342	-.392	-.291	-.412	-.387	-.285

can reduce their teens' likelihood of delinquency by holding regular family prayer, scripture reading, and family home evening. Finally, feelings of being accepted by peers in the Church as well as by Church leaders and ward members in general are also associated with lower rates of delinquency.

TESTING THE DELINQUENCY MODEL

Testing the multivariate model illustrated in Figure 1 allows the various peer, religious, family, personality, and school factors to shed light on a student's delinquency. The model will identify the relative strengths of each of the factors and show how much of the delinquency is explained by the combination of factors.[1]

Table 21 presents the observed variables included in the Utah County boys and girls models. We present the Utah County results as an example of a measurement model.[2]

Figure 2 shows the model fit indices for delinquency among Utah County boys in the lower right-hand corner. A good fit was found between the observed data and the hypothesized model.[3]

Because of space constraints, we have summarized all of the model fit indices for each model tested for boys and girls in each of the geographical regions (see Table 22). As can be seen, the model fit indices tested show a good fit of the data to the model.

The structural equation model also estimates a structural model that identifies the factors associated with delinquency and their relative strength. Figure 2 presents the structural model for young men in Utah County as an example. As expected, the strongest predictor of delinquency was peer pressure, with a beta of .45. Religiosity was second, with a beta of −.21, followed by peer example (.19).

Interestingly, parental connection has a significant direct effect on delinquency, with a beta of −.13. The betas for religiosity and parental connection are negative, which means the stronger the ties between parent and youth and the stronger the religiosity, the lower the delinquency. In addition, parental

Table 21. Factor Loading and R^2 Values for Latent Variable for Measurement Model
(Utah County Boys' and Girls' Models)

Latent Variables/Scales	Factor		R^2	
	Boys	Girls	Boys	Girls
Delinquency				
Offenses against others	.787	.745	.620	.569
Offenses against property	.777	.809	.603	.654
Status offenses	.660	.697	.435	.485
Religiosity				
Religious belief	.655	.717	.428	.515
Private religiosity	.760	.784	.578	.615
Public religiosity	.533	.663	.284	.440
Religious commitment	.931	.967	.866	.936
Spiritual experiences	.686	.712	.471	.507
Church integration	.529	.582	.280	.339
Peer Pressure				
Offenses against others	.660	.687	.435	.472
Offenses against property	.833	.775	.694	.601
Status offenses	.764	.830	.539	.689
Peer Example				
Offenses against others	.884	.889	.782	.791
Offenses against property	.876	.906	.767	.821
Status offenses	.889	.895	.791	.802
Rebellion				
Rebellion	.988	.980	.975	.960
Risk	.699	.736	.489	.542
Parental Connection				
Father's connection	.854	.737	.730	.542
Mother's connection	.713	.657	.509	.432
Parental Regulation				
Father's regulation	.695	.738	.487	.545
Mother's regulation	.713	.742	.763	.551
Parental Autonomy				
Father's autonomy	.727	.765	.529	.586
Mother's autonomy	.680	.737	.462	.543

Figure 2. *Model of Significant Estimates for Delinquency*
(Utah County Boys)

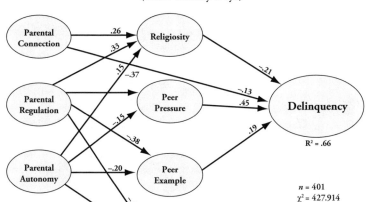

connection, parental regulation, and parental psychological autonomy have strong indirect effects on delinquency. Parental regulation especially has a strong indirect impact on delinquency. It is no surprise that families who set rules, monitor compliance, and discipline where appropriate have teens with lower rates of delinquency. Finally, these six factors account for 66% of the delinquency reported by young men living in Utah County ($R^2 = .66$).

The beta weights from the structural models and the explained variance (R^2) are presented in Table 22 for each to the populations of LDS students. Consistent with past research, the strongest predictor of delinquency in every region for both young men and young women was peer pressure. Because the error terms for peer pressure and delinquency are so highly correlated from asking about the same activities, this strong relationship may be at least partially a result of the questions asked. Regardless, these results tell us that the more peer pressure and association with delinquent friends, the greater the youth's delinquency.

Table 22. Significant Estimates for Predicting Delinquency, by Geographic Region

	Utah County		Castle Dale, UT		East Coast		Pacific Northwest		Great Britain		Mexico	
	Boys (n = 411)	Girls (n = 543)	Boys (n = 156)	Girls (n = 198)	Boys (n = 619)	Girls (n = 738)	Boys (n = 227)	Girls (n = 343)	Boys (n = 152)	Girls (n = 219)	Boys (n = 587)	Girls (n = 635)
Religiosity	-.21	-.27	—	-.26	-.26	-.24	-.27	-.23	-.47	-.33	-.23	-.23
Peer influence	.45	.54	.40	.70	.39	.52	.50	.59	.63	.28	.30	.36
Peer example	.19	—	—	—	.12	.12	—	—	—	.32	.11	—
Rebellion	—	—	—	—	.27	.16	—	.23	—	—	.22	.30
Parental connection	-.13	—	—	—	x	x	—	—	.23	—	—	—
Parental regulation	—	—	—	-.30	x	x	—	—	—	—	—	—
Parental autonomy	—	—	—	—	x	x	—	—	—	—	—	—
Mother's employment	—	—	—	—	—	—	—	—	—	.13	—	.09
R²	.66	.70	.62	.87	.62	.73	.46	.72	.72	.72	.39	.46
χ²	427.9	420.3	353.6	314.9	336.2	326.4	318.6	359.4	327.9	343.2	523.0	376.9
df	200	200	200	200	109	107	204	201	201	201	201	201
TFI	.941	.961	.901	.947	.944	.959	.944	.950	.922	.941	.921	.957
CFI	.957	.972	.928	.961	.960	.971	.959	.964	.943	.957	.942	.969

In contrast, adolescents who were less delinquent had peers who rarely put pressure on them to participate in delinquent acts.

Although not as strong, peer example also significantly predicted delinquency in about half of the models. Having friends who commit delinquent acts influenced delinquency independent of whether or not these friends pressured the youth to do so.

As we confidently predicted to our doubting friends, religiosity also had a strong direct effect on delinquency, even after controlling for peer and family influences. Beta weights for this relationship ranged from $-.21$ to $-.47$, indicating that as religiosity increases, involvement in delinquency decreases. Youth who held strong religious beliefs, participated in public and private religious behavior, had spiritual experiences, placed high importance on religion in their lives, and felt accepted in their Church congregations reported less participation in delinquency (except for the Castle Dale boys).

Other factors that were significant in some models are the personality trait of rebellion and the family characteristics of parental connection, parental regulation, and the mother's employment. A rebellious personality tendency was a significant predictor for both boys and girls living along the East Coast and in Mexico. The family factors emerged as significant only in a few isolated cases. Because some of these factors were strongly correlated to the other significant measures in the model, their influence on delinquency may be limited by or mediated through peer influences, religiosity, and parenting practices. For example, the importance of maternal employment in predicting delinquency may be insignificant as long as parenting practices, such as family connection, parental regulation, and psychological autonomy, are found in the home.

The explained variance (R^2) in delinquency for each of the models is also shown in Table 22. These are very impressive with the lowest variance at .39 (Mexico boys) and the highest at .87 (Castle Dale girls). Among the Castle Dale young women, the model accounts for an amazing 87% of the delinquency.

It was anticipated that the parental practices would have both direct and indirect effects on delinquency. In two of the models (Utah boys and Great Britain boys) parental connection was found to have a significant direct effect. Strangely, one is positive and the other negative.

The negative beta weight found among the Great Britain boys may represent a statistical anomaly because of its high correlation with other variables in the model. In structural equation analysis, this type of outcome happens once in a while and is attributed to a phenomenon known as suppression (Collins & Schmidt, 1997). Parental connection had a negative relationship to delinquency and a positive one in the structural model. This is a good indication of suppression effect. Finally, we found a direct relationship between parental regulation and delinquency among the Castle Dale girls (.30).

More importantly are the strong indirect effects that parents have on delinquency through peer pressure and religiosity (see Table 23). The data for the young men and young women living along the East Coast is missing because this study was the first conducted in our research program, and we used measures of family support and control rather than parental connection, regulation, and autonomy. The splitting of control into regulation and psychological autonomy was discovered by researchers later. Regulation and psychological control are more sophisticated measures of family processes, so we substituted them for the measure of control we had earlier used with East Coast youth.

Family connection, or youth's feelings of closeness with their parents, had a strong positive relationship with religiosity, which in turn was negatively related to delinquency. This outcome was found in every group except Castle Dale youth. Surprisingly, family connection was significantly related to peer pressure among only the Mexican boys and to peer example only among the British girls. Connection was also related to rebellion in several regions.

Table 23. *Significant Estimates of the Indirect Effects of Parental Connection, Regulation, and Autonomy on Delinquency, by Geographic Region*

	Utah County		Castle Dale, UT		East Coast		Pacific Northwest		Great Britain		Mexico	
	Boys	Girls	Boys	Girls	Boys	Girls	Boys	Girls	Boys	Girls	Boys	Girls
Connection												
Religion	.26	.28	—	.27	N/A	N/A	.25	.32	.19	.33	.26	.18
Peer presure	—	—	—	—	N/A	N/A	—	—	—	—	.16	—
Peer example	—	—	—	—	N/A	N/A	—	—	—	-.24	—	—
Rebellion	—	-.19	-.24	-.27	N/A	N/A	-.19	-.22	—	-.30	—	—
Regulation												
Religion	.33	.21	.28	.44	N/A	N/A	.28	.29	.38	.20	.32	.35
Peer pressure	-.37	-.38	-.39	-.36	N/A	N/A	-.44	-.28	-.32	—	-.24	-.24
Peer example	-.38	-.29	—	-.53	N/A	N/A	-.36	-.33	-.32	—	-.19	-.20
Rebellion	-.44	-.27	-.26	-.39	N/A	N/A	-.48	-.38	-.42	-.26	-.38	-.38
Autonomy												
Religion	.15	.22	—	—	N/A	N/A	—	.22	—	—	—	.12
Peer pressure	-.15	-.29	—	—	N/A	N/A	—	-.39	—	-.28	—	-.11
Peer example	-.20	-.25	—	—	N/A	N/A	—	-.23	—	—	—	—
Rebellion	-.30	-.38	-.42	-.17	N/A	N/A	—	-.36	-.36	-.23	-.26	-.20

Parental regulation produced the strongest indirect effects on delinquency through religiosity, peer influences, and rebellion. Compared to the other parenting variables, it is clear that parental regulation has the strongest influence in deterring delinquency through its positive influence on religion and its impact on helping youth resist peer pressure and select less-delinquent friends. The importance of parents setting rules, monitoring compliance, and disciplining when appropriate is fairly obvious (see Table 23). Another interesting finding is that based on the high correlation found between family connection and parental regulation, it seems that families who are highly connected are also more likely to have parents who regulate their children's activities. This relationship may account for the lack of an effect of parental connection on peer influences.

Likewise, parental psychological autonomy had strong indirect effects on delinquency, mainly among youth in Utah County and girls in the Pacific Northwest. For these groups, parental psychological autonomy, like parental regulation, had a strong positive influence on religiosity and a strong negative influence on peer pressure, peer example, and rebellion—all of which predicted delinquency. In other words, parents who allowed their children freedom of thought and expression raised youth who were more religious and less influenced by negative peer influences and rebellious attitudes.

CONCLUSION

The analysis presented in this lengthy chapter provides rather convincing evidence that religion plays a major role in the lives of LDS teenagers, especially in the teens' involvement in delinquency and other antisocial behavior. LDS teens who have stronger religiosity, as indicated by accepting Christian and LDS beliefs, by attending church meetings, by engaging in personal prayer and scripture reading, and by sincerely trying to live their religion engage in significantly less delinquency than do non-LDS teens. Those LDS high school students with the strongest involvement in the Church have the lowest rate of delinquent and immoral behavior.

We found that religion has this powerful influence on LDS youth even within the context of peer pressures and friends setting inappropriate examples. Through the gospel and through Church programs, parents have the means to combat the destructive influence of less-religious, sinful, or immoral friends or associates. The data leaves little doubt that the gospel is a shield against the negative pressures of friends and associates that LDS youth experience in the high school environment.

We were not surprised by the strong support between family and religion in preventing delinquency. The Church's emphasis on family life and parents' responsibility to teach and nurture children in the gospel weaves family and religion together. Those social scientists who argue that parents have little impact on how their teenage children behave away from their parents have missed the direct effects and the powerful indirect impacts of family processes on religiosity and on the ability of teens to withstand negative influence of peers—and ultimately on delinquency. Those families in which parents and teenagers share a loving relationship have the foundation for the family to exercise appropriate regulation of the teens' behavior. Within a warm, supportive relationship, parents and youth can work together to establish family rules and the appropriate discipline for disregarding them. When discipline occurs within a loving relationship, the youth are not alienated from their parents but accept the discipline as a learning experience which was motivated by the parents' love and concern.

The importance of parents encouraging their teenage children to develop their own set of guiding principles (psychological autonomy) is clearly evident in the results. Parents need to foster in their teenage children the internalization of beliefs, opinions, principles, values, and attitudes that are consistent with gospel and societal values. Youth who internalize their own guiding principles become independent young adults.

Finally, we were gratified to discover that the gospel's influence operates within the lives of LDS high school students residing in a variety of religious climates and in different cultures. The same general results emerged across the United States, in Great Britain, and in Mexico. LDS teenagers and LDS families are the same regardless of where they reside. Gospel principles are timeless and apply among all cultures.

All things said, the gospel and a gospel-centered home nurture youth who emerge as competent young adults in whom parents take joy. Religion is clearly a powerful deterrent to delinquency among LDS high school students. In subsequent chapters we will ascertain the gospel's impact on a variety of other behaviors, such as academic achievement and feelings of self-worth.

This chapter was coauthored by Janice Garrett Esplin, who at the time of this research was a graduate student in sociology at BYU. After obtaining a master's degree, Garrett worked for the Research and Evaluation Department of The Church of Jesus Christ of Latter-day Saints.

Notes

1. Structural equation modeling first computes a measurement model to identify measurement error. The measurement model tests the relationship between the specific questions asked of the students and "latent" variables such as religious beliefs or self-esteem, which are based on several questions. The measurement model used confirmatory factor analysis based on twelve questions to test the appropriateness of the observed variables as indicators for the latent variables like offenses against others.

2. An acceptable factor weight is .35, while an acceptable R^2 is .30. The results for Utah County show that according to the factor weights and the R^2s, the observed variables are all strong indicators of the latent variables. This outcome is the case for the boys and girls models in every geographical region. As a side note, because delinquency, peer pressure, and peer example each refer to the same activities (if the teens had performed the activity, if their friends had pressured them, or if their friends engaged in the activity), correlations between the corresponding items' error terms (theta epsilons) were freed in the measurement model to separate item-specific relationships from underlying construct relationships. In spite of the similarity in the questions, three independent scales emerged from the factor analysis.

3. The delinquency model produced a χ^2 of 428 with 200 degrees of freedom mainly due to the large sample size. This high χ^2 raises some concern about the

fit of the data to the model. However, when considering the degrees of freedom, the Comparative Fit Index (CFI) of .957 also indicates an acceptable match between observations and latent variables. Moreover, the model's Tucker-Lewis model fit index (TFI) of .941 indicates a relatively good fit between the data and the model. The root mean square residual (RMSR) of .017 further suggests that the revised model is well designed. All of the different measures of fit taken together indicated a good correspondence between the hypothesized model and the observed data.

REFERENCES

Agnew, R. (1991). The interactive effects of peer variables on delinquency. *Criminology, 29*(1), 47–72.

Akers, R. L. (1998). *Social learning and social structure: A general theory of crime and deviance*. Boston: Northeastern University Press.

Albrecht, S. L, Chadwick, B. A., & Alcorn, D. S. (1977). Religiosity and deviance: Application of an attitude-behavior contingent consistency model. *Journal for the Scientific Study of Religion, 16*(3), 263–274.

Bachman, J. G., Johnston, L. D., & O'Malley, P. M. (1993). *Monitoring the Future: Questionnaire responses from the nation's high school seniors, 1990*. Ann Arbor, MI: University of Michigan.

Bahr, S. J., Marcos, A. C., & Maughan, S. L. (1995). Family, educational, and peer influences on the alcohol use of female and male adolescents. *Journal of Studies on Alcohol, 56*(4), 457–469.

Bahr, S. J., Maughan, S. L., Marcos, A. C., & Li, B. (1998). Family, religiosity, and the risk of adolescent drug use. *Journal of Marriage and Family, 60*(4), 979–992.

Barber, B. K. (1997). Adolescent socialization in context: The role of connection, regulation, and autonomy in the family. *Journal of Adolescent Research, 12*(1), 5–11.

Barber, B. K. (1996). Parental psychological control: Revisiting a neglected construct. *Child Development, 67*(6), 3296–3319.

Barber, B. K., Olsen J. E., & Shagle, S. C. (1994). Associations between parental psychological and behavioral control and youth internalized and externalized behaviors. *Child Development, 65*(4), 1120–1136.

Barber, B. K., & Shagle, S.C. (1992). Adolescent problem behaviors: A social-ecological analysis. *Family Perspective, 26*(4), 493–515.

Barber, B. K., Thomas, D. L., & Proskauer, S. (1997). *Refining parent-child research: Identifying central dimensions and testings for independent and interactive effects.* Manuscript submitted for publication.

Barnes, G. M., & Farrell, M. P. (1992). Parental support and control as predictors of adolescent drinking, delinquency, and related problem behaviors. *Journal of Marriage and Family, 54*(4), 763–776.

Baumrind, D. (1991). The influence of parenting style on adolescent competence and substance use. *Journal of Early Adolescence, 11*(1), 56–95.

Benda, B. B., & Corwyn, R. F. (1997). Religion and delinquency: The relationship after considering family and peer influences. *Journal for the Scientific Study of Religion, 36*(1), 81–92.

Brody, G. H., & Forehand, R. (1993). Prospective associations among family form, family processes, and adolescents' alcohol and drug use. *Behavior Research and Therapy, 31*(6), 587–593.

Brownfield, D., & Sorenson, A. M. (1991). Religion and drug use among adolescents: A social support conceptualization and interpretation. *Deviant Behavior: An Interdisciplinary Journal, 12,* 259–276.

Centers for Disease Control and Prevention. (1995). Youth risk behavior surveillance—United States, 1993. *Morbidity and Mortality Weekly Report 44* (SS-1), 1–58. Retrieved from http://www.cdc.gov/mmwr/PDF/ss/ss4401.pdf.

Chadwick, B. A., & Top, B. L. (1993). Religiosity and delinquency among LDS adolescents. *Journal for the Scientific Study of Religion, 32*(1), 51–67.

Cochran, J. K., & Akers, R. L. (1989). Beyond hellfire: An exploration of the variable effects of religiosity on adolescent marijuana and alcohol use. *Journal of Research in Crime and Delinquency, 26*(3), 198–225.

Cochran, J. K., Wood, P. B., & Arneklev, B. J. (1994). Is the religiosity-delinquency relationship spurious? A test of arousal and social control theories. *Journal of Research in Crime and Delinquency, 31*(1), 92–123.

Collins, J. M., & Schmidt, F. L. (1997). Can suppressor variables enhance criterion-related validity in the personality domain? *Educational and Psychological Measurement, 57*(6), 925–936.

Dishion, T. J., Andrews, D. W., & Crosby, L. (1995). Antisocial boys and their friends in early adolescence: Relationship characteristics, quality, and interactional processes. *Child Development, 66*(1), 139–151.

Dornbusch, S. M., Ritter, P. L., Leiderman, P. H., Roberts, D. E., & Fraleigh, M. J. (1987). The relation of parenting style to adolescent school performance. *Child Development, 58*(5), 1244–1257.

Elliot, D. S., Huizinga, D., & Ageton, S. S. (1985). *Explaining delinquency and drug use.* Beverly Hills, CA: Sage.

Evans, R. C., Levy, L., Sullenberger, T., & Yvas, A. (1991). Self-concept and delinquency: The on-going debate. *Journal of Offender Rehabilitation, 16*(3/4), 59–74.

Finn, J., Stott, M., & Zarichny, K. (1988). School performance of adolescents in juvenile court. *Urban Education, 23*(2), 150–161.

Free, M. D., Jr. (1994). Religiosity, religious conservatism, bonds to school, and juvenile delinquency among three categories of drug users. *Deviant Behavior: An Interdisciplinary Journal, 15*, 151–170.

Gerstein, L. H., & Briggs, J. R. (1993). Psychological and sociological discriminants of violent and nonviolent serous juvenile offenders. *Journal of Addictions and Offender Counseling, 14*(1), 2–13.

Gough, H. G. (1965). *California psychological inventory.* Palo Alto, CA: Consulting Psychologists Press, Inc.

Harris, J. R. (1998). *The nurture assumption.* New York: The Free Press.

Hillman, S. B., Sawilowsky, S. S., & Becker, M. J. (1993). Effects of maternal employment patterns on adolescents' substance use and other risk-taking behaviors. *Journal of Child and Family Studies, 2*(3), 203–219.

Hirschi, T. (1969). *Causes of delinquency.* Berkeley: University of California Press.

Hirschi, T., & Stark, R. (1969). Hellfire and delinquency. *Social Problems, 17*(2), 202–213.

Jarjoura, R. G. (1993). Does dropping out of school enhance delinquent involvement? Results from a large-scale national sample. *Criminology, 31*(2), 149–171.

Johnson, R. E. (1979). *Juvenile delinquency and its origins: An integrated theoretical approach.* Cambridge, MA: Cambridge University Press.

Johnson, V., & Pandina, R. J. (1991). Effects of the family environment on adolescent substance use, delinquency, and coping styles. *American Journal of Drug and Alcohol Abuse, 17*(1), 71–88.

Johnston, L. D., Bachman, J. G., & O'Malley, P. M. (1995). *Monitoring the future: Questionnaire responses from the nation's high school seniors, 1993.* Ann Arbor, MI: Institute for Social Research, University of Michigan, 250, 277.

Krueger, R. F., Schmutte, P. S., Caspi, A., Moffitt, T. E., Campbell, K., & Silva, P. A. (1994). Personality traits are linked to crime among men and women: Evidence from a birth cohort. *Journal of Abnormal Psychology, 103*(2), 328–338.

Kurdek, L. A., & Fine, M. A. (1994). Family acceptance and family control as predictors of adjustment in young adolescents: Linear, curvilinear, or interactive effects? *Child Development, 65*(4), 1137–1146.

Lamborn, S. D., Mounts, N. S., Steinberg, L., & Dornbusch, S. M. (1991). Patterns of competence and adjustment among adolescents from authoritative, authoritarian, indulgent, and neglectful families. *Child Development, 62*(5), 1049–1065.

LeFlore, L. (1988). Delinquent youths and family. *Adolescence, 23*(91), 629–642.

Litchfield, A. W., Thomas, D. L., & Li, B. D. (1997). Dimensions of religiosity as mediators of the relations between parenting and adolescent deviant behavior. *Journal of Adolescent Research, 12*(2), 199–226.

McBride, A. A., Joe, G. W., & Simpson, D. D. (1991). Prediction of long-term alcohol use, drug use, and criminality among inhalant users. *Hispanic Journal of Behavioral Sciences, 13*(3), 315–323.

McCord, J. (1979). Some child-rearing antecedents of criminal behavior in adult men. *Journal of Personality and Social Psychology, 37*(9), 1477–1486.

Nowicki, S., & Strickland, B. R. (1973). A locus of control scale for children. *Journal of Consulting and Clinical Psychology, 40*(1), 148–154.

Ollendick, T. H., Elliott, W., & Matson, J. L. (1980). Locus of control as related to effectiveness in a behavior modification program for juvenile delinquents. *Journal of Behavior Therapy and Experimental Psychiatry, 11*, 259–262.

Orthner, D. K. (1990). Parental work and early adolescence: Issues for research and practice. *Journal of Early Adolescence, 10*(3), 246–259.

Patterson, G. R., & Stouthamer-Loeber, M. (1984). The correlation of family management practices and delinquency. *Child Development, 55*(4), 1299–1307.

Rollins, B. C., & Thomas, D. L. (1979). Parental support, power, and control techniques in the socialization of children. In W. R. Burr, R. Hill, F. I. Nye, & I. L. Reiss (Eds.), *Contemporary Theories about the Family* (Vol. 1). New York: The Free Press.

Rosenberg, M. (1965). *Society and the adolescent self-image.* New Jersey: Princeton University Press.

Rosenberg, F. R., & Rosenberg, M. (1979). Self-esteem and delinquency. *Journal of Youth and Adolescence, 7*(3), 279–291.

Rosenberg, M., Schooler, C., & Schoenbach, C. (1989). Self-esteem and adolescent problems: Modeling reciprocal effects. *American sociological review, 54*(6), 1004–1018.

Rowe, D. C., & Flannery, D. J. (1994). An examination of environmental and trait influences on adolescent delinquency. *Journal of Research in Crime and Delinquency, 31*(4), 374–389.

Schaefer, E. (1965). Children's reports of parental behavior: An inventory. *Child Development, 36*(2), 413–424.

Smith, G. M., & Fogg, C. P. (1979). Psychological antecedents of teenage drug use. *Research in Community and Mental Health: An Annual Compilation of Research, 1*, 87–102.

Steinberg, L. (1987). Single parent, stepparents, and the susceptibility of adolescents to antisocial peer pressure. *Child Development, 58*(1), 269–275.

Steinberg, L., Fletcher, A., & Darling, N. (1994). Parental monitoring and peer influences on adolescent substance use. *Pediatrics, 93*(6), 1060–1064.

Thornberry, T. P., Lizotte, A. J., Krohn, M. D., Farnworth, M., & Jang, S. J. (1994). Delinquent peers, beliefs, and delinquent behavior: A longitudinal test of interactional theory. *Criminology, 32*(1), 47–83.

Tygart, C. E. (1992). Do public schools increase juvenile delinquency? *Urban Education, 26*(4), 359–370.

Warr, M., & Stafford, M. (1991). The influence of delinquent peers: What do they think or what do they do? *Criminology, 29*(4), 851–865.

Wells, L. E., & Rankin, J. H. (1991). Families and delinquency: A meta-analysis of the impact of broken homes. *Social Problems, 38*(1), 71–93.

Wood, P. B., Cochran, J. K., Pfefferbaum, B., & Arneklev, B. J. (1995). Sensation-seeking and delinquent substance use: An extension of learning theory. *Journal of Drug Issues, 25*(1), 173–193.

Four

EDUCATION

Since the earliest days of the Restoration, Church leaders and members alike have placed a high premium on learning—secular as well as spiritual. The revelations of the Lord make it clear that education is necessary both on earth and in eternity. Education is seen as a spiritual pursuit as much as a practical necessity for earthly life.

Education, according to LDS teachings, is not antagonistic to spirituality but is a unique and important aspect of both the doctrinal teachings and the religious life of Latter-day Saints. "The glory of God is intelligence," the Lord declared to the Prophet Joseph Smith in 1833 (Doctrine and Covenants 93:36). Earlier, the Prophet had been directed to establish schools for the education of both children (see Doctrine and Covenants 55:4) and adults (see Doctrine and Covenants 88:127–41). Such schools, whether they were for children or adults, were a unique blend of the secular and the spiritual. The Lord said, "And as all have not faith, seek ye diligently and teach one another words of wisdom; yea, seek ye out of the best books words of wisdom; seek learning, even by study and also by faith" (Doctrine and Covenants 88:118).

For members of the Church, gaining intelligence through study and faith is a religious pursuit, not just an intellectual exercise. Latter-day Saint theology teaches that education affects not just the mind in mortality, but also the spirit and the destiny of the soul beyond this life. "Whatever principle of intelligence we attain unto in this life, it will rise with us in the resurrection. And if a person gains more knowledge and intelligence in this life through his diligence and obedience than another, he will have so much the advantage in the world to come" (Doctrine and Covenants 130:18–19).

Latter-day prophets and apostles continue to counsel members of the Church, young and old, to get as much formal education as they can and to make learning a lifetime pursuit. "We have in the Church a strong tradition regarding quality education," President Gordon B. Hinckley observed (1997). He then further admonished Latter-day Saints: "Get all the education you can. . . . Education is the key to opportunity. The Lord has placed upon you, as members of this Church, the obligation to study and to learn of things spiritual, yes, but of things temporal also. Acquire all the education that you can, even if it means great sacrifice while you are young. You will bless the lives of your children. You will bless the Church because you will reflect honor to this work" (pp. 169, 172).

This chapter explores the influence that religion has on educational attainment and whether LDS teens and young adults with higher religiosity do better in school and further their education more than less-religious members do. In addition, we will ascertain whether higher education challenges faith and results in members drifting into inactivity. In other words, do those members of the Church who have graduated from college, especially those who have completed graduate school or earned professional degrees, have a lower rate of Church activity than do less-educated members?

RELIGIOUS AFFILIATION AND EDUCATION

Early research linking religion and education compared members of different denominations and found that those belonging to fundamentalist denominations such as Pentecostals and Jehovah's Witnesses have less education than members of mainline and liberal denominations. For example, Rhodes and Nam (1970) examined census data for the United States collected in 1965 and found that children with a Jewish mother were the most likely to attend college, followed by children with a mainstream Protestant mother, while children with mothers belonging to fundamentalist denominations were the least likely to attend college.

The most plausible explanation for the more limited education of members in fundamentalist churches is that their doctrine discourages it. Leaders and members alike are convinced that education challenges religious faith, which leads to members reducing the number of years they attend college and perhaps even dropping out. It is assumed that the religious values and doctrine taught by the more fundamentalist denominations are critical of higher education and that fewer of their members continue beyond high school.

Darnell and Sherkat (1997) examined the writings of popular conservative Protestant authors to ascertain if they actually do preach against higher education. They found that conservative ministers do, in fact, oppose "secular" education because it threatens religious beliefs, such as the belief that the Bible is inerrant. Fundamentalists point to the shift from teaching about the creation of the earth under God's hand to teaching evolution devoid of God in public schools as an example of religious beliefs being replaced with secular ones.

The fundamentalist writers, according to Darnell and Sherkat, perceive secular humanist values taught in the public schools as a serious threat to religious beliefs. They found that fundamentalists are especially fearful of higher education because colleges, with their secular humanist orientation, tend to be anti-God and to promote moral relativism.

Darnell and Sherkat (1997) also analyzed data collected from a large national sample of youth to test the relationship between fundamentalist affiliation and educational achievement. Information was obtained from nearly 1,800 high school seniors in 1965 and 1973, and then again in 1982, when they were adults approaching their mid-30s. The researchers discovered that conservative Protestant affiliation and fundamentalist beliefs both had a significant and substantial negative influence on educational attainment.

Sacerdote and Glaeser (2001) analyzed data from the General Social Survey (GSS) from 1972 through 1998. The GSS surveys a random sample of approximately 1,500 adults across the United States every two years. By combining the data from the surveys conducted during this 26-year period, they obtained a large sample of men and women belonging to a wide variety of religious denominations. Unfortunately, they placed the LDS Church with fundamentalist Protestant denominations such as Pentecostals and Jehovah's Witnesses in an "other Protestant" category. The data reveal that members of these "other Protestant" denominations have less education than members of a mainline Protestant church such as the Methodist Church or a liberal Protestant denomination such as the Episcopal Church.

Lehrer (1999) tested a multivariate model predicting educational attainment using data from the large National Survey of Families and Households conducted in 1987–88. She included several factors along with religious denomination in her model to predict educational attainment. She discovered that Jews had the highest education, followed by Catholics and mainline Protestants, while fundamentalist Protestants had the least. Interestingly, Lehrer called for additional study of the "other religious populations," including the LDS Church.

One study looked specifically at the relationship between religion and postsecondary education for men and women. The authors felt the relationship may be different because of traditional sex roles (Keysar & Kosmin, 1995). They hypothesized that religion, due to its influence on the choice between marriage and participation in the labor force, has an indirect effect on women's educational attainment.

According to the researchers, women who belong to conservative religious groups such as Baptist, Evangelical, and Pentecostal churches tend to marry younger and are less likely to work outside the home. Both of these trends reduce higher education. Information was obtained via a telephone survey in 1990 from 19,274 women. The researchers compared the percentage of women from different religious groups who had obtained higher education. They were surprised to learn that as many women belonging to conservative groups had post–high school training—including business school, vocational school, junior college, or college—as women from the liberal denominations. Sixty-one percent of the LDS women had obtained some post–high school education, as compared to 84% of Jewish women, 77% of liberal religions, 77% of Eastern religions, 69% of Episcopalian women, and 67% of Presbyterian women. The women belonging to more conservative religions had married younger and had remained in the home more often.

LDS women had a higher educational level than did conservative Protestants, Pentecostals, Baptists, Lutherans, Catholics, Methodists, and women with no religion. Researchers discovered that religious identification had significant direct and indirect relationships to higher education.

Finally, a more recent study of nearly 3,000 adults in the United States also confirmed that religious affiliation has an effect on educational attainment (Beyerlein, 2004). He found that members of mainline and Evangelical Protestant denominations were 2.5 times more likely to have graduated from college than fundamentalist Protestants and 5 times more likely than Pentecostal Protestants (both very conservative denominations).

In previous studies, the relationship between religion and education in conservative denominations was often assumed to apply to members of the LDS Church, since the studies usually grouped the Church with the conservative denominations. However, revelations revealed in the Doctrine and Covenants, as well as the statements made by prophets discussed earlier in this chapter, make it clear that there is no antieducational bias taught within the LDS Church. Rather, the Church endorses education and encourages its members to pursue as much of it as possible.

LDS EDUCATIONAL ATTAINMENT

Although many non-LDS observers anticipate that members of the LDS Church have less education than members of other churches, such is not the case. Actually, Latter-day Saints have significantly more education than the general public.

Albrecht and Heaton (1984) compared the educational achievement of a large national sample of LDS to that of the general population. They found that 54% of the LDS men had some post–high school education, as compared to 37% for the general population. LDS women's post–high school educational attainment significantly exceeded the national average, at 44% compared to 28% (Albrecht & Heaton, 1984).

More recently, McClendon and Chadwick (2004) compared the educational attainment of men and women who have served missions to that of men and women in U.S. society of the same age. They examined the education of missionaries who had been home from the mission field for 17 years because almost all of this 35- to 44-year-old age-group had completed their formal education. Since returned missionaries are very strong members of this conservative Church, most social scientists would predict they would have significantly less education than the national group of the same age.

*Table 1. Educational Attainment of LDS Returned Missionaries
Compared with National Rates in 1998, by Percentage*

Education Level 1999	Returned Missionaries Ages 35–44			United States Ages 35–44
	Men (n = 453)	Women (n = 308)	Combined (n = 761)	Combined (n = 44,462)
Did not finish high school	0	0	0	15
High school	4	3	4	41
Some college/skill training	26	38	31	18
College	37	45	40	18
Graduate/Professional school	33	14	25	8

Question: "Please circle the highest grade in year of school that you have completed."
Possible answers: "none," "elementary school," "high school," "some college or skill training," "college," "graduate/
professional school"

The study soundly rejects this hypothesis. The educational advantage of the returned missionaries is evident in Table 1. Over 40% of these LDS men and women graduated from college, compared to only 18% of the general population at the same age. An additional 25% of the LDS young adults completed professional school or graduate school, while the national average of such attainment for this age-group is only 8%. These are not trivial differences, and they clearly document that many active members of the LDS Church are highly educated.

Additional evidence of higher LDS educational attainment was obtained by comparing the level of education of fathers and mothers of high school seniors. The Monitoring the Future project collects data from a very large national sample of high school seniors each year. We compared the results from the seniors in this study to the senior students in our samples. The results for fathers' and mothers' education are presented in Tables 2 and 3. The differences are substantial. For example, nearly 30% of the fathers of the LDS young men have a graduate degree, which is more than double the 13.8% for non-LDS fathers of young men.

Interestingly, significantly fewer young women, both LDS and non-LDS, report that their fathers have completed such

Table 2. Educational Level of Fathers of LDS Youth and National Sample of Seniors, by Percentage

	Young Men		Young Women	
Education Level 1999	LDS	National Sample[1]	LDS	National Sample
	(*n* = 326)	(*n* = 7,125)	(*n* = 419)	(*n* = 7,650)
Grade school or less	3.8	3.9	3.1	5.9
Some high school	7.4	11.1	10.7	11.4
High school graduate	8.5	28.8	11.2	30.6
Some college	24.6	18.9	37.2	18.0
College graduate	25.8	23.5	31.6	20.1
Graduate degree	29.9	13.8	6.6	13.9

1. National sample from Johnston, Bockman, & O'Malley (1995), p. 17.
Question for national sample: "What is the highest level of schooling your father completed?"
Question for LDS sample: "How much education did your father complete?"

Table 3. Educational Level of Mothers of LDS Youth and National Sample of Seniors, by Percentage

	Young Men		Young Women	
Education Level 1999	LDS	National Sample[1]	LDS	National Sample
	(*n* = 260)	(*n* = 7,459)	(*n* = 356)	(*n* = 8,061)
Grade school or less	0.4	3.4	0.3	4.4
Some high school	1.9	9.4	1.4	11.9
High school graduate	10.9	34.8	13.3	34.5
Some college	38.1	21.8	43.3	20.7
College graduate	39.7	21.7	34.8	19.6
Graduate degree	8.9	9.3	6.8	8.9

1. National sample from Johnston, Bockman, & O'Malley (1995), p. 17.
Question for national sample: "What is the highest level of schooling your mother completed?"
Question for LDS sample: "How much education did your mother complete?"

degrees. We don't know the reason why sons have different perceptions of their fathers' education than daughters have. In spite of such gender differences, the trend is the same: LDS

Table 4. Grades Received in High School by LDS Youth
and National Sample of Seniors, by Percentage

Grades	Young Men		Young Women	
	LDS	National Sample[1]	LDS	National Sample
	(*n* = 260)	(*n* = 7,398)	(*n* = 356)	(*n* = 8,101)
A	24.6	9.1	33.1	14.3
A–	15.9	10.6	18.1	14.7
B+	15.7	15.8	18.1	19.3
B	16.0	19.3	15.5	20.2
B–	9.1	15.4	5.7	12.7
C+	8.9	14.4	5.6	10.2
C	3.5	9.8	2.8	5.6
C–	3.9	4.0	0.8	2.3
D or below	2.2	1.6	0.3	0.8

1. National sample from Johnston, Bachman, & O'Malley (1995), p. 20.
Question for national sample: "Which of the following best describes your average grade in high school?"
    Possible answers: A, A–, B+, B, B–, C+, C, C–, D or below
Question for the LDS sample: "What grades do you receive in high school?"
    Possible answers: "Mostly A's," "A's and B's," "Mostly B's," "B's and C's," "Mostly C's," "C's and D's," "Mostly D's," "D's and F's"

fathers have significantly more education than do the fathers of non-LDS high school seniors in this national sample.

The educational differences are not as large for mothers of the high school seniors. Nevertheless, significantly more LDS mothers had some college or had graduated from college than the other mothers. But the percentages who had completed graduate or professional degrees actually favor the national sample a little. Perhaps, as Keysar and Kosmin (1995) suggested, the LDS emphasis on women's roles of wife and mother reduced the number of LDS women who pursued graduate degrees.

Comparing the grades earned by LDS high school seniors to those of non-LDS high school seniors provides insight into the relationship between religious affiliation and educational performance of students. Both the LDS young men and young

Table 5. Hours of Homework Each Week for LDS Youth and National Sample of Seniors, by Percentage

Hours per Week	Young Men		Young Women	
	LDS	National Sample[1]	LDS	National Sample
	(*n* = 260)	(*n* = 804)	(*n* = 356)	(*n* = 931)
0	9.8	15.5	4.1	5.6
1–4	0.0	47.8	0.0	45.1
5–9	49.6	20.3	36.8	24.2
10–14	22.6	6.1	33.6	12.7
15–19	10.2	4.5	15.7	5.7
20–24	3.8	3.2	3.1	3.4
25 or more	4.0	2.6	6.7	3.4

1. National sample from Johnston, Bachman, & O'Malley (1995), p.126.
Question for national sample: "About how many hours do you spend on the average week on all of your homework, including both in school and out of school?"
Question for LDS sample: "About how many hours do you spend on school work outside of class each day?"

women who were seniors in high school reported significantly higher grades than did non-LDS seniors. Twice as many LDS young men as non-LDS students claimed they earned As as did non-LDS students, and the difference was almost as large for the young women. An examination of the table reveals that LDS students are more clustered at the higher end of the GPA scale than students in the national sample.

Students in the national sample were asked how many hours of homework they do each week. We asked in our study how many hours they do each day. To make the data comparable, we multiplied the replies of the LDS students by 5. We used 5 days rather than 7 to calculate a conservative estimate of hours of homework completed each week. Because of this multiplication, the 1–4 hours category for the LDS students is blank. Nevertheless, the overall trend is that LDS seniors spend more time doing homework than do their national peers. The difference appears among both the young men and the young women.

Table 6. Feelings about School as reported by LDS Youth and National Sample of Seniors, by Percentage

Feeling about School	Young Men		Young Women	
	LDS	National Sample[1]	LDS	National Sample
	(*n* = 360)	(*n* = 1,267)	(*n* = 356)	(*n* = 1,340)
I like it very much	28.1	12.5	32.0	10.3
I like it some	41.1	27.7	38.8	28.6
Mixed feelings	23.5	42.7	23.6	45.7
I dislike it	5.0	10.6	4.8	11.4
I dislike it very much	2.3	6.5	0.8	4.0

1. National sample from Johnston, Bachman, & O'Malley (1995), p. 96.
Question for national sample: "Some people like school very much, others don't. How do you feel about going to school?
   Possible answers: "like very much," "like quite a lot," "like some," "don't like very much," "don't like school at all"
Question for LDS sample: "Some people like going to school very much while others don't. How do you feel about going to school?"
   Possible answers: "like very much," "like some," "mixed feelings," "dislike very much"

Table 7. Post–High School Educational Expectations of LDS Youth and National Sample of Seniors, by Percentage*

Educational Level	Young Men		Young Women	
	LDS	National Sample[1]	LDS	National Sample
	(*n* = 260)	(*n* = 7,708)	(*n* = 356)	(*n* = 8,310)
Technical/Vocational school	3.5	8.7	2.0	7.5
Two-year college	7.7	14.2	7.0	18.4
Four-year college	27.7	47.8	60.4	36.7
Graduate/Professional school	57.7	15.7	28.9	21.9

* Total percentages do not add up to 100 because some planned on military service and entering the work force.
1. National sample from Johnston, Bachman, & O'Malley (1995), p. 96.
Question for national sample: "How likely is it that you will do each of the following after high school?"
   Possible answers: "attend a technical or vocational school," "graduate from a two-year college," "graduate from college,"
   "attend graduate or professional school after college"
Question for LDS sample: "What are your educational expectations?"
   Possible answers: "not finish high school," "only finish high school," "trade or vocational school," "some college,"
   "graduate from college," "advanced degree after college"

One of the major reasons students drop out of high school or limit their education is because they have developed a dislike for school and academics. The feelings about school reported by students in the two samples are presented in Table 6.

The middle of the five response categories used in the two studies was a little different in the two samples. We used "mixed feelings," while the national sample had "I like school some." The other categories were the same, or very similar, and reveal that significantly more LDS seniors, both young men and young women, like school "very much." Over 28% of the LDS boys like school "very much," as compared to only 13% of the national sample of boys. The percentage for young women is 32% for LDS and only 10% for the national sample.

The reverse pattern appears for the other extreme category of "disliking school very much." In other words, more non-LDS students were turned off by school. Even though the data are not exactly parallel, the trend of LDS students liking school is readily apparent. Such feelings probably motivate more LDS youth to complete high school and to seek post–high school training.

The influence of LDS teachings about and support for education is evident in the educational expectations of the youth. It is amazing that over half of the LDS young men who are seniors in high school expect to obtain a graduate or professional degree (see Table 7). These young men expect to complete a master's degree or PhD or to attend professional school and become a doctor, dentist, accountant, business manager, or lawyer. This compares to only 15% of the national sample. This is a dramatic difference!

Interestingly, the differences are not nearly as large for the young women. LDS young women in the last year of high school do expect to obtain a little more education than their national peers, but the gap is not nearly as large as it is for the young men. Significantly more LDS young women than non-LDS young women plan on a college degree, but the difference is smaller for young women than for young men. This may be due in part to the Church's emphasis on men being the primary provider for the family.

It is clear that LDS doctrine strongly encourages the pursuit of knowledge, both secular and sacred. Church leaders encourage young people to stay in school and to seek higher education. In addition, leaders invite members to make learning a lifelong adventure. The data demonstrates that members of the LDS Church are educated beyond their national peers. The higher education of LDS people is obtained in spite of the supposedly conservative nature of their doctrine.

INDIVIDUAL RELIGIOSITY AND EDUCATION

Although the educational differences between members of various denominations are substantial, they may be the consequence of factors other than religious beliefs and values. Some researchers have pointed out that social class and minority culture greatly impact educational attainment. They go on to suggest that members of fundamentalist churches tend to be from the lower classes and from minority populations. Thus, social class and race rather than religious affiliation may account for their lower educational attainment. One strategy to eliminate these class and ethnic factors as explanations of educational attainment is to focus on the relationship between individual religiosity and educational attainment within a single denomination.

A number of studies examine the association between personal religiosity and educational aspirations and attainment. Dai (1996) examined data collected in 1989 from the Monitoring the Future study. The major focus of the analysis was on the links between race, political orientation, and educational plans after high school. He found that religious involvement was also related to strong aspirations for higher education among members of different races and among those with divergent political orientations.

Trusty and Watts (1999) studied 13,000 high school seniors who had been surveyed in 1988 and then again in 1992. They found seniors who reported that religion was important in their lives had a more positive attitude toward school, fewer attendance problems, spent more time on homework, and received better grades than did seniors for whom religion was not important.

Jeynes (1999) analyzed data from the same large sample of students and identified a religious work ethic among religious black and Hispanic students, which fostered higher academic achievement. He also noted that religious youth engaged significantly less in risky behavior that endangers academic performance. These effects were observed even after he controlled for the influence of social class, sex, and whether the students attended a private or public school.

Regnerus and Elder (2001) suggest an alternative explanation of the religiosity-education link. They hypothesize that social capital provided by membership and activity in a church leads to stronger academic achievement. They argue that activity in a church provides a youth with positive role models who help with homework, provide encouragement, and give guidance on how to deal with teachers. All of these are considered "social capital" by the researchers. They found among a national sample of 13,500 high school students that the church functions as a stable community for youth living in an "otherwise disorganized world." Activity in a church provided social and emotional support, which in turn kept youth from engaging in risky behavior. In their view, it is the social capital component of religious activity, rather than the spiritual component, that fosters education.

Muller and Ellison (2001) used the same study as Jaynes (1999) and Trusty and Watts (1999) to test this social capital model and found that activity in a church was related to higher academic performance. Importantly, they also found that even after the effects of social capital have been removed, personal religious involvement remained modestly linked with desired school behaviors. They attribute this residual impact to spiritual or psychological benefits derived from religious activity. Thus, in their study, both the social and spiritual components of church membership were found to be related to academic achievement.

Finally, Loury (2004) examined data collected from a sample of youth in 1979 and then fourteen years later in 1993. She found a relationship between church activity as a teenager and educational attainment in later life. Those individuals who were active in their church when they were teenagers had obtained more education than had those who were less active. However, she attributes most of the difference in education to parents rather than to church activity. She argues that parents of religious youth are different from other parents in that they more vigorously encourage their children to do well in school. After analysis of the data, she concludes that religious activity includes both family and religious influences, and both contribute to performance in school.

EDUCATIONAL ACHIEVEMENT OF LDS YOUTH

In light of all this research, the important question is if active LDS students do better in school than less-active members and if active LDS adults have more education than less-active peers in the Church. Albrecht and Heaton (1984) provided an initial answer to this question. They collected data from 3,500 LDS adults living in the United States and found a positive link between religious activity and education. They rejected the social capital model for their sample of adults, as religion had a stronger relationship with education than it did with income or occupational success.

The same data suggested that the Church's policy of a lay ministry contributes to the link between religiosity and education. It may be that educated members are more likely to be called to leadership positions in the Church and that leaders have spiritual experiences that maintain, or most likely strengthen, their religiosity. Whatever the reasons, they found that active LDS people had higher educational attainment than did those who were less active in the Church.

We have collected information from LDS teens and young adults of different ages, which allows us to follow the relationship between religiosity and education.

RELIGIOSITY AND ACADEMIC ASPIRATIONS OF HIGH SCHOOL STUDENTS

To test the religion-education link, we analyzed data from LDS high school students to ascertain the relationship between religiosity and educational performance and aspirations. In Appendix A, we describe the large sample of LDS high school students selected from four different regions in the United States and from Great Britain and Mexico.

We first computed bivariate correlations between the various dimensions of religiosity and educational aspirations. *Educational aspirations* combined the responses to three questions. The first question was "Some people like school very much, while others don't. How do you feel about going to school?" The five responses ranged from "I like school very much" to "I dislike school very much."

The second question was "How important is it to you to get good grades in school?" The five response categories varied from "Extremely important" to "Not important."

The third question was "What are your educational expectations?" The six response categories ranged from "I don't expect to finish high school" to "I expect to get an advanced degree after graduation from college."[1]

The questions used to create the six *dimensions of religiosity* are described in detail in Appendix B. Bivariate correlations shown in Tables 8 and 9 demonstrate the relationship between religiosity and educational plans when all other factors are ignored. Obviously other factors such as peer pressure and the father's education are important, but it is informative to determine the relationship between religiosity and educational

Table 8. Bivariate Correlations between Seven Dimensions of Religiosity and Educational Aspiration for Male LDS High School Students, by Region

	Utah County (n = 417)	Castle Dale, UT (n = 152)	East Coast (n = 576)	Pacific Northwest (n = 225)	Great Britain (n = 128)	Mexico (n = 587)
Belief	.280	.309	.258	.164	.182	.206
Public	.293	.416	.253	.116	.201	.261
Private	.491	.368	.275	.205	.266	.276
Spiritual experience	.507	.344	.393	.322	.276	.313
Acceptance in church	.269	.373	.278	.254	.272	.230
Family religious behavior	.127	.276	.120	NS	.256	.176

Table 9. Bivariate Correlations between Seven Dimensions of Religiosity and Educational Aspiration for Female LDS High School Students, by Region

	Utah County (n = 555)	Castle Dale, UT (n = 192)	East Coast (n = 700)	Pacific Northwest (n = 328)	Great Britain (n = 167)	Mexico (n = 628)
Belief	.295	.262	.272	.180	.339	.089
Public	.367	.197	.256	.147	.275	.149
Private	.359	.220	.332	.288	.354	.269
Spiritual experience	.415	.255	.362	.288	.384	.215
Acceptance in church	.269	.195	.256	.256	.334	.191
Family religious behavior	.141	.164	.117	NS	.244	.127

aspirations, with all other things held constant. Frankly, we were surprised at the magnitude of the correlations for both young men and young women. Thirty-six correlations are reported in each table, and all but one for men and one for women were statistically significant.

For some reason, family religiosity was not related to education among either the boys or the girls living in the Pacific Northwest. Family religiosity had the weakest relationship to education, perhaps because it is not a direct measure of the students' personal religious beliefs and behaviors.

Spiritual experiences and private religiosity produced higher correlations with education than did the other dimensions. The correlation between spiritual experiences and educational aspirations produced by the young men in Utah County is remarkable. The strength of spiritual experiences and private religious behaviors to predict education is similar to the superior ability to predict delinquency by the lack of religiosity, as was discussed in Chapter 3. Personal religious commitment, as evidenced by private religious behavior and by spiritual

Figure 1. Model of Significant Estimates
of Educational Aspirations

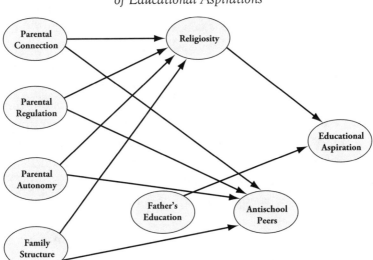

experiences, has a greater impact in the youth's daily life than more public religious activities.

These rather sizable correlations reveal that the six dimensions of religiosity are strongly related to the educational performance and plans of LDS teenagers. Religious parents, a religious work ethic, the Church's doctrine concerning education, and social capital provided by Church participation all combine to significantly enhance the education of LDS high school students.[2]

Sociology has produced several rather sophisticated models of how young people gain entrance into class structure. Interestingly, religion is rarely included in these models, and when it is, it usually identifies only the young adult's religious denomination.

Figure 1 identifies the seven factors included in our model to explain educational aspirations. *Antischool peers* combined the responses to four questions about how friends engaged in disruptive and disrespectful behavior at school. The behaviors included "Purposely damaged or destroyed things at school," "Openly defied a teacher or official at school," "Skipped school without a legitimate excuse," and "Been suspended or expelled from school."[3] It was anticipated that antischool friends would place powerful peer pressure on the LDS teens to engage in similar behavior, which would most likely interfere with school performance.

Religiosity combined the students' responses to the six dimensions of beliefs, public and private behaviors, spiritual experiences, acceptance in Church, and family religious practices. We expected religiosity to predict educational aspirations.

Parental connection, parental regulation, and *parents granting psychological autonomy* were also included in the model. The items used to create these scales are reported in Appendix B. Such parental behaviors were expected to contribute to educational performance.

Family structure determined if the teens lived in a home with two parents or only one. The question we asked was:

"Who do you live with?" The responses included "Mother and father," "Mother and stepfather," "Father and stepmother," "Mother alone," "Father alone," and "Other." Two-parent homes included stepfathers and stepmothers. Single-parent families in this study had been created mostly by divorce, but a few were the result of the death of a mother or father. We anticipated that high school students living with two parents would do better in high school and would desire more higher education than those raised by a single parent.

Research on status attainment in American society has identified the fathers' education as a powerful factor in the educational and occupational accomplishments of their children. We asked the students: "How much education did your father (mother) complete?" See Tables 2 and 3 for the distribution of responses from men and women to this question. The responses ranged from "Grade school (grades 1–6)" to "Advanced degree (master's, PhD, or doctor)." We anticipated that fathers' and

Figure 2. Model of Significant Estimates for Educational Aspirations (Utah County Boys)

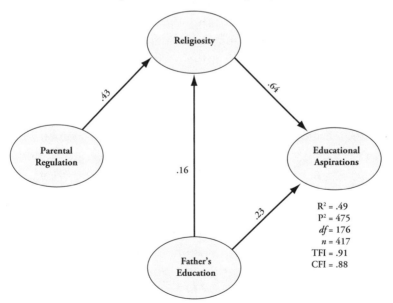

Figure 3. *Model of Significant Estimates for Educational*
Aspirations (Utah County Girls)

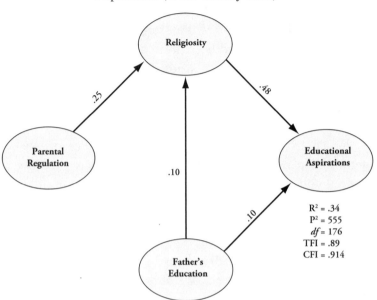

mothers' education would make a positive contribution to educational desires among LDS high school students.

The initial model included the mothers' education and maternal employment, but the bivariate analysis and the initial modeling made it clear that these two variables were not significant, and they were deleted.

The model for the young men living in Utah County reasonably fit the data (see Figure 2). The range and meaning of these indicators are discussed in the previous chapter. The findings surprised us. First, only two factors emerged from the competition to explain educational aspirations. The strength of the relationship between religiosity and education is truly amazing. The only other factor to contribute was the fathers' education. These two factors combined to explain nearly half of the variation in educational aspirations among these young men. It should be noted that parental regulation and the fathers' education both made a significant indirect contribution to

Table 10. *Summary of Structural Equation Modeling Linking Religiosity to Educational Aspirations among Male LDS High School Students*

Dimensions of Religiosity	Utah County (n = 417)	Castle Dale, UT (n = 152)	East Coast (n = 576)	Pacific Northwest (n = 225)	Great Britain (n = 128)	Mexico (n = 587)
Religiosity	.635	.268	.435	.277	*	.437
Antischool peers	*	*	-.221	*	-.363	*
Family connection	*	.523	**	.278	*	*
Family regulation	*	*	**	*	*	*
Family autonomy	*	*	**	*	*	*
Father's education	.226	.179	.303	.188	.217	*
Two–parent family	*	*	*	*	*	*
R²	.494	.634	.390	.285	.314	.379
χ²	475	279	288	230	239	299
df	178	176	90	176	145	162
TLK	.878	.890	.899	.953	.903	.943
CFI	.906	.916	.924	.964	.926	.956

* Not significant.
** No data.

understanding education through religiosity. We were very surprised to see that peer pressure to misbehave in school was not significant.

Figure 3 demonstrates that the same factors that influenced the boys emerged as significant predictors for the young women in Utah County. Religiosity was the strongest factor, which combined with the fathers' education to account for a strong contribution to the girls' educational aspirations.

Table 10 presents summary data for the models, predicting educational aspirations among young men in all six geographical regions. The young men living in Great Britain were the only group among which religiosity did not emerge as a significant predictor. We don't have any explanation for this finding other than the fact that British society is very secular, and religion has a tough time having much influence. Also, the British educational system is more structured than it is in the United States, and religion may be limited in the influence it exerts.

Among the other five samples, religiosity made a very strong contribution. Overall, the results support the hypothesis that individual religiosity is a powerful predictor of educational achievement among LDS male high school students.

The fathers' education proved an influential factor in all of the models except for the boys living in Mexico. The British young men fit the more traditional model of adolescent behavior, in which peer pressures dominate. Peers were important to the boys living along the East Coast, but their influence was not nearly as strong as that of religiosity.

Another surprise finding was the association of family connection with educational aspirations among young men living in rural Castle Dale, Utah. Those boys who felt close to their parents had much stronger desires for education than those boys who felt their parents were less interested in them. While these unique findings are interesting, they do not detract from the importance of the influence of religiosity on educational aspirations among LDS high school students.

Table 11. *Summary of Structural Equation Modeling Linking Religiosity to Educational Aspirations among Female LDS High School Students*

Dimensions of Religiosity	Utah County (n = 555)	Castle Dale, UT (n = 192)	East Coast (n = 700)	Pacific Northwest (n = 328)	Great Britain (n = 167)	Mexico (n = 628)
Religiosity	.479	.293	.436	.292	.425	.435
Antischool peers	*	*	-.173	*	*	*
Family connection	*	*	**	.294	.337	**
Family regulation	*	*	**	*	*	.254
Family autonomy	*	*	**	*	*	*
Father's education	.099	.146	.144	.146	*	*
Two-parent family	*	*	*	*	*	*
R^2	.349	.189	.304	.294	.406	.269
χ^2	555	310	233	371	307	352
df	178	176	90	176	176	162
TLK	.889	.889	.941	.891	.889	.927
CFI	.914	.915	.956	.917	.911	.944

* Not significant.
** No data.

The results for the young women living in the different regions are presented in Table 11. The model fit the data nicely for all six samples. Among the young women, religiosity was the strongest factor predicting educational aspirations for all six samples. Interestingly, the fathers' education emerged as a significant factor among the four samples in the United States, but not in the British or Mexican samples. Perhaps the importance of the fathers' education for daughters is culturally determined and is more important in the United States.

Family connection had a strong direct effect among the girls in the Pacific Northwest and Great Britain. Teens with involved parents desired more education than those teens with more distant parents.

An important finding is that in none of the samples of either men or women did family structure make a contribution. These results indicate that single parents are able to foster educational desires in their children as strong as those found in teens living with two parents.

In summary, the strength of individual religiosity in comparison to family and peer influences in predicting educational aspirations is remarkable. In all six regions, among both men and women, religiosity was associated with doing better in school and desiring a higher education. It seems that religious values that encourage education are one reason for this strong association. Other reasons are a religious work ethic, social capital obtained by church activity, and religious students' tendency to engage in less risky behavior.

ACADEMIC ACHIEVEMENT OF LDS COLLEGE STUDENTS

College is a time when young adults, away from the steadying influence of their parents and other significant adults, struggle with their religious beliefs. They must decide if they still believe in God and whether or not they will attend religious services, pray, and read their scriptures.

In addition, liberal and secular ideas in the classroom challenge the students' religious beliefs. Media attention to the recreational activities of some college students, such as hanging out and hooking up (casual sex), keg parties, and recreational drug use add to the belief that college students are fairly nonreligious.

Astin and Astin (2004) are coprincipal investigators of a national study of the Spiritual Development of American College Students. The study is being conducted by the Higher Education Research Institute at the University of California, Los Angeles, and funded by the Templeton Foundation. The initial survey, interviewing 3,680 freshmen attending 46 colleges and universities across the country, was conducted in the fall of 2000, and a follow-up survey was obtained in the spring of 2003. The final follow-up took place in the fall of 2004. Several reports from this study have been posted on the project's Web site, www.spirituality.ucla.edu. Analysis has not been completed, but tentative findings have been reported for the 2000 to 2003 period, in which the students were followed from their freshman through their junior years.

We compared the information about the religiosity of this sample of college students across the country to data we collected from BYU students at both the Provo and Idaho campuses. We conducted a study of dating and courtship among BYU students attending both of these campuses. The details are presented in Appendix A. We included in the mail survey several questions about educational goals and aspirations, peer and family pressures to do well in college, and religious beliefs and activities. Thus, we are able to test a model in which religiosity competes with family characteristics, peer pressures, and family pressures to explain educational performance and aspirations.

The major limitation with this analysis is that all of the BYU students have rather high religiosity. A lack of variation in religiosity limits its ability to predict education. In order to provide insights about the religiosity of BYU students, their religious beliefs and activities were compared to the findings from the national study.

The strong religious behavior found among non-LDS students in the national study surprised the researchers. Seventy percent of the students in the national study had attended church services the previous year, and 52% had attended regularly. The authors of the national study indicated that the level of religiosity was higher at Evangelical colleges affiliated with Baptist and Church of Christ denominations. They did not report the beliefs and activity of students attending Evangelical colleges, but we are very confident that the church attendance of the BYU students is significantly higher than even this group of students. Our data showed that 95% of the BYU students attended sacrament meeting every week, and another 4% attended three or four times a month.

Over three-fourths (77%) of the students in the national study reported that they pray. The researchers did not ask how often the students prayed but just if they did so. Over 99% of the BYU students said they prayed. A large majority (78%) of the BYU students said they pray every day, and another 16% pray several times a week.

Table 12. Bivariate Correlations between Five Dimensions of Religiosity and Three Academic Factors or Attitudes among Students Attending BYU and BYU–Idaho

College experience	Religious beliefs	Public behavior	Private behavior	Spiritual experience	Acceptance in congregation	Total religiosity
	(n = 2,372)	(n = 2,374)	(n = 2,371)	(n = 2,356)	(n = 2,370)	
Satisfaction with college	.076	.165	.237	.192	.242	.108
Cumulative GPA	.145	.126	.192	.111	.086	.131
Educational expectations	*	*	.054	*	*	*

*Not significant.

Finally, 74% of the students in the national study reported that their religious or spiritual beliefs had provided them with strength, support, and guidance. It is encouraging that over three-fourths of the college students across this country derive strength and comfort from the Spirit. In comparison, all of the BYU students "strongly agreed" that they have felt the Spirit guide or comfort them. As stated, those conducting the national study were impressed with the level of religiosity of college students, especially those attending Evangelical colleges.

It is also important to ascertain the relationship between the religiosity of college students and their academic performance. In a limited study of 251 students, Zern (1989) found that belief in God, self-perception of righteousness, and "ritual" observances such as baptisms and religious holidays were not related to grade point average. However, when he controlled for the students' religiousness during their youth, he found that those who had become more religious had significantly higher GPAs than did the rest of the sample.

Astin and Astin (2004) found that high school grades were the strongest predictor of a student's college grade point average. In addition, students who worked or who partied a lot in high school had lower-than-average grades. Nevertheless, spiritual/religious factors affect academic performance in college (Astin & Astin, 2004). Students who read sacred texts and other religious materials, who went to church, and who engaged in religious singing had higher-than-expected grades. In addition, religious students were more satisfied with their college experience, had stronger self-esteem, lower psychological distress, and higher self-rated physical health.

The bivariate correlations between the five dimensions of religiosity and three measures of school performance among BYU students are presented in Table 12. Family religiosity was deleted from the questionnaire because most BYU students live away from home. The correlations in the table are fairly modest, probably because there is so little variation in religiosity among

BYU students. Even so, private religious behavior (personal prayer, scripture reading, and fasting) is significantly related to positive feelings about college, a high cumulative GPA, and ambitious educational aspirations. The other four dimensions of religiosity produced significant correlations with both satisfaction and GPA. For some reason, educational expectations are more independent of religiosity.

EDUCATION AND ENDURING RELIGIOSITY

As discussed at length above, research has demonstrated the positive impact of religion on educational attainment. However, a reverse relationship—that education erodes religious beliefs and practices—is also plausible.

Secularization, or the increase of worldliness, is used by members of conservative denominations to justify fear of advanced secular education. The significant question is whether or not advanced education influences members of the LDS Church to replace their religious beliefs with scientific beliefs and, in turn, to decrease their religious involvement. Do reason and rationality replace faith and activity among educated members of the Church? The logic is so pervasive that a "secularization hypothesis" has been widely accepted by both social scientists and the general public. A recent article complained that social scientists "have long ceased troubling themselves with exclusive investigations of the relationship between formal education and religious belief. . . . They could simply assume as a matter of course that formal education induces a weakening of faith" (Johnson, 1997, p. 231).

COLLEGE STUDENTS

Many observers, religious leaders, and members of the general public assume that the college experience leads to secularization. College allows freedom from family, so that teens who went to church to please Mom and Dad can now stay away. In addition, students are exposed to secular ideas in many of the classes they attend.

An early study tracked college students from 1948 to 1974 and concluded that college attendance was associated with a shift from orthodox religious beliefs to more liberal and humanistic viewpoints and was also associated with a decline in church attendance up to 1967 (Hastings & Hoge, 1976). The authors caution that the decline in religiosity they observed may be the consequence of the political and social alienation that occurred in the 1960s, rather than the college experience alone. Additional analysis convinced them that the age when religious views are formed had shifted down from college to the high school, and that after the mid-1960s college students' religiosity remained fairly constant. According to them, any shifts in belief and activity had already taken place in high school.

On the other hand, Johnson (1997) examined the national General Social Survey (GSS) study for the years 1988 through 1993. He found that each year of schooling beyond high school decreased belief in God among the young people in the study.

The national study of college students (Astin & Astin, 2004) found that 52% of the freshmen regularly attended religious services prior to attending college, and that the percentage had declined to 29% by their junior year. It is unfortunate that the study does not have information about the frequency of attendance during the students' freshman year. It may be that most of this decline in attendance occurred when the students left home and entered college.

We do not have data from BYU students, but we did compare the attendance and personal prayer of freshman students to that of juniors. Ninety-four percent of both freshman and juniors reported weekly attendance at Church. A few more juniors than freshmen revealed they prayed daily, at 78% versus 74%. Obviously, exposure to BYU had not decreased religious activity. One probable reason there was no decrease in religiosity between freshmen and juniors at BYU is that many of the latter, especially the young men, are returned missionaries.

Self-reported spirituality also declined among the students in the national sample during their first three years of college. Twenty percent of the students claimed to be more spiritual in 2003 as compared to 2000, while 36% acknowledged their spirituality was lower (Astin and Astin, 2004). There was a loss in the spirituality of this sample of college students during the three-year period.

We did not ask the same question, but instead used responses to the question: "I have a strong testimony of the gospel," to represent spirituality. Just over 80% of the freshmen at BYU "strongly agreed" with this statement, as compared to 86% of the juniors. Again, the juniors' religiosity is actually stronger than that of freshman. Attendance at BYU certainly was not associated with a decline in religiosity.

Interestingly, 39% of the students in the national sample reported that their religious or spiritual beliefs were strengthened by "new ideas encountered in class" (Bonderud and Fleischer, 2003). Over half, at 53%, felt their classroom experience had no impact on their religiosity, and only 8% reported that exposure to secular ideas and theories in the classroom reduced their religiosity. This should calm some of the fear among conservative denominations about the consequences of secular education. We did not ask any questions about the impact of classroom material, but given that religiosity did not decline between freshmen and juniors, it seems that what is taught in the BYU classrooms did not threaten religiosity.

We tested the relationship between education and religion by computing the bivariate correlations between three measures of educational attitudes and five dimensions of religiosity. The relationships between satisfaction with college, cumulative grade point average, educational expectations, and the measures of religiosity are presented in Table 12.

If college education secularizes students, then the correlations between college experience and religion should be negative which means that as education increased, religiosity declined. However, the opposite is the case. All of the significant correlations are positive, which argues that for BYU students, success in college and desire for more education are associated with stronger religiosity. Only private religious behavior has a positive relationship to educational expectations. But importantly, none of the correlations support the notion of college reducing religiosity.

As stated earlier, it is difficult to rigorously test the secularization hypothesis among BYU students because all of the students have such strong beliefs and high level of Church activity. The comparison of religious attitudes and behavior between the students in the national sample and BYU students also reveal the extremely high religiosity of BYU students. But all the analysis we were able to conduct not only refuted the secularization hypothesis but also indicated that attendance at BYU strengthened religiosity.

Young Adults

The analysis of the educational achievement of young adults provides potential evidence about the secularizing effect of a college education. Men and women in their middle and late thirties have finished their education, and it has had time to work its effect on their religiosity. We have two different groups of LDS young adults whose educational attainment can be studied. We collected data in 1994 from a sample of 6,000 men who had served missions for the Church. One-fourth of the subjects (1,500) had been home from their missions one year, one-fourth had been home 5 years, one-fourth had been home 10 years, and the final one-fourth had been home for 17 years. We also surveyed a sample of 4,000 young women who had been home the same number of years.

Two years later we conducted a companion study of LDS young men and women who had not served a mission. They

Table 13. *Bivariate Correlation between Family, Friends, and Religiosity and Educational Attainment for Adult LDS Men and Women*

Family/Religiosity/Peers	Men		Women	
	Returned Missionaries	Non-Missionaries	Returned Missionaries	Non-Missionaries
	(*n* = 1,874)	(*n* = 336)	(*n* = 1,341)	(*n* = 540)
High school years				
High school grades	.301	.364	.333	.383
Father's education	.130	.292	.215	.275
Family connection	*	*	*	.108
Family regulation	.053	.194	.121	.175
Family autonomy	.079	*	.097	.150
Religiosity	.092	*	.112	.249
Post-mission/college				
Friends attending college	.219	**	.244	**
Religiosity	.119	.185	*	.177
Current				
Marital status (single)	*	*	*	.109
Religiosity	.080	.113	*	.141
Public	.075	*	*	.124
Private	.051	.133	*	.101

* Not significant.
** No data.

were in the same four age categories as the missionaries. A high proportion of the men in the study refused to participate, as they argued they were no longer affiliated with the Church. Not serving a mission was part of their separation from the Church, which in many cases had started when they were much younger. Young women have no obligation to serve a mission, and those who do not serve are treated much differently than are young men who do not go on missions. This difference was evident in that we obtained a much higher response from women than from men. Details of the data collection for both studies are presented in Appendix A.

The educational attainment of the returned missionaries is compared to a national sample in Table 1. The educational accomplishment of the members of the Church is remarkable. The bivariate correlations between educational achievement, family, peer, and religious factors are presented in Table 13. Some family, peer, and religious factors are from when the young adults were in high school. Others are from the first couple of years after the missionaries returned from their missions. For the non-missionaries, the factors refer to when they were finishing college. Some are current characteristics.

The most important correlations are those between educational attainment and current religiosity. If education reduces religiosity, then the correlations should be negative. The opposite is the case. Three of the four correlations are positive, which means that the higher the education, the stronger the person's religiosity.

The correlation between education and current religiosity for young women who served a mission is not significant, but is not a negative correlation. These results are very strong evidence that for both LDS men and women, higher education does not reduce religious beliefs and activities. This is true even among those who did not serve missions and have fairly low levels of religiosity.

Sacerdote and Glaeser (2002) found interesting mixed results concerning education's impact on religiosity among adults. They discovered that education is positively related to church attendance, but is negatively related to religious beliefs. Thus, the more education a person attains, the higher will be their attendance at church, but the weaker will be their religious beliefs and values. They explain this inconsistency by observing that church attendance is a social activity and that education tends to enhance social participation.

On the other hand, their study found that education may erode fundamental religious beliefs, which are replaced by

Table 14. Bivariate Correlation between Background, Peer Pressure, Religiosity, and Educational Attainment among LDS Returned Missionaries Ages 35–50

Characteristics	Men (n = 1,442)	Women (n = 1,548)
High school grades	.397	.333
Friends seeking higher education	.268	.244
Father's education	.212	.215
Youth religiosity	.148	.112
Religiosity prior to mission	.133	.072
Religiosity following mission	.160	*
Current religiosity	.138	*

* Not significant.

Figure 4. Model of Significant Estimates for Educational Attainment for Male Returned Missionaries over Age 32

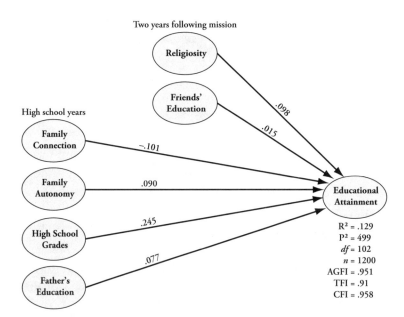

Figure 5. Model of Significant Estimates for Educational
Attainment for Female Returned Missionaries over Age 32

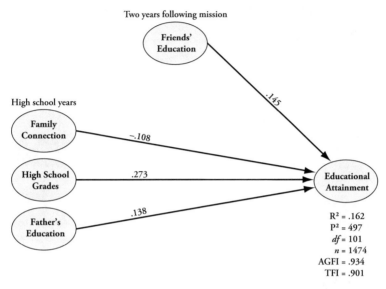

Figure 6. Model of Significant Estimates for Educational Attainment
for Young Women over Age 32 Who Did Not Serve a Mission

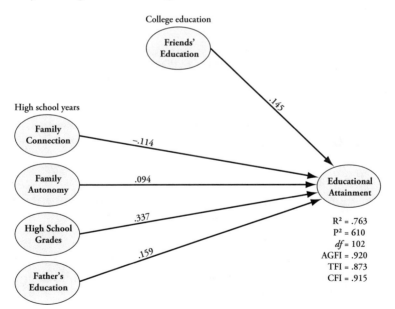

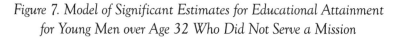
Figure 7. Model of Significant Estimates for Educational Attainment for Young Men over Age 32 Who Did Not Serve a Mission

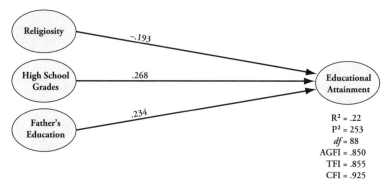

science and secular beliefs. They suggest that educated men and women resolve this inconsistency by gravitating to less "fervent" religions, where they can be involved socially while still holding to their weak religious beliefs.

Our study also calculated the association between educational attainment and current public and private religious behavior. We wanted to test Sacerdote and Glaeser's idea that education increases church attendance (public behavior) and reduces religious beliefs and private behavior.

This differential effect did not appear among the four samples of LDS men and women. Education was not negatively related to private religious behavior, which included personal prayer, personal scripture reading, and thinking about religion. Actually, three of the four correlations were positive, and the fourth was not significant.

It is interesting that high school religiosity and religiosity following a mission were significantly associated with eventual educational achievement. The higher the religiosity among teens and returned missionaries, the more education they obtained.

High school grades reflect intellectual ability and a commitment to education, and it is not surprising that grades were the strongest predictor of eventual educational achievement.

Consistent with the other studies, the father's education had a strong relationship to educational attainment.

The structural equation models predicting educational achievement for each of the four samples are presented in Figures 4 through 7. We actually should have run the models with current religiosity as the dependent variable to show any secularizing effect of education. Given the time frame of the other variables in the model, this was not reasonable. The models in these four figures confirm the findings of the bivariate correlations that educational attainment did not reduce the religiosity of LDS men and women. Current religiosity did not emerge as a negative correlate of education in any of the four models.

The negative score between high school religiosity and educational attainment among young men who did not serve a mission may at first glance raise some interesting conjectures. But the correlation between high school religiosity and educational attainment for these men is not significant. In other words, high school religiosity is so strongly related to high school grades and the father's education that in the model it appears to have a negative influence. However, it does not.

CONCLUSION

This chapter is long and complex, as is nature of the relationship between religion and education. We have compared LDS teens and young adults to non-LDS students of the same ages. All these analyses make it absolutely clear that members of the LDS Church have significantly more education than the general public. Among LDS youth, individual religiosity is associated with academic success and aspirations. Finally, the structural equation modeling demonstrates that advanced education does not lead to a decrease in religiosity among LDS adults. Education does not replace religious beliefs or erode religious activities and practices.

NOTES

1.   These three questions produced a fairly strong scale as factor analysis produced an Eigenvalue of 1.60 and the factor weights for the three items were .70 and higher. The Cronbach's alpha coefficient was .55, which is a little low. The limited number of only three items likely reduced the alpha.

2.   We discussed in Chapter 3 the information provided by structural equation modeling. This statistical procedure allows all the various family, peer, and religious factors to compete to provide an explanation of educational aspirations. The R^2 reveals the percent of the variation in educational desires predicted by the combination of factors in the model. The level of individual contribution made by each factor is revealed in its beta coefficient. Structural equation modeling also calculates the indirect effects of family factors on education through peers and religious factors. This interaction between the various influences approximates real life much more closely than bivariate correlations. In our study of the relationship between religion and education, we are not interested in developing a comprehensive model of status attainment. Rather, we have included the major factors from the status attainment models with religiosity to determine whether religion makes an independent contribution while competing with these other variables.

3.   The items produce a strong scale with an Eigenvalue of 2.27 and factor weights greater than .74. The Cronbach's alpha reliability coefficient was .74.

REFERENCES

Albrecht, S. L., & Heaton, T. (1984). Secularization, higher education, and religiosity. *Brigham Young University Review of Religious Research, 26*(1), 43–58.

Astin, A. W., & Astin, H. S. (2002–2005). The Spirituality in Higher Education Project, Higher Educational Research Institute, UCLA. Retrieved from www.spirituality.ucla.edu.

Astin, A. W., & Astin, H. S. (2004). Spiritual development and the college experience. Internet release April 5, 2004, by the Spirituality in Higher Education Project, Higher Educational Research Institute, UCLA. Retrieved from www.spirituality.ucla.edu.

Beyerlein, K. (2004). Specifying the impact of conservative Protestantism on educational attainment. *Journal for the Scientific Study of Religion, 43*(4), 505–518.

Bonderud, K., & Fleischer, M. (2003, November 21). College students show high levels of spiritual and religious engagement, but new study finds colleges provide little support. Internet release by the Spirituality in Higher Education Project, Higher Educational Research Institute, UCLA. Retrieved from www.spirituality.ucla.edu.

Darnell, A., & Sherkat, D. E. (1997). The impact of Protestant fundamentalism on educational attainment. *American Sociological Review, 62*(2), 306–315.

Dai, Y. (1996). Educational plans after high school: A national survey of high school seniors. *Journal of Research and Development in Education, 30*(1), 22–30.

Doctrine and Covenants of The Church of Jesus Christ of Latter-day Saints (1981). Salt Lake City: The Church of Jesus Christ of Latter-day Saints.

Hastings, P. K., & Hoge, B. R. (1976). Changes in religion among college students, 1948 to 1974. *Journal for the Scientific Study of Religion, 15*(3), 237–249.

Hinckley, G. B. (1997). *Teachings of Gordon B. Hinckley.* Salt Lake City: Deseret Book.

Jeynes, William H. (1999). The effects of religious commitment on the academic achievement of Black and Hispanic children. *Urban Education, 34*(4): 458–479.

Johnson, D. C. (1997). Formal education vs. religious belief: Soliciting new evidence with multinomial logit modeling. *Journal for the Scientific Study of Religion, 36*(2), 231–246.

Keysar, A., & Kosmin, B. A. (1995). The impact of religious identification of differences in educational attainment among American women in 1990. *Journal for the Scientific Study of Religion, 34*(1), 49–62.

Lehrer, E. L. (1999). Religion as a determinant of educational attainment: An economic perspective. *Social Science Research, 28*, 358–379.

Loury, L. D. (2004). Does church attendance really increase schooling? *Journal for the Scientific Study of Religion, 43*(1), 119–127.

McClendon, R. J., & Chadwick, B. A. (2004). Latter-day Saint returned missionaries in the United States: A survey on religious activity and post-mission adjustment. *BYU Studies, 43*(2), 131–157.

Muller, C., & Ellison, C. G. (2001). Religious involvement, social capital, and adolescents' academic progress: Evidence from the National Education Longitudinal Study of 1988. *Sociological Focus, 34*(2), 155–183.

Regnerus, M. D. (2000). Shaping schooling success: Religious socialization and educational outcomes in metropolitan public schools. *Journal for the Scientific Study of Religion, 39*(3), 363–370.

Regnerus, M. D., & Elder, G. H., Jr. (2001). Staying on track in school: Religious influences in high- and low-risk settings. *Journal for the Scientific Study of Religion, 42,* 633–649.

Rhodes, A. L. & Nam, C. B. (1970). The religious context of educational expectations. *American Sociological Review, 35*(2), 253–267.

Sacerdote, B., & Glaeser, E. L. (2002). Education and religion. Working paper 8080, National Bureau of Economic Research, Cambridge, MA, 02138.

Sherkat, D. E. & Darnell, A. (1999). The effect of parents' fundamentalism on children's educational attainment: Examining differences by gender and children's fundamentalism. *Journal for the Scientific Study of Religion 38*(1), 23–35.

Trusty, J. & Watts, R. E. (1999) Relationship of high school seniors' religious perceptions and behavior to educational, career and leisure variables. *Counseling and Values, 41*(1), 30–40.

Zern, D. S. (1989). Some connections between increasing religiousness and academic accomplishments in a college population. *Adolescence, 24*(93), 141–154.

Five

SELF-ESTEEM

elf-esteem, self-worth, self-concept, and similar terms describe aspects of self-evaluation. Individuals seem to seek their "true" nature by searching for an identity or sense of being. Social scientists usually define the self as the combination of one's physical appearance, memories, and sensory images. Gecas (1982) conceptualized the self as "the concept the individual has of himself as a physical, social, and spiritual or moral being" (p. 3).

Logic, theory, and research have linked high self-esteem to a host of positive behaviors and low self-esteem to maladaptive ones. As popular enthusiasm for self-esteem swelled during the 1970s and 1980s, many came to see self-esteem as a social vaccine that increases desirable behaviors and decreases negative ones. The optimistic promise of self-esteem has appeared on the covers of many popular magazines, in numerous self-help books, in personal-improvement seminars, and on the Internet (Hillman, 1992; Burns, 1993; Branden, 1994; Sorensen, 1998; Emler, 2001). The assurance is that as self-esteem is raised, desirable behavior will increase while inappropriate behavior will diminish.

The self-esteem story is entertainingly illustrated in the George Bernard Shaw play *Pygmalion*, which was later adapted into the popular Broadway musical and motion picture *My Fair Lady*. Professor Henry Higgins reshaped the self-image of Eliza Doolittle by teaching her to speak proper English, schooling her in etiquette of high society, and dressing her in stylish gowns. The reactions of acquaintances to the "new" Eliza altered her self-concept. This miraculous metamorphosis fashioned a confident young woman from a cocoon of self-disdain. She had previously viewed herself as a coarse, lower-class flower vendor on the streets of London. Later she sees herself as a lovely, desirable young lady of society.

The pioneering research testing the Pygmalion effect, as it is known, was reported in the enthusiastically received book *Pygmalion in the Classroom* (Rosenthal & Jacobson, 1968). In 1964, researchers tested all the students in an elementary school in northern California with a standard nonverbal test of intelligence. Then 20% of the students were randomly selected as experimental subjects, while the other 80% served as the control group. At the start of the school year, teachers were shown a list of the randomly assigned "bloomers" in class, students that they were told were exceptionally bright. The only difference between the so-called bloomers and other students was actually in the teachers' minds. The average IQ scores for students in the two groups were identical.

Nothing more was said to the teachers about the bloomers during the school year. The children were retested with different versions of the same intelligence test twice the following year. The IQ gains of the bloomers at the end of the school year were extraordinary! Twenty-one percent of the bloomers in the first and second grades increased their IQs by 30 or more points, 48% increased by 20 or more points, and 78% increased by at least 10 IQ points. Although the IQs of the students in the control group had also increased a little, the difference between them and the experimental group was remarkable.

The researchers argued that the modest increase in IQ gains by the students in the control group was a "spillover effect" from the positive classroom influence of the bloomers. The researchers speculated that teachers had acted differently towards the bloomers by giving them more help, greater approval, additional opportunities, and other classroom perks, which altered the students' self-concepts. The high self-esteem of the students was manifest in their schoolwork, including performance on the IQ test.

The Pygmalion study has been replicated literally hundreds of times by other researchers. These studies focused on elementary, junior high, and high school students of many different demographics. Unfortunately, the literature is so varied that different scholars claim to have proven or disproven the Pygmalion effect (Rosenthal, 1973; Hansford & Hattie, 1982). Researchers have analyzed the data over and over again and have been unable to identify any theoretical explanation as to why the Pygmalion effect is so inconsistent. Importantly, even when the effect of self-esteem on academic achievement appeared in some of the replications, the correlation was rather weak.

In spite of sparse evidence, the belief in the efficacy of self-esteem mobilized the California state legislature to improve the quality of life in the state by enhancing its citizens' feelings of self-worth. In 1986 the California legislature created the Task Force to Promote Self-Esteem and Personal and Social Responsibility. The politicians, scholars, and other members of the task force were convinced that raising self-esteem would reduce crime, delinquency, drug and alcohol use, school dropouts, poor academic performance, unemployment, discrimination, out-of-wedlock births, divorce, family violence, and a host of other undesirable behaviors. In addition, increasing self-esteem was expected to increase a variety of positive behaviors, such as academic achievement, work effort, productivity, and a relatively stable family life. In other words, self-esteem was seen as a panacea for a large number of social and personal problems.

The task force produced a rather insightful manual outlining ways that parents, teachers, school officials, community leaders, and clergymen could strengthen self-esteem (California Task Force to Promote Self-Esteem and Personal and Social Responsibility, 1990). In most California counties, committees were established to launch programs to foster feelings of self-worth.

The task force also assembled a team of scholars to review the research linking self-esteem to the relevant behaviors. The findings of the study group were disappointing, as they failed to support the high hopes of the task force (Mecca, Smelser, & Vasconcellos, 1988). The correlations between self-esteem and behaviors such as academic achievement, delinquency, crime, and job performance were too weak to offer support to the theory that increasing self-esteem would affect them. Because of this lack of scientific evidence for the efficacy of self-esteem, the task force was quietly disbanded in 1995.

Although the research support is weak, the enthusiasm for self-esteem as an antidote for many social problems has been unrelenting. In response to the persistence of the self-esteem movement, the American Psychological Association commissioned a team to systematically review the vast self-esteem literature, especially its relationship to important social behaviors (Baumeister, Campbell, Kreuger, & Vohs, 2003). This team examined over 15,000 publications focusing on self-esteem and tried to make sense of the findings while considering important methodological issues concerning the measurement of self-esteem and the direction of causation.

Self-esteem poses measurement problems because it is a subjective emotional state and, as such, is difficult to accurately assess. In addition, researchers have struggled with whether self-esteem is a perception of one's entire life or if a person has different levels of self-esteem for different aspects of his or her life. For example, is it possible that a teen has very high self-esteem about athletic ability but low self-esteem about academic talents? Or does the teen incorporate athletic and academic accomplishments into a single sense of self-esteem?

After an initial review of the studies, the research team decided to include only those that used a global measure of self-esteem. It is difficult to assess which is the cause and which is the result; success in school, sports, or other endeavors may increase self-esteem just as high self-esteem may influence such behaviors.

In the Pygmalion and similar experiments, the impact of raising self-esteem on school performance was obvious; self-esteem was systematically varied and the effects on behavior were then observed. In addition to experiments, longitudinal studies where self-esteem and academic achievement or other behaviors are measured at different points in time offer some insight into the direction of causation.

An example of such a study was conducted by Rosenberg, Schooler, and Schoenbach (1989). They compared the self-esteem of nearly 1,900 boys in the tenth grade to the boys' academic achievements when they were seniors in high school. They found that the relationship between tenth-grade self-esteem and twelfth-grade performance was not statistically significant. However, they did find a statistically significant relationship between academic achievement in the tenth grade and self-esteem as seniors, although the relationship was weak.

Most of the studies reviewed by the team were surveys where the level of self-esteem, delinquency, school achievement, or initiation of sexual behavior were all measured at the same time. Causation is difficult to determine when all of the relevant variables are measured at the same time.

This exhaustive review by the American Psychological Association concluded that the effects of self-esteem on various behaviors are very limited. For example, they found that the impact of self-esteem on youths' school performance is negligible. The association reported:

The modest correlations between self-esteem and school performance did not indicate that high self-esteem leads to good performance. Instead, high self-esteem is partly the result of good school performance. Efforts to boost the self-esteem of pupils have not been shown to improve performance and may sometimes be counterproductive. (Baumeister et al., 2003, p. 1)

In addition, it was discovered that high self-esteem had mixed results in preventing delinquent behavior. "Overall, there is some support for the traditional view that low self-esteem may predispose a person to participate in antisocial behavior" (p. 1). However, the correlations were rather weak. These findings suggest that self-esteem generally is associated with lower delinquency, but the effect is very limited.

Interestingly, the review noted that some studies such as Salmivalli, Kaukiainen, Kaistaniemi, and Lagerspetz (1999) discovered that high self-esteem appeared among both those who were perpetrators of bullying and those who defended victims. Similarly, Lobel and Levanon (1988) discovered that self-esteem was strongest in both the highest cheating and lowest cheating groups of students. Baumeister et al. (2003) speculated, "Quite possibly, the actual effect of high self-esteem per se is to support initiative and confident action, for good or ill" (pp. 24–25).

Surprising findings emerged concerning alcohol and drug abuse. It appears that high self-esteem facilitates teenagers' participation in behaviors like drinking and drug abuse. They also cautioned that the relationship between drinking and drug abuse is complicated, which makes it hard to draw any hard and fast conclusions.

Similar negative findings appeared concerning sexual activity. Studies revealed that teens with high self-esteem tended to have lower inhibitions and were more disposed to engage in risky behavior, including sexual activity. Researchers warn against accepting the relationship between self-esteem and sex as fact, since "popularity could cause both high self-esteem and more sex" (Baumeister et al., 2003, pp. 33–34).

Not surprisingly, their findings indicate that high self-esteem has a strong relationship to feelings of happiness and that "low self-esteem is more likely than high to lead to depression under some circumstances" (p. 1). In other words, those who feel good about themselves sometimes tend to be happier with their lives.

A rather disturbing concern was raised by the review. The research suggested that parents, teachers, and others who have endeavored to raise self-esteem in young people may have unintentionally fostered narcissism in their children. Young people thought to have high self-esteem are actually rather self-absorbed and conceited. These narcissistic youth feel that they are so special they deserve special treatment by others and that the rules of society don't apply to them. Narcissism is certainly not a trait parents and teachers wish to cultivate in their children.

At the conclusion of this meticulous review of the many studies, the research team suggested a low-profile approach when fostering self-esteem:

> Hence, we think self-esteem should be used in a limited way as one of a cluster of factors to promote positive outcomes. It should not be an end in itself. Raising self-esteem will not by itself make young people perform better in school, obey the law, stay out of trouble, get along better with their fellows, or respect the rights of others, among many other desirable outcomes. However, it does seem appropriate to try to boost people's self-esteem as a reward for ethical behavior and worthy achievements. Although that may sound banal, we think it will require a basic change in many self-esteem programs, which now seek to boost everyone's self-esteem without demanding appropriate behavior first. (p. 39)

ADOLESCENT SELF-ESTEEM

Although the scientific support is weak, some social scientists, school officials, and parents are convinced that feelings of self-worth are especially important during adolescence. This is a time when teens are seeking to establish independence from their families and are struggling to discover who and what they are.

Extensive research has established that peer pressure has enormous influence during adolescence. The high school years are also a pressure-packed time when many critical decisions about education, career, and marriage are made by these somewhat insecure youth. Some assume that youth with high self-esteem will perform stronger in high school, will more often seek admittance to college, will pursue professional careers, and will establish happier and more stable marriages. Because of this concern about adolescent self-esteem, we will first review the data we have collected concerning the level of self-esteem of LDS high school students in comparison to that of other students. Then, we will explore the effect of family, religion, and school on self-esteem. Finally, remembering the concern about causation, we will examine the relationship between the self-esteem of LDS high school students, academic achievement, and delinquency.

SELF-ESTEEM AMONG LDS YOUTH

Self-esteem among LDS youth was measured using ten items from the popular Rosenberg scale (Rosenberg, 1979). This scale includes items such as, "I feel that I have a number of good qualities," or "Sometimes I feel like I am no good at all." The students' responses ranged along a five-point scale from *strongly agree* to *strongly disagree*. The answers to ten questions were summed into a measure of self-esteem.

Each year a very large national study of high school seniors, Monitoring the Future, is conducted to ascertain what the seniors plan to do following graduation (Bachman et al., 1997). The survey includes five of the ten Rosenberg self-esteem items we asked of the LDS students. We compared the responses to these five questions of the national sample of seniors to the LDS seniors from different regions of the United States and from Great Britain and Mexico. Data from the national study collected in 1994 were used because that year was in the middle of the time frame in which we surveyed the different LDS samples. The results are presented in Table 1.

A couple of interesting findings appear. First, the LDS seniors reported somewhat lower scores on the self-esteem items than did the seniors in the national sample. Weaker self-esteem scores appeared for both the positive and negative phrasing of questions. Two alternative explanations may explain these lower self-esteem scores. One common explanation is that the gospel and the Church place very high expectations and demands on its youth, which may foster feelings of inadequacy or not measuring up. This lack of perfection impacts the teens' sense of self and is then expressed in response to the self-esteem items. This explanation is also frequently invoked to account for Utah's high rate of prescriptions for antidepressant medication.

The alternative explanation is that LDS youth are taught to be humble and avoid pride, so they might be more modest in answering questions praising themselves. This avoidance of pride guards against the narcissism that was discovered in studies reviewed by the American Psychological Association. We do not have the necessary data to test these proposed explanations. We hope it is the latter explanation. Whatever the reason(s), LDS high school seniors report somewhat lower self-worth than U.S. youth of the same age.

Another interesting item in Table 1 was the high self-esteem reported among the Mexican LDS students, especially on the positive items. As can be seen, on the three items praising the self, their scores approximate those of the national sample. Interestingly, the Mexican youth were not as confident about themselves when they responded to the two negatively phrased items. We have no reasonable explanation for this cultural difference.

Table 1. Self-Esteem of LDS High School Students in the U.S., Great Britain, and Mexico, by Gender

Self-esteem	U.S. National Sample		LDS Seniors, United States		LDS Seniors, Great Britain*		LDS Seniors, Mexico	
	Males (n = 1,154)	Females (n = 1,416)	Males (n = 372)	Females (n = 971)	Males (n = 66)	Females (n = 63)	Males (n = 179)	Females (n = 182)
I have a positive attitude about myself								
Agree	83%	78%	70%	61%	65%	44%	78%	66%
Neutral	9%	8%	20%	27%	21%	38%	12%	19%
Disagree	8%	14%	10%	12%	14%	18%	10%	15%
On the whole, I am satisfied with myself								
Agree	78%	78%	69%	63%	65%	48%	74%	34%
Neutral	12%	10%	21%	25%	21%	31%	15%	20%
Disagree	10%	12%	10%	12%	14%	21%	11%	16%
I feel that I am a person of worth at least on an equal plane with others								
Agree	88%	83%	79%	74%	62%	64%	84%	81%
Neutral	8%	10%	15%	20%	28%	30%	8%	11%
Disagree	4%	7%	6%	6%	10%	6%	8%	8%
At times I think I am no good at all								
Agree	18%	30%	26%	36%	73%	29%	34%	40%
Neutral	16%	14%	20%	24%	22%	24%	16%	16%
Disagree	66%	56%	64%	40%	5%	47%	50%	44%
I feel I do not have much to be proud of								
Agree	13%	15%	14%	11%	18%	18%	31%	25%
Neutral	14%	10%	17%	21%	23%	26%	16%	18%
Disagree	73%	75%	69%	68%	59%	56%	53%	57%

* Data based on the U.S. equivalent of a high school senior.

It should be noted that among all the samples, young men reported significantly stronger feelings of self-worth than did young women. There is intriguing research literature that shows that young women's self-perception declines dramatically during junior and senior high school. One explanation for this is the finding that girls do very well in math and science until they enter junior high, but then they fall considerably behind young men by the time they graduate from high school. It should be noted that at this time when girls' math scores are falling, their verbal skills are increasing (Tavris & Wade, 2001).

Mary Pipher, a clinical psychologist who works with young women, provides a discerning discussion of the eroding self-confidence of young women:

> Some girls do well in math and continue to like it, but many who were once good at math complain that they are stupid in math. Girl after girl tells me, "I'm not good in math." My observations suggest that girls have trouble with math because math requires exactly the qualities that many junior-high girls lack—confidence, trust in one's judgment, and the ability to tolerate frustration without becoming overwhelmed. Anxiety interferes with problem solving in math. A vicious cycle develops—girls get anxious, which interferes with problem solving, and so they fail and are even more anxious and prone to self-doubt the next time around. (Pipher, 1994, p. 63)

However, feminists are convinced that sexism in school is producing this effect. They argue that girls are counseled into educational tracts that move them away from the sciences and toward nurturing disciplines. Because of the difference in self-esteem between young men and young women, we have analyzed their data separately.

In summary, we found that LDS high school seniors have lower self-esteem as measured by the Rosenberg scale than do other youth across the nation. The lower self-esteem appeared among all three LDS samples. It also was discovered that in accord with many other studies, young men have higher self-esteem than young women.

RELIGION AND SELF-ESTEEM

Our second objective in this study of the self-esteem of LDS teens was to ascertain the relationship between religion and self-esteem. We utilized the same five dimensions of religiosity discussed in previous chapters. We related religious beliefs, private religious behavior, public religious behavior, importance of religion, and acceptance at Church to self-esteem. (The specific items are presented in Appendix A.)

Religious beliefs were measured by ten statements about traditional Christian beliefs, as well as beliefs unique to Latter-day Saint theology. Examples of the questions are "Jesus Christ is the divine Son of God," and "Joseph Smith actually saw God the Father and Jesus Christ."

Private religious behavior was gauged by the frequency of personal prayer, personal scripture reading, fasting, and payment of tithing.

Public religious behavior included five questions about attendance at sacrament meeting, Sunday School, priesthood or young women meeting, and participation in church activities.

Importance of religion was determined by answers to 12 questions about the role of religion in each teen's life and how often he or she has felt the Holy Spirit. Sample questions are "My relationship with God is an important part of my life," and "I have been guided by the Spirit with some of my problems or decisions."

Finally, *acceptance at church* was ascertained by three questions about how the student felt he or she fit in at church. "I am well liked by members of my ward," is an example of one of these questions. All these questions were answered with the same five-point scale used for self-esteem. The responses were

Table 2. Correlations between Measures of Religiosity and Self-Esteem

	United States		Great Britain		Mexico	
	Males (*n* = 721)	Females (*n* = 968)	Males (*n* = 199)	Females (*n* = 274)	Males (*n* = 814)	Females (*n* = 879)
Religious belief	0.205	0.303	0.038	0.158	0.133	0.193
Public religious behavior	0.214	0.308	0.070	0.064	0.222	0.232
Private religious behavior	0.298	0.380	0.116	0.189	0.266	0.330
Importance of religion	0.258	0.414	0.076	0.227	0.281	0.356
Acceptance at church	0.354	0.431	0.257	0.363	0.356	0.376

summed to compute scale scores on each of the measures of religiosity. The correlations are presented in Table 2.

Obviously self-esteem is formed from many sources, including parents, friends, teachers, religious leaders, and from experiences in the home, school, and church. Bivariate correlations were examined because they isolate the relationships between the measure of religiosity and feelings of self-worth. Perhaps the most important finding from this analysis is that all three of the samples produced strong correlations between all the dimensions of religiosity and self-esteem. All five dimensions were significantly related to feelings of self-worth in the United States and Mexico for both young men and young women. Four of the five dimensions were significant for young women in Great Britain, but for some reason only the dimension of acceptance at church was significant for British young men.

The magnitude of the correlations with *acceptance in church* was most surprising. Table 2 reveals that for every sub-sample of LDS high schools students, feelings of acceptance, warmth, and belonging in church were associated with feelings of self-esteem. On deeper reflection, this relationship is not so surprising. Church leaders, advisors, teachers of youth, and friends at church make a significant contribution to young people's self-worth, as do other members of the ward, by helping youth feel welcome and valued.

Importance of religion includes not only the salience of religion in a young person's life, but also their spiritual experiences. This dimension of religiosity also produced rather strong correlations with self-esteem for all samples except British young men. It seems that a teen's feelings about his or her relationship with God and affirming spiritual experiences authenticate feelings of personal worth.

Private religious behavior was also a strong predictor of self-esteem. One possible explanation is that those youth who engaged in personal prayer and scripture reading experienced validation of their self-worth because these activities also foster a personal relationship with their Heavenly Father.

Public religious behavior, primarily attendance at church meetings, and *religious beliefs* had significant, but somewhat weaker, correlations with self-esteem. One reason for these lower correlations found in previous research is that attendance is an inadequate measure of religiosity because young people frequently attend their meetings for nonreligious reasons, such as associating with friends or gaining parental permission to use the family car. Also, we have reported elsewhere that Latter-day Saint youth with strong religious beliefs sometimes have difficulty translating their beliefs into their daily lives (Top & Chadwick, 1998). This data suggests that teens also do not fully transfer their religious beliefs into their feelings of self-worth.

In sum, we are amazed at the powerful correlations between the various measures of religiosity and self-esteem among LDS teenagers. It is suggested that the relationship is reciprocal, with both being the cause and effect of the other. Although the effects are probably weaker than the religion and self-esteem link, feelings of self-esteem probably contribute to religiosity.

MULTIVARIATE MODELS OF SELF-ESTEEM

The third objective of this chapter was to test the power of religion to predict self-esteem while competing with other factors in a multivariate model. To accomplish this we used structural equation modeling, which assesses several factors predicting self-esteem at the same time. This analysis, where religiosity competed with other variables to explain self-esteem, more closely approximates real-world conditions than do bivariate correlations.

Another advantage of structural equation modeling is that it identifies not only the direct effects of a factor on self-esteem, but also indirect effects. For example, the model will test not only whether a mother's connection to a teen has a direct effect on self-worth, but also whether it has an indirect effect on self-esteem through private religiosity. In other words, the model will recognize that a mother has an impact on a teen's private religiosity, which in turn is related to the teen's self-esteem. The conceptual model we tested is presented in Figure 1 and shows potential direct and indirect relationships.

In addition to the five dimensions of religiosity, we included several family variables in the model. *Family structure* asked with whom the teen lived and identified single-parent families. *Maternal employment* ascertained whether a youth's mother worked part time or full time outside the home. *Family process*

Figure 1. Model Predicting Self-Esteem
among LDS Students

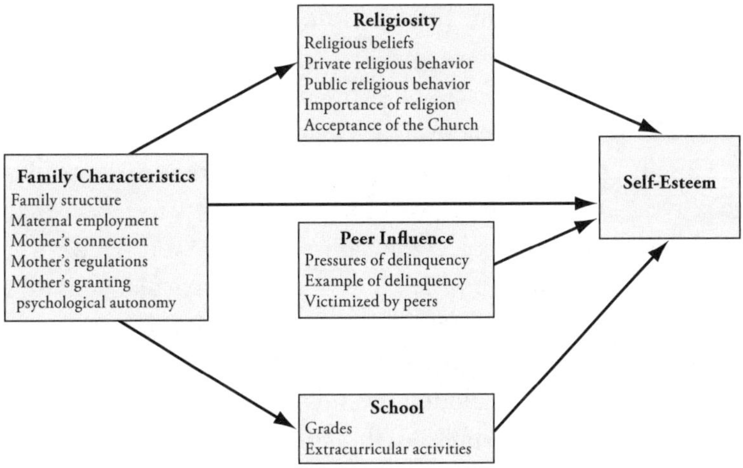

included three aspects of the parent-teenager relationship: connection, regulation, and psychological autonomy.

Mother's/father's connection involves the degree of affection, attention, and closeness the youth feels with his or her parents. It was measured by fifteen questions asking about the parents' involvement in their teens' lives. Two sample questions are "My mother makes me feel better after talking over my worries with her," and "My father makes me feel like the most important person in his life."

Mother's/father's regulation focused on the parent establishing family rules, monitoring teens' compliance, and applying appropriate discipline. Regulation was determined by six questions about parents' awareness of their teens' activities. Sample questions are "Does your mother know who your friends are?" and "My father is very strict with me."

Mother's/father's psychological autonomy is the parent's use of psychological control, such as withholding love to control a teen's thoughts, opinions, or feelings. This involves controlling thoughts rather than behavior. This factor is sometimes called "psychological control" because it is measured by ten questions about how often parents use psychologically controlling tactics. Sample questions are "My mother will avoid looking at me when I have disappointed her," and "My father says if I really cared about him, I would not do things that cause him to worry."

Two measures of school performance were added to the model. Previous research has suggested that getting good grades and participating in extracurricular activities contribute to self-esteem. Therefore, we asked the students to report their cumulative high-school grade point average (GPA). We also asked them to indicate which of eight extracurricular activities, such as sports or student government, they participated in and the number of hours devoted to these activities each week.

Peer influences included friends who engaged in delinquency, friends who pressed the students to engage in such

activities, and peers who bullied them. We assumed that delinquent friends and peer pressure to engage in delinquent behavior would contribute to lower self-esteem. The rationale was
that such deviance would likely result in the disapproval of
important adults, including parents, teachers, religious leaders,
and even other peers, and would lower self-esteem.

Peer example was assessed by asking the teens if their friends
participate in 40 different delinquent activities ranging from
cheating in school to being in a gang fight. *Peer pressure* was
measured by asking if friends pressured them to participate in
the same 40 activities.

Victimization was the degree to which the LDS teen was
bullied or victimized by his or her peers, which was thought
to lower self-esteem. The measure of victimization was determined by eight questions about how often peers at school verbally or physically attacked them. Sample questions are "How
often has someone picked a fight with you?" and "How often
has someone forced you to engage in sexual activities?"

In the initial analysis we discovered that the responses the
teens gave about their relationships with their mothers and
fathers were so similar that it was statistically problematic to
create independent scales. Because of this, we used the data
about only one of the parents. Since more teens live with their
mothers than their fathers, we used relationships with mothers
in the model. We removed the father's connection, regulation,
and granting of psychological autonomy from the analysis.

We encountered another problem with importance of
religion and private religious behavior. Essentially, these two
dimensions of religiosity were measuring the same thing. Not
surprisingly, those students who have private prayer and read
their scriptures are also the ones who value the gospel and have
had spiritual experiences. We therefore deleted private religious
behavior from the analysis and chose to include importance
of religion, knowing that private religiosity was also related to
self-esteem.

*Figure 2. Model Predicting Self-Esteem
among LDS Young Men in the U.S.*

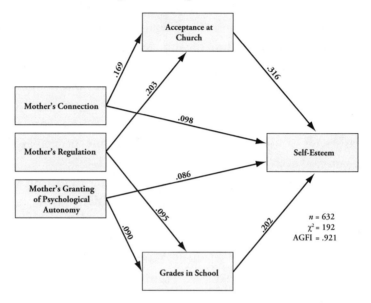

*Figure 3. Model Predicting Self-Esteem
among LDS Young Women in the U.S.*

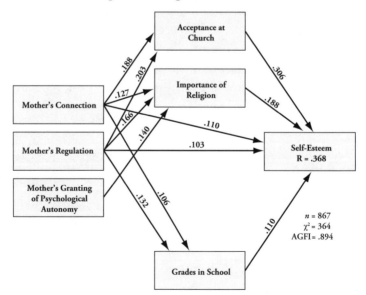

Table 3. Summary of Structural Equation Models Predicting Self-Esteem of LDS High School Students

	United States		Great Britain		Mexico	
	Males	Females	Males	Females	Males	Females
Model Characteristics						
n	632	867	153	224	530	571
χ^2	192	364	108	156	117	140
AGFI	0.921	0.894	0.854	0.847	0.947	0.941
Religiosity						
Acceptance	0.316	0.306	0.398	0.326	0.257	0.262
Importance	*	0.188	*	*	0.101	*
Family						
Mother's connection	*	0.11	*	0.297	0.145	0.112
Mother's regulation	0.098	0.103	*	*	0.144	0.221
Mother's granting psychological autonomy	0.086	*	*	*	0.177	—
School						
Grades	0.202	.011	0.148	0.146	0.122	*
Peers						
Victimization	*	*	*	*	*	0.108

* Not significant.

Figures 2 and 3 present the results for young men and young women in the United States. The results for the United States, Great Britain, and Mexico are summarized in Table 3.

Findings from the structural equation model show that religiosity has a powerful direct effect on self-worth for both young men and young women in the United States, Great Britain, and Mexico. Insignificant factors were trimmed from the models shown in Figures 2 and 3.

Acceptance at church produced by far the strongest link with self-esteem for both men and women. It is not surprising to find that feeling accepted is closely linked to how adolescents value themselves. What is unique for these Latter-day Saint youth is where and with whom they feel comfortable. It is not acceptance by peers at school, but rather, it is within their wards and branches with leaders, teachers, and fellow members that acceptance has such a powerful relationship to feelings of self-worth.

In addition to the influence of acceptance at church, *importance of religion* was also significantly related to self-esteem for young women in the United States and young men in Mexico. This measure represents how teens feel about the gospel and the level of spirituality they have experienced in their lives. For these two groups, both acceptance at church and importance of religion make important independent contributions to explaining self-esteem. In the other groups, acceptance was so strong as to diminish the relationship of importance. Although acceptance has a stronger association with feelings of self-esteem, importance of religion can make a meaningful contribution, especially among youth who feel less accepted in the ward.

This analysis focused on religion's relationship to self-esteem. But it is also informative to note the contribution that school success, as measured by grades, had on self-esteem. Grades were an important predictor of self-worth among both men and women in all three countries. It is clear that approval of teachers, as well as the sense of accomplishment associated with good grades, significantly impacts the feelings of self-esteem among Latter-day Saint youth.

The structural model was created so that acceptance at church is a predictor of self-esteem. However, we recognize that the association is probably cyclical. In other words, not only does acceptance lead to strong self-esteem but, at the same time, feelings of self-worth contribute to acceptance by others at church. Theoretically, however, it seems most likely that the strongest direction of the relationship flows from acceptance to self-esteem.

Although not the primary focus of this chapter, the influence of parent-teenager relations on self-esteem should be recognized. As mentioned earlier, because the feelings of connection, regulation, and psychological autonomy reported by the youth about their mothers and fathers were similar, we could include only the mother's data in the model. Just to make sure, we ran the model with only the fathers' data and found that the results were almost identical.

Mother's connection, the emotional ties the youth felt to their mothers, had a direct relationship with self-esteem for all three samples of young women and one sample of young men. *Mother's regulation*, the setting of rules, monitoring compliance, and administering discipline, was significantly related to self-esteem for young men and young women in the United States and Mexico.

Perhaps because the youth in the British sample were older and many of them had left home, mothers did not appear to have as much influence in children's lives, and it appears that mothers' regulation was not related to self-esteem for these young adults.

These findings are interesting because most research finds a fairly modest relationship between a parent's behavior and a teenager's self-esteem. Among LDS youth, parents' emotional connections and regulation of teens' behavior were both significant factors in understanding the teens' feelings of self-esteem.

The structural equation models also identified the indirect effects of the three parenting behaviors on the youths' self-worth. The results are presented in Table 4, which reveals that mothers' regulation makes an especially significant indirect impact on their teens' self-esteem. As can be seen in both the models in Figures 2 and 3 and in Table 4, regulation has an effect through acceptance at church, both for young men and young women in all three countries.

This same regulation makes an indirect effect through the academic grades of both young men and young women in the United States and Mexico. Parents who sit down with their teenage children and discuss family rules, such as responsibility for helping around the home, curfews, completion of home-work, and so on, score high on regulation.

These parents are also involved enough in their teens' lives to notice when the teens fail to obey the family rules. When rules are violated, these parents administer the agreed-upon discipline, usually some type of grounding, loss of privilege, or extra chores. Parents who provide this type of structure in the lives of their children help them realize the consequences of their behavior and also promote higher self-esteem.

Building self-esteem in this way is consistent with the suggestions made by the American Psychological Association team. Parents who express love and acceptance and then encourage their teens to freely express their opinions and feelings indirectly contributed to self-esteem among some of the sample of young men and young women in the three countries. But it is clear that mother's connection and psychological autonomy were not significant nearly as often as parental regulation.

Table 4. Indirect Effects of Mother's Connection, Regulation, and Psychological Autonomy

Indirect Effects	United States		Great Britain		Mexico	
	Males	Females	Males	Females	Males	Females
Mother's connections through						
Acceptance	0.169	0.188	*	*	*	*
Importance	*	0.127	*	*	0.109	*
Grades	*	*	*	*	0.113	*
Mother's regulation through						
Acceptance	0.203	0.166	0.274	0.198	0.227	0.233
Importance	*	0.203	*	*	0.306	*
Grades	0.095	0.106	*	*	0.110	0.181
Mother's granting of psychological autonomy through						
Acceptance	*	*	0.209	*	0.088	*
Importance	*	0.140	*	*	—	—
Grades	—	—	—	—	—	—

* Not significant.

Conclusion

The results of this complex analysis make it clear that parents and Church leaders really do matter in the lives of the youth of the Church, including how teens feel about themselves. What leaps out from the analysis is that parents and Church leaders must do more than increase young people's understanding of gospel principles. The main goal should be to make sure teens feel a spirit of love, acceptance, and warmth in the home and in the community of Saints. Parents must take the time and energy to monitor the activities of their teenage children and provide guidance in living gospel principles. Parents and Church leaders must work together to make sure youth feel welcome in seminary, institute, priesthood quorums, Scout groups, young women classes, Sunday School, sacrament meetings, and other Church-sponsored activities. Such acceptance is important in helping young people develop positive feelings about themselves.

This finding about the importance of feeling accepted adds to an earlier study that showed that young men who felt close to their priesthood leaders were more likely to serve a mission and to marry in the temple (Key to strong young men, 1984). The feelings of acceptance by adult leaders and youth peers help create a fertile seedbed for nurturing faith. Parents should work with youth leaders to help create this type of environment.

In response to the fear raised about narcissistic youth, parents and Church leaders need to help youth come to know the Savior for themselves. Youth need to feel like children of God and feel his infinite love for them. This is a personal journey of gospel internalization, rather than participation only in programs focused on outward behavior.

Ultimately, parents should help their children gain a personal testimony of who they really are, what the gospel can mean to them, and that they are loved by the Savior. Youth should be taught that as the Savior loves them, they must love and serve others. These feelings of self-worth will prevent the arrogance and self-centeredness feared by the American Psychological Association team.

As parents work to help their teens follow this spiritual path, teens will strengthen their feelings of self-worth. This is not the way to enhanced self-esteem as embraced by the world and many pop psychologists, but it is the Lord's way. Following the Lord's way will give Latter-day Saint teens the kind of self-worth that will strengthen their confidence and character, enable them to resist temptations, and give them the desire to be caring of others.

References

Bachman, J. G., Johnston, L. D., & O'Malley, P. M. (1997). *Monitoring the future: Questionnaire responses from the nation's high school seniors, 1994.* Ann Arbor, MI: Institute for Social Research, University of Michigan.

Baumeister, R. F., Campbell, J. D., Krueger, J. I., & Vohs, K. D. (2003). Does high self-esteem cause better performance, interpersonal success, happiness, or healthier lifestyles? *Psychological Science in the Public Interest, 4*(1), 1–44.

Branden, N. (1994). *The six pillars of self-esteem.* New York: Bantam.

Burns, D. D. (1993). *Ten days to self-esteem.* New York: William Morrow.

California Task Force to Promote Self-Esteem and Personal and Social Responsibility. (1990). *Toward a state of self-esteem.* Sacramento: California State Department of Education.

Emler, N. (2001). *Self-esteem: The costs and causes of low self-worth.* York, England: Joseph Rowntree Foundation.

Gecas, V. (1982). The self-concept. *Annual Review of Sociology, 8,* 1–33.

Hansford, B. C., & Hattie, J. A. (1982). The relationship between self and achievement/performance measures. *Review of Educational Research, 52*(1), 123–142.

Hillman, C. (1992). *Recovery of your self-esteem: A guide for women.* New York: Fireside.

Key to strong young men: Gospel commitment in the home. (1984, December). *Ensign, 14*(12), 66–68.

Lobel, T. E., & Levanon, I. (1988). Self-esteem, need for approval, and cheating behavior in children. *Journal of Educational Psychology, 80*(1), 122–123.

Mecca, A. M., Smelser, N. J., & Vasconcellos, J. (Eds.). (1989). *The social importance of self-esteem*. Berkeley: University of California Press.

Pipher, M. (1994). *Reviving Ophelia: Saving the selves of adolescent girls*. New York: Ballantine.

Rosenberg, M. (1979). *Conceiving the self*. New York: Basic Books.

Rosenberg, M., Schooler, C., & Schoenbach, C. (1989). Self-esteem and adolescent problems: Modeling reciprocal effects. *American Sociological Review, 54*(6), 1004–1018.

Rosenthal, R. (1973). The Pygmalion effect lives. *Psychology Today, 7*(4), 56–63.

Rosenthal, R., and Jacobson, L. (1968). *Pygmalion in the classroom: Teacher expectations and pupils' intellectual development*. New York: Holt, Rinehart and Winston.

Salmivalli, C., Kaukiainen, A., Kaistaniemi, L., & Lagerspetz, K. M. J. (1999). Self-evaluated self-esteem, peer-evaluated self-esteem, and defensive egotism as predictors of adolescents' participation in bullying situations. *Personality and Social Psychology Bulletin, 25*(10), 1268–1278.

Sorensen, M. (1998). *Breaking the chain of low self-esteem*. Sherwood, OR: Wolf Publishing.

Top, B. L., and Chadwick, B. A. (1998). *Rearing righteous youth of Zion: Great news, good news, not-so-good news*. Salt Lake City: Bookcraft.

Tavris, C., and Wade, C. (2001). *Psychology in perspective* (3rd ed.) Upper Saddle River, NJ: Prentice Hall.

Six

SEXUAL PURITY

In the early days of The Church of Jesus Christ of Latter-day Saints, the Prophet Joseph Smith prophesied that members of the Church "would receive more temptations, be more buffeted, and have greater difficulty" with sexual immorality than with any other single challenge (Brigham Young, 1860).

That prophecy is being fulfilled today. The so-called sexual revolution that started in the 1960s continues to impact society. Young and old alike are bombarded with images of immodesty and immorality. Youth are engaging in premarital sex at earlier and earlier ages. That which was once considered sacred, or at least private, is now spoken of casually and with little reverence. Those who speak up for moral values and advocate chastity before marriage and fidelity within marriage are often put down as being provincial and unsophisticated.

Unfortunately, many parents, school officials, and government leaders seem less concerned with the immorality of premarital sexual behavior than with the social ills that often come with it—teen pregnancies, abortion, and sexually transmitted diseases. Although these are very serious and damaging ramifications of a sexually permissive society, there are yet other sobering consequences, such as the negative influence early premarital sexual activity has on the ability to form long-term relationships later in life (McIlhaney & Bush, 2008).

Numerous studies chronicle this pervasive culture of sexuality and the damaging effects of premarital sexual activity among teenagers and young adults. One study found that among 15-year-olds, 13% of girls and 21% of boys have engaged in sexual intercourse (Abma, Martinez, Mosher, & Dawson, 2004). The percentages steadily increase with age, so that 70% of unmarried 19-year-old girls were sexually active. Interestingly, fewer boys (65%) were sexually experienced at the same age.

A slight decrease in premarital sex was noted in the Abma report during more recent years. The percent of sexually experienced teenage girls ages 15 to 19 dropped from 49% in 1997 to 46% in 2002. The decline was more significant for boys, dropping from 55% in 1997 to 46% in 2002. While this modest change is welcome news, parents should not hold out hope that the frequency of teen sex will diminish. The emphasis on sexuality in general society and in the media messages bombarding teenagers will ensure that their level of sexual activity will remain high (Levin & Kilbourne, 2008).

These frightening trends generate questions about how Latter-day Saint teens are faring in this morally polluted environment. What is their level of participation in premarital sexual activities? What are the factors that discourage teenage sex? What, if anything, can be done to help strengthen LDS youth against the many influences that compromise personal purity? This chapter seeks to answer these questions.

Our study compares the premarital sexual behavior of LDS high school students to that of other youth in the United States. To provide meaningful information for parents, Church leaders, and other adults, we tested the correlation between premarital sex among LDS youth and the factors of friends, religion, and family. We used a structural equation model that included peer, family, and religious factors to test how these factors predicted premarital sexual behavior.

THE INFLUENCE OF FRIENDS

Peer pressure is the most significant predictor of delinquency, including early sexual activity. The extensive literature linking friends' attitudes, examples, and pressure to sexual behavior is persuasive. Miller and Moore (1990) reviewed the literature of the antecedents of premarital sex among adolescents for the 1980s. Based on seven studies, they concluded that peer influences were the most significant predictors of adolescent sexual behavior.

Research in the 1990s continued to support the significance of friends' influence in initiating (participating in for the first time) sexual behavior. For example, a study of 1,496 students attending ten private high schools scattered across the United States tested four competing theories of teen sexual activity (Benda & DiBlasio, 1991). Differential association theory, one of the four theories, focuses largely on peer pressure. This theory accounted for two-thirds of the variance in sexual activity among these young people. This variance is very high for social science research and provides powerful support for the importance of peers. Interestingly, the authors suggested that future research should examine the effects of family characteristics on youths' susceptibility to peer pressure for sexual involvement.

Whitbeck, Yoder, Hoyt, and Conger (1999) attempted to unravel the relationship between peer and family influences on the premarital sexual activity of adolescent girls. Panel data (collected from the same students at two different times) were obtained from a sample of 451 two-parent families with seventh-grade students attending schools in a midwestern state. The initial data were collected in 1989.

In addition to peer pressure, the study analyzed the influence of older sisters within four years of the respondents' age.

Older sisters served as role models for a substantial number of girls. Data on sexual activity was collected one year after the initial data collection concerning friends and sisters. The model revealed that friends' sexual experience was the strongest predictor of girls' sexual initiation. Results also showed that girls with a sexually active older sister were more likely to engage in sexual activity and to respond to peer pressure to have sex.

In a later study, Whitbeck, Simons, and Goldberg (1996) attempted to identify the processes whereby peer characteristics influence adolescent sexual behavior. They used information obtained from 499 girls in the Iowa Youth and Families Project and the Iowa Single Parent Project. They included association with deviant peers along with several family-related measures. They found that girls who associated with friends who were breaking the law, who had been arrested, who were fighting with their parents, or who were not doing well in school were significantly more likely to have initiated sexual activity. It appears that delinquent peers included premarital sex among their delinquent behaviors.

An ecological risk-factor model was tested by Perkins, Luster, Villarruel, and Small (1998). This model included factors in a youth's family, neighborhood, school, and peer environments that put him or her at risk for engaging in sex. Data was collected from a sample of over 15,000 youth ages 12 to 17 in a large midwestern state. The model included a three-item peer delinquency scale that asked if the teen's closest friends drink, use drugs, and get into trouble at school. Association with delinquent friends was the strongest predictor of sexual experience for both boys and girls.

Whitbeck and his associates (1999) tested a multivariate model that included peer influences, family influences, and self-esteem to predict premarital sex. Nearly 500 adolescents in the eighth and tenth grades participated in two panel studies. The initial wave of data was collected in 1989, and the second wave in 1993.

Steady dating, a form of peer influence, increased the likelihood of having sexual intercourse by five times. This finding underscores prophetic counsel for youth to delay dating until age 16 and then to avoid steady dating. In addition, association with delinquent friends increased the chances of sexual activity by one and a half times. Interestingly, general delinquency of friends was more significant than friends' sexual activity.

In 1994, an interesting study interviewed 2,436 young people who were sexually inexperienced, and then these young people were interviewed again in 1996 (Sieving, Eisenberg, Pettingell, & Skay, 2006). Those who had initiated sex during this two-year period between interviews were compared to those who had remained virgins. The strongest influences on engagement in premarital sex were sexually active peers and friends who approved, encouraged, and lauded sexual involvement. For example, 42% of those who had sex hung out with sexually active friends, while only 28% of the virgins had sexually involved friends.

We could add dozens of other studies supporting the importance of friends in the initiation of adolescent sexual activity. The few reviewed in this chapter merely illustrate the extensive literature documenting the importance of peers in understanding why teens engage in premarital sexual behavior.

Recent studies have focused on a particularly pernicious type of extreme peer pressure—strong physical force. In such cases young women are literally forced to engage in sex. Miller, Monson, and Norton (1995) found that nearly 10% of young women included in the 1987 National Survey of Children had been forced to have sex. Significantly, they discovered that the girls who had been forced into sex had more permissive sexual attitudes and had engaged in voluntary sex at a younger age than those girls who had not been forced. This suggests that once initiated, even by force, the girls become more accepting of such behavior.

Abma et al. (2004) analyzed data from the 2002 National Survey of Family Growth. One-fourth of the girls under age 14 indicated that their first intercourse had been involuntary. About 10% of the 14- and 15-year-old girls and about 5% of the 16- to 18-year-old girls reported they had been forced to have sex.

The young women were also asked to rate from one to ten the "wantedness" (or desire) of their first intercourse. Even among young women who had voluntary intercourse, about half rated the desire rather low (in the four-to-seven range) rather than in the upper end of the scale. They also found that the greater the age difference between the young girl and her partner, the higher the likelihood that force had been involved.

We suspect that LDS girls, because of their religious values and training, are more hesitant to engage in sex and so are at risk of being forced at a rate higher than the national average. In addition, we observed that LDS girls who date older non-LDS young men are most likely at greater risk of being forced into having sex.

MEASURING PEER PRESSURE

Based on this literature, we include five measures of peer influence in our model. First, we include the example of friends who have experienced sexual activity. These friends may not pressure the LDS youth to have sex, but they serve as negative role models.

Second, we included friends' pressure to participate in premarital sex. This was the proportion of friends who encouraged, teased, and pressured the teen to have sexual activity.

The third measure of peer influence was friends' pressure to engage in a range of light delinquent activities such as cheating on tests, smoking, drinking, and skipping school.

As noted earlier, some researchers have reported that peer pressure for general delinquency was more significant than pressure specifically focused on sex. We also included in the model the proportion of friends who were fellow members of the LDS Church. The rationale is that those with more LDS friends receive lower levels of pressure to participate in sexual activity. Hopefully the teens actually receive pressure from their LDS friends to abstain from such behavior.

Finally, given the finding by Abma and her associates (2004) about coercion, we added whether or not LDS teens reported that they had been forced to participate in sexual activities.

THE INFLUENCE OF FAITH

Cochran and Beeghley (1991) reviewed a substantial number of studies testing the relationship between religion and premarital sexual behavior. They concluded that evidence of direct or indirect effects of religion and/or religiosity on nonmarital sexual attitudes and behavior can be found in more than 80 studies conducted during the past several decades (pp. 45–46). Research conducted since this review has confirmed religion's link to lower levels of premarital sexual behavior.

Religious affiliation or preference has frequently been noted as a significant predictor of premarital sexuality. Those youth belonging to, or identifying with, a religious denomination report lower rates of nonmarital sex than do the unchurched (Beck, Cole, & Hammond, 1991; Cooksey, Rindfuss, & Guilkey, 1996; Brewster, Cooksey, Guilkey, & Rindfuss, 1998; Smith & Denton, 2005).

These same studies have noted that teenagers belonging to Christian fundamentalist denominations participate in less premarital sex than do members of more liberal denominations (Cooksey, Rindfuss, & Guilkey, 1996; Brewster, Cooksey, Guilkey, & Rindfuss, 1998; Smith & Denton, 2005). This is not surprising, as fundamentalist denominations look upon unwed sexual activity as a much more serious sin than do liberal denominations.

Beck, Cole, and Hammond (1991) analyzed data from the National Longitudinal Surveys of Youth collected in 1979 and in 1983. They found that both young men and young women who belonged to Pentecostal, Mormon, and Jehovah's

Witnesses denominations had lower rates of premarital sex than members of mainstream denominations.

We did not test the relationship between denominational affiliation and premarital sex, because we collected data from LDS youth only. If we had data from other denominations, we are confident that LDS teens would have a lower rate, as Church doctrine emphasizes that sex before marriage is a serious sin. In addition, to help LDS youth avoid sexual participation at a young age, youth are encouraged to delay dating until they are 16 and even then to avoid steady dating. We do compare the rates of sexual behavior of LDS students to national non-LDS averages, a comparison which provides some evidence that LDS youth are significantly less sexually active than their peers.

Church attendance, or public religiosity, has been found to be a strong predictor of premarital sex among teenagers (Studer & Thornton, 1987; Thornton & Camburn, 1989; Miller & Moore, 1990; Petersen & Donnenwerth, 1997). Attendance at religious services is assumed to be an indicator of the importance of religion in a teenager's life and thus is associated with lower premarital sexuality.

Day (1992) analyzed data from the National Longitudinal Survey of Labor Market Experience of Youth, which was collected in 1979. This sample included over 12,000 white, black, and Hispanic teens. The model revealed that attendance at church was a significant predictor of lower premarital sex for all three samples of young women and for white young men. Perkins et al. (1998) discovered among a large sample of 15,000 adolescents living in a large midwestern state that attendance at church services, along with involvement in church activities and feelings of the importance of religion, was related to lack of sexual experience among white, black, and Hispanic teenagers.

Private religiosity, as indicated by personal prayer and feeling that religion is important, is also a significant predictor of lower initiation of sexual activity. Schroeder (1997) analyzed data from the 12,000 teens in the 1994–95 National Study of Adolescent Health. He found that those young men and women who reported that they prayed often and that religion was important to them were less likely to engage in premarital sexual behavior.

Similar results linking private religiosity to delayed sexual behavior from the same data set were reported by Resnick et al. (1997). They combined affiliation, frequency of prayer, and a religious self-perception into a variable they labeled "religious identity," and they found that it was significantly related to a higher age of sexual debut.

The National Survey of Youth and Religion collected data from a national sample of nearly 3,300 youth ages 13 to 17 (Smith & Denton, 2005). They grouped the youth into four groups according to their religiosity: devoted, regular, sporadic, and disengaged. The sexual attitudes and behaviors of these four groups were compared. The results revealed that religion had a powerful relationship to premarital sexuality. For example, 95% of the devoted teens plan on saving sex for marriage as compared to only 24% of the disengaged. Among the devoted teens, 18% had participated in petting, compared to 43% of the sporadic and disengaged teens. Finally, only 9% of the devoted teens had engaged in sexual intercourse as compared to 23% of the sporadic and 26% of the disengaged.

The authors noted that "again, we see across a variety of sexual outcome measures noticeable correlations between the degree of teen religious seriousness and cautious teen sexual attitudes and behaviors" (Smith & Denton, 2005, p. 235).

MEASURING RELIGIOSITY

Appendix A describes in detail the methodology for data collection and the kinds of questions that were included in the extensive questionnaire that was used in our study.

As seen in Appendix B, we examined five dimensions of religiosity in the statistical model predicting premarital sexual behavior. They are (1) religious beliefs, (2) public religiosity (church attendance), (3) importance of religion, (4) family religious activities (family prayer, home evening, and scripture reading), and (5) acceptance in their ward by leaders and ward members.

THE INFLUENCE OF FAMILY

Family structure has frequently been linked to early sexual behavior of teenagers. Most of the studies have focused on single-parent families. The argument is that a single parent has less time and energy than two parents to devote to monitoring teens' behavior. Consequently, teens living in single-parent families have more opportunities for sexual exploration. A second argument is that the single parent may be involved in a dating relationship and thus may be a role model of permissive sexual attitudes and behavior.

Miller and Moore (1990), in their review of the research from the 1980s, concluded that "adolescents—daughters in particular—from single-parent families are more likely to begin sexual intercourse at younger ages than their peers from two-parent families" (p. 1028).

Additional support for family structure as an influence on sexual activity has been found in a large number of studies, such as Hayes (1987), Newcomer and Udry (1984), Forste and Heaton (1988), Miller and Bingham (1989), Flewelling and Bauman (1990), Day (1992), Feldman and Brown (1993), Small and Luster (1994), and Upchurch et al. (1999).

Related research has also revealed that youth living with stepparents exhibit greater premarital sexual behavior than children in two-parent families, but less than youth in single-parent families (Rodgers, 1983; Thornton & Camburn, 1987; Miller & Bingham, 1989).

Interestingly, Capaldi, Crosby, and Stoolmiller (1996) examined "parental transitions" rather than single versus two-parent families. A teenager living with a single parent because of a divorce was scored "one transition," while living with a stepparent following divorce was scored as "two transitions." Higher transition scores were assigned to teens whose parents had experienced multiple divorces and remarriages. They found that the greater the number of transitions, the more frequent the premarital sexual activity of the teenagers.

Limited support has linked maternal employment to early sexual activity among teenagers. Ku, Sonenstein, and Pleck (1993) found among 1,880 young men in the National Survey of Adolescent Males that those without a mother present in the home during the day had experienced sexual intercourse at an earlier age than those with a stay-at-home mother.

Brewster, Billy, and Grady (1993) reported that adolescent sexual activity was higher in neighborhoods where a relatively high percentage of women worked full time. They concluded that adolescents lack adequate adult supervision in such neighborhoods and thus are freer to engage in sexual activity.

On the other hand, Thornton and Camburn (1987) found that neither part- nor full-time employment of mothers was related to premarital sexual behavior. Although previous results have been inconsistent, we include maternal employment in our model.

Three parent-teenager relationships have been linked to early sexuality among adolescents. The first is the feeling of closeness or connection between parents and their teenage children. The second is regulation—the degree to which parents set rules of conduct for teens, monitor their compliance, and discipline disobedience. The third process is the use of psychological control over adolescents rather than encouraging them to develop their own psychological autonomy.

Weinstein and Thornton (1989) reported that children who had a close relationship (connection) with their parents adopted attitudes similar to their parents' and thus engaged in sexual behavior less frequently than children who did not have a close relationship with their parents. Resnick et al.

(1997) analyzed the National Longitudinal Study of Adolescent Health, which included data from over 12,000 youth in the seventh through ninth grades. They reported that family connection was protective against early sexual behavior.

Whitbeck, Conger, and Kao (1993) found by using panel data that parental support (connection) was indirectly related to later sexual activity through a "depressing affect." A strained relationship between parents and teens was linked to depression, which in turn influenced the teens' sexual activity and their likelihood to have sexually active friends.

Feldman and Brown (1993) also analyzed panel data to test whether self-restraint was a mediating variable between family closeness (connection) and lower sexual activity. They found that connection was both directly linked to lower sexual behavior and indirectly through self-restraint. In the latter, distance between parents and teen led to lack of self-restraint, which in turn led to sexual initiation.

Family regulation includes setting family rules, monitoring teens' compliance to them, and disciplining when appropriate, and has been found to be associated with lower adolescent sexual activity. Moore, Peterson, and Furstenberg (1986) analyzed the National Survey of Children, which was collected in 1976. They discovered that adolescents whose parents knew their teenage children's friends had a lower rate of sexual behavior. Wu and Martinson (1993) noted among young men studied in the National Survey of Adolescent Males that strict family rules were related to delayed sexual activity. Hovell et al. (1994) found that family rules governing dating were associated with lower sexual behavior.

Interestingly, Small and Kerns (1993) discovered that youth whose parents failed to monitor their behavior were more often recipients of unwanted sexual attention. Studies by Small and Luster (1994) and Miller, Forehand, and Kotchick (1999) reported that parental monitoring of adolescents' activities was related to lower sexual activity.

Harris et al. (2006) studied the relationship between assets, including positive role models, family communication, school connection, constructive use of time, and aspirations for the future to sexual experience. They interviewed over 1,000 parent/teenager pairs in two midwestern cities. They discovered that youth with parental supervision were less likely to have engaged in sexual behavior.

In addition, a self-care youth's sexual experience was significantly reduced by access to these assets, especially supervision by adults. Overall, the evidence suggests rather strongly that parental regulation of teens' behavior is an important deterrent to early sexual initiation.

A growing literature emphasizes the importance of adolescents developing psychological autonomy from their parents in the process of becoming competent adults (Barber, Olsen, & Shagle, 1994). Autonomy fosters teens' confidence in their own ideas, feelings, and perceptions. This in turn enables them to make more rational decisions about their sexuality. Small and Kerns (1993) found that psychological overcontrol (lack of autonomy) by parents was associated with greater unwanted sexual contact. Upchurch, Aneshensel, Sucoff, and Levy-Storms (1999) also found that youth who experienced excessive psychological control from their parents were at greater risk of sexual activity.

MEASURING FAMILY FACTORS

Based on this literature, we included family structure, maternal employment, parental connection, parental regulation, and parental granting of psychological autonomy to their teens in the model predicting premarital sexual behavior. The theoretical model predicting premarital sex that was tested in our study is presented in Figure 1. As can be seen, we included several measures of friends' influence, religiosity, and family factors that competed to explain premarital sexual behavior. Family factors were placed in the model so as to test both direct and indirect effects on the teens' sexual activity.

Many of the studies observed different causes of sexual activity among young women as compared to young men. For example, Rodgers (1999) noted that family processes seem to impact girls more than boys. Therefore, we tested the model for young men and young women separately.

The data collection procedures and the response rates for the various samples are reported in Appendix A. In addition to the questionnaire that was completed by thousands of LDS youth, we interviewed 50 young women in Utah County who were under the age of 20 and who had given birth to a baby out of wedlock.

This source of data provides a unique and interesting perspective. Researchers are very concerned about the validity, or truthfulness, of answers from teens in a questionnaire about their sexual experiences. The birth of a child prior to marriage was adequate evidence that these young women were sexually experienced before they married. These interviews provide valuable insights into the sexual initiation of LDS young women.

Figure 1. Conceptual Model Predicting Premarital Sex

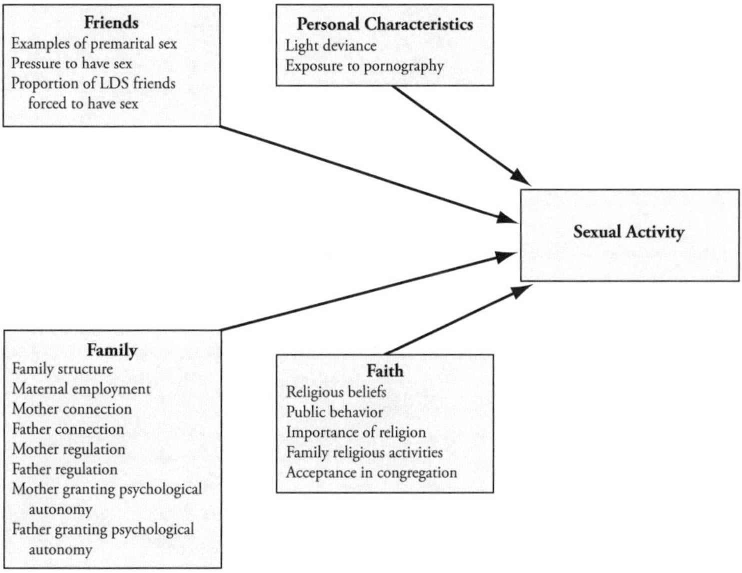

MEASURING PREMARITAL SEXUAL BEHAVIORS

Premarital sexual activity was measured by asking the students if they had ever read pornographic materials, watched pornographic movies or videos, participated in heavy petting, or engaged in sexual intercourse. Those who indicated yes to any of these activities were asked how often they had ever done so. Since LDS youth have rather low rates of these sexual behaviors, it was necessary to ask if they had *ever* engaged in the activities rather than if they had done so during the previous year.

Table 1. Percent of Young People Who Have Ever Had Sexual Intercourse, by Religious Affiliation and Age

Religious Affiliation & Age	Young Men		Young Women	
	Number	Percent	Number	Percent
Ages 15–17				
LDS Youth				
1990–99	1,511	8	1,977	11
General Population*				
1995	5,658	43	5,293	38
2002	5,726	31	5,815	30
Age 18				
LDS Youth				
1990–99	298	11	407	19
General Population**				
1995	1,608	59	1,690	65
2002	1,891	58	2,006	54

* Abma, J. C., Martinez, G. M., Mosher, W. D., Dawson, B. S. (2004). *Teenagers in the United States: Sexual activity, contraceptive use, and child bearing, 2002*. National Center for Health Statistics, *Vital Health Statistics 23*(24), 2004.

** Although the studies of LDS youth and the general population defined the age-groups differently (9- to 12-grade students and high school seniors, and 15- to 17-year-olds and 18-year-olds respectively), we felt the parameters were close enough to make a valid comparison. The Abma report gave the number of 18- and 19-year-olds combined. We divided that number by two to obtain the closest approximation to the age of high school seniors.

At the time we were studying these LDS youth, Internet pornography had yet to appear, and pornography was primarily confined to books, magazines, movies, and videos. Thus we did not include a question about exposure to this pervasive source of pornography. Since pornography was not included as part of the measure of sexual behavior, and since it is such a visible force in society, we included it in the model as an independent variable predicting sexual behavior.

The factor analysis also revealed a problem with teens' relationships with their mothers and fathers. The teens' reports of their connection with parents, the regulation of parents, and parents granting of psychological autonomy were almost identical. When both parents' data were included, the model would not specify or calculate. To eliminate this problem, we used only the mothers' connection, regulation, and granting of autonomy in the model predicting premarital sex.

FREQUENCY OF PREMARITAL SEX

The percent of LDS high school students who have ever had sexual intercourse is compared to the percent of high school students examined in a very large national study in Table 1. The influence of affiliation in the LDS Church, with its unique moral values, is readily apparent in the substantially lower rates of premarital sexual behavior for both young men and young women. The national rate for young men in 1995, which is most comparable to the LDS youth, is six times larger than the rate for LDS young men. The gap is not as large for young women, but the LDS rate is still four times lower than that among the young women in the national sample. It should be noted that the national sample includes some 19-year-olds, which probably inflates its rate a little. Nevertheless, the differences are amazing.

The LDS seniors and the 18-year-olds in the national sample are a very dramatic contrast. The percentages are greatly different—11% versus 58% for boys and 19% versus 59% for young women. Interestingly, 2002 is the first year that a higher percentage of young women than young men are shown to be sexually experienced in a sizable national sample.

The greater sexual experience of women as compared to men appeared among the LDS students much earlier. At the time of our study, we speculated that some LDS young women were frequently dating older nonmember men who were sexually experienced. Thus, LDS young women were at greater risk of being allured into sexual behavior than LDS young men. While this is an interesting trend, the important point made in the table is the powerful influence of religious affiliation in reducing teenage sexual activity.

The frequencies of specific sexual activities—heavy petting, and intercourse—are presented in Table 2. About 20% of the LDS high school students have participated in heavy petting but have not had intercourse. Only 8% of the boys and 10% of the girls had participated in sexual intercourse. In all cases, those who had experienced intercourse had first engaged in petting.

BIVARIATE CORRELATIONS WITH PREMARITAL SEX

A bivariate correlation measures the relationship between one variable, such as peer pressure, and premarital sex, while holding all the other variables constant. The bivariate correlations between the various personal, peer, religious, and family factors with premarital sex are presented in Table 3. Not surprisingly, pressure from friends to engage in sex produced the strongest bivariate correlation with sex for both young men and young women.

Table 2. Sexual Activity among LDS High School Students

Sexual Activity	Young Men (n = 1,518)	Young Women (n = 1,946)
Heavy petting only	19%	19%
Intercourse	8%	10%

Having friends who are sexually active also strongly correlated with sexual activity. For the young women, being forced to have sex was strongly related to premarital sex. Not surprisingly, among young men, sexual coercion was a relatively unimportant factor.

The proportion of friends who were LDS was only weakly related to premarital sex. This relationship was expected to be stronger, because it is assumed that LDS friends do not pressure the youth as often to have sex as non-LDS friends do. This finding suggests that it is not the religious affiliation of friends that is important; rather it is the moral values of friends.

Both participation in light deviance and exposure to pornography were strongly related to premarital sex. Those youth who were smoking, drinking, and skipping school probably had adopted a "hedonistic" or thrill-seeking lifestyle that included sexual activity. In addition, they seemed to be in rebellion against parents, school officials, and Church leaders. As for pornography, it is suspected that it heightens sexual arousal and thus enhances motivation for sex.

All the dimensions of religiosity except acceptance in their congregation were inversely related to premarital sex. The correlations all have a minus sign, which means that the higher the religiosity, the lower the probability of engaging in sex. The correlation between the importance of religion and sexual activity is strong for both young men and young women. Public religiosity (attendance) is also strongly related to such behavior. Family religious activity has a modest relationship to the sexual activity of teenagers. However, family structure is significantly related to sexual behavior, as youth living in single-parent families were more sexually experienced. A similar modest relationship was observed between a mother's employment and sexual activity.

Family structure and maternal employment produced weak but significant relationships with initiation of sex for both young men and young women. Among the parent/teenager relationships, mothers' regulation had the strongest relationship to premarital sex. The correlations for both young women and young men were the same. Those parents who set rules, observed compliance, and disciplined when appropriate had children who engaged in sex less often as compared to children raised in families with limited regulation.

Parents' granting psychological autonomy was not related to premarital sexual behavior. This finding was somewhat anticipated, as early studies had reported that lack of autonomy is more often related to internal states of mind, such as depression and thoughts of suicide as contrasted to behavior (Barber et al., 1994).

MODEL PREDICTING PREMARITAL SEXUAL BEHAVIORS

The structural model indicates the strength of the relationships between the predictor variables and premarital sexual behavior. The results for the young men are presented in Figure 2. One indicator from each of the four domains of peer influences, personal characteristics, religiosity, and family emerged as significant predictors in the trimmed model.

As anticipated, peer pressure for boys to engage in premarital sex was by far the strongest predictor of such behavior. Unfortunately, we do not know how much of the peer pressure to have sex came from other young men and how much came from young women. It is suspected that most of the pressure came from male friends, but it is likely that some pressure came from the girls with whom the boys associated and perhaps dated.

Public religious behavior has a significant inverse relationship to premarital sex. Thus, the more often young men attended church and participated in religious activities, the less likely they had initiated sex. In the earlier chapter on delinquency, the importance of religion in a boy's private life made a stronger contribution than did church attendance. Perhaps the social support against premarital sex obtained in church meetings, as well as the association with adult leaders and

Figure 2. Model Predicting Premarital Sex among LDS Young Men

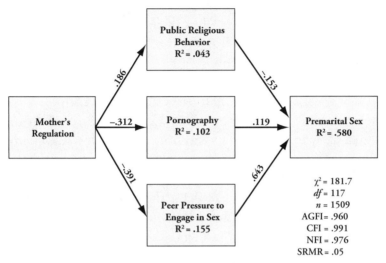

other young people with similar values and behavior, was more important in explaining participation in premarital sex than were religious feelings. It is suspected that as youth started to participate in inappropriate sexual behaviors they withdrew from church fellowship.

As we all know, pornography has become more readily available to teens in high school. Access to the Internet places hardcore pornography into the hands of youth. In addition to the Internet, youth have ready access to soft pornography in videos and movies on cable or satellite. It appears that LDS young men struggling to understand and cope with hormonal changes of puberty are sexually aroused by pornography to participate in activities contrary to their values and behavioral intentions.

In our study, none of the family characteristics had a direct relationship to premarital sexual behavior. But mothers' regulation of their sons' behavior had a fairly strong indirect link to sex through the other three factors in the model. Regulation, as explained earlier, involves parents setting family rules, monitoring compliance to the rules, and disciplining noncompliance.

Also, mothers' regulation represents both mothers' and fathers' regulation of their teenage children.

The strongest indirect effect of mothers' regulation flows through peer pressure. The more that mothers regulated their teens' behavior, the lower the impact of peer pressure in the teens' lives. Mothers' regulation probably influenced the selection of friends as well as their teens' ability to resist peer pressure. Mothers' regulation also had a strong indirect effect on sexual activity through exposure to pornography. It is pretty obvious how a mother monitoring Internet use reduces access to porn. Finally, mothers' regulation had a modest indirect impact of their children's sexual activity through public religious behavior. In this case, teens whose mothers encouraged and monitored their church attendance were less likely to have initiated sexual behavior.

These four factors explained 58% of the variance in premarital sexual activity among LDS young men. This means that over half of the sexual activity of these boys is accounted for by these four variables. Friends were a powerful social influence in the lives of young men and pressured some of them to participate in premarital sex. On the other hand, faith, as represented by church attendance, was a social influence against early sexual activity. Participation in pornography had an obvious impact on such behavior. Finally, parents' regulation of their teenage sons did have a strong indirect effect through peer pressure, church attendance, and exposure of pornography.

The trimmed model predicting premarital sexual activity among LDS young women is presented in Figure 3. The model is very similar to that for young men, with the exception that pornography dropped out of the model. The results make it clear that young women initiate sexual behavior as a consequence of external pressures rather then personal desires.

Comments from three sexually active LDS young women illustrate the influence of pressure. When asked, "Why did you engage in sex for the first time?" they replied:

I had a boyfriend who pressured it on me a lot. And I thought, "Well, maybe I should." I wasn't thinking right. I don't know. And one night I thought, "Well, maybe I want to do this." But I didn't really want to. But he wouldn't stop. He just kept doing it. I was like, "No," but he just kept doing it.

'Cause everyone else was doing it. I think that is why I did it. Everyone was like, "I have, I have!" It was just like at that moment, I said, "Okay." It wasn't like I even thought about it.

It was when I was fifteen. Really I just felt pressure. Mostly pressure. I just went to a friend's house, and she was having a party. And I was left alone with this guy, and one thing kind of led to another.

The last comment illustrates the casualness of some of the young women's first sexual activity. This young woman was pressured into having sex by "this guy" she was not even dating.

Figure 3. Model Predicting Premarital Sex among LDS Young Women

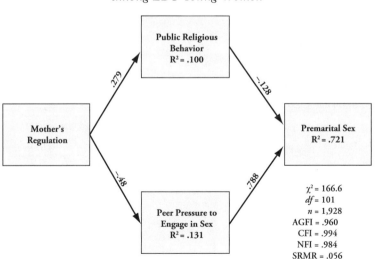

Table 3. Correlations between Friends, Religion, and Family Characteristics and Premarital Sex for LDS Young Men and Women

Independent Variables	Young Men	Young Women
Personal Behaviors		
Light deviance*	.455**	.496**
Exposure to pornography	.364**	.308**
Friends		
Examples of having sex	.351**	.472**
Pressure to have sex	.473**	.595**
Pressure for light deviance	.298**	.376**
Proportion of lds friends	−.187**	−.220**
Forced to have sex	.193**	.406**
Religiosity		
Beliefs	−.269**	−.243**
Public behavior (church attendance)	−.263**	−.350**
Importance of religion	−.367**	−.397**
Family religion activities	−.171**	−.202**
Acceptance in congregation	−.010**	−.034**
Family		
Single-parent family	.140**	.068**
Maternal employment	.104**	.090**
Mother's connection	−.132**	−.132**
Father's connection	−.093**	−.093**
Mother's regulation	−.275**	−.275**
Father's regulation	−.154**	−.154**
Mother granting psychological autonomy	−.065**	−.065**
Father granting psychological autonomy	−.019†	−.019†

* Defined in this study as cheating on tests, smoking, drinking, shoplifting, and skipping school without an excuse.
** Significance probability < .01
† Significance probability < .05

Involvement in church activities had a modest inhibiting effect. As with the young men, it was public religious behavior rather than private religious behavior that was most significant to delayed sexual initiation. This is not to say that personal beliefs, prayer, and scripture reading were not important. But in the multivariate model, church attendance emerged as a stronger predictor. Typical comments about church activities from the unwed mothers revealed that such behavior declined before the initiation of sex:

> I was really active in the Church until my folks divorced. My dad was in the bishopric. I haven't been since they broke up. But I still pray every day and think and talk about the Church with people. I just don't go to church.

> My mom always forced me to go to church. We're LDS. I was baptized and all that. But my mom got sick of fighting me, so that after maybe age twelve, I just stopped going very often.

> I grew up Mormon, and I don't consider myself Mormon right now. I think I started trying to figure out what I believed around thirteen or fourteen. That also had a lot to do with my parents being pretty strong Mormons. I've always prayed. I have my personal beliefs. I don't really believe in an organized religion.

Mothers' regulation has a strong indirect effect on the daughters' sexual behavior through both peer pressure and church attendance. This is somewhat smaller than that for the young men. The lack of parental regulation and the inconsistency between mother and father are illustrated in the following comments:

> The rules depended on the mood they were in. Sometimes they'd come up with this rule: "Now you have to be home at eight on a school night." That never worked. "You

have got to have the house clean before you leave." That never worked. My mother could never stick to the rules.

They tried to have a lot of rules. But after a while they just gave up. 'Cause I'd never follow them. They tried. Everything I'd do, they'd come up with a new rule. They finally just gave up. My dad would try to ground me, and I'd just fight it. I'd get my mom, and it was kind of like they were two separate parents. I could get them to disagree, which helped me.

Peer pressure, public religious behavior, and mothers' regulation accounted for 72% of the variance in premarital sexual activity among LDS young women. This means that nearly three-fourths of the sexual initiation of this sample of LDS young women is accounted for by these three variables. LDS young women engaged in sex because their friends pressured them. This pressure came from young men they were dating, from those they were associating with, and even from their girlfriends.

As noted earlier, the interviews with the young unwed mothers shed some interesting insights about the power of external pressure to engage in sex. The reasons they gave in

Table 4. Reasons for Sexual Activity Reported by LDS Unwed Mothers

Question: "Why did you decide to have sex the first time?"	
Reason	Percent ($n = 45$)
Don't know, just happened	48
Coerced or raped	25
To be wanted	17
In love/special gift	5
Planning marriage	3
Wanted to do it	2

response to the question of why they had sex for the first time are presented in Table 4 and illustrate their susceptibility to forces they faced.

When asked why they had sex the first time, half of the unwed mothers replied, "I don't know." When pressed by the interviewer for a more insightful answer, they very emphatically replied, "I don't know!" Two young women expressed this lack of understanding.

> I don't know! It just happened! I didn't really at the time . . . like, I always told myself that I wouldn't do it until I was married. And one night it just happened. It was almost like I did not care anymore, I guess. We just did it.

> I became sexually active when I was sixteen. I don't know why. Just all of a sudden I decided. I don't even know why myself. A lot of guys had wanted to, and I always said no. And then all of a sudden I just did it.

It is remarkable that half of these young women initiated sexual activity, which has had such a drastic consequence in their lives, for reasons they do not understand.

It is obvious from these two comments that many of the girls who did not understand why they became involved in intimacy were pressured by boyfriends. An additional 25% clearly reported that they had been coerced to have sex, or in other words, they were raped. The young women made it clear that they were not just encouraged by their partners, but that they were strongly pressured into sex.

A substantial number of girls, 17%, engaged in sex for the first time because they wanted to feel accepted or to have a boyfriend. Pipher (1994), a clinical psychologist, argued that American culture poisons young women's feelings about themselves so that their only source of self-worth is attachment to a boyfriend. The powerful self-conformation that they hoped to gain from having a boyfriend was evident in their comments.

I don't have really low self-esteem, but probably the feeling of having a man, like the relationship or whatever, not wanting him to leave me. So I thought that by giving him some sort of pleasure maybe he would stay around longer. I don't know how to explain it, but probably for security reasons I guess. If that makes any sense.

I like being with someone. You know, someone just to be with, to hold hands. And it was just a cool thing, "I have a boyfriend." Especially if he is cute and popular. It's like "I'm dating so and so, and this is a cool thing." My first boyfriend was a cowboy; he rode bulls. That was real cool. I like the attention of a guy. I like getting attention from guys, because I never had any male give me attention in my home because I did not have a dad. It was just attention from guys that I like that made me have sex.

Feeling accepted. That is why I did it. That's always been important to me. I always wanted to feel accepted by boys.

Sadly, these LDS girls confused sex with affection, acceptance, and belonging. They felt that giving a boy sex would somehow create a lasting relationship with him. Unfortunately, the girls discovered that the enduring relationships they sought did not materialize from their sexual generosity.

The final 10% of the unwed mothers stated that they engaged in sex as a way to show their love to their partner. Several stated their "love" for their boyfriend motivated them to give him this special gift. Others reported that they were planning on marrying, and thus it was okay to have sex. Finally, only one young woman reported that she participated in sex for the first time because she was sexually aroused to the point that she wanted to engage in sexual relations.

Among these 45 LDS unwed mothers, all but one initiated sexual activity for reasons other than their own sexual feelings. These findings do not deny that young women have sexual desires, but that in making the decision to have sex for the first time, such feelings are relatively unimportant. Most were pressured to participate, while others wanted acceptance and self-validation derived from having a boyfriend.

CONCLUSION

This study reveals that initiation of sexual activity among LDS youth is influenced by a variety of social, religious, and personal characteristics. The social influence of friends, not surprisingly, appears to be the strongest predictor of LDS youths' participation in premarital sex. Although not as powerful as peer influences, religion does have a direct effect. The multivariate analysis suggests that significant religious effect is more a social effect than a strictly personal or spiritual effect.

However, the correlations do indeed show a strong inverse relationship between the different dimensions of religiosity and involvement in premarital sex. As a result, we can conclude that the more religious an LDS teenager is, the less likely that he or she will engage in immoral behaviors.

Finally, although parents' behavior does not have a direct relationship to the sexual behavior of their teenagers, parents do have a strong indirect effect on such behavior. Thus parents can affect the choice of their adolescent children's friends and positively influence their religious activity and spiritual development.

The major implications for parents from the analysis in this chapter appears to fall into three main areas. First, there is a need for parents, both mothers and fathers, to be actively involved in their teens' lives by what the literature refers to as "family regulation." This involves setting family rules, such as how late the teens can stay out at night; when, who, and where they can date; and how much they can be alone with members of the opposite sex. Equally important, parents need to monitor their teens' compliance to family rules. Sometimes a casual word with a teacher or parent of a friend about how things are going with the son or daughter and his or her friends will produce revelations about obedience to family rules. When rules are violated, parents must step forward and discipline their teens. This practice is sometimes hard for parents to do, but as our study discovered, teens expect appropriate discipline and feel unloved when it is neglected.

The second major implication for parents is that they should do all they can to involve their teens with friends and peers who share similar values and standards. Granted, teens have their own criteria for picking friends, but parents can create conditions that maximize the selection of good ones. Parents can encourage their teens to participate in extracurricular activities, such as debate, chess club, band, and other clubs or organizations. Generally, such participation will surround a teen with potential friends who have shared values.

Lastly, the power of religiosity cannot be overlooked. Parents can strengthen their children and minimize the negative effects of peer pressure by creating a home environment where youth can not only learn gospel principles but also feel the Spirit in their lives. Family religiosity is strengthened through activities such as prayer, scripture study, and family home evening.

While it is indeed daunting to raise righteous and responsible teenagers in these challenging times, it is not impossible. Although there were some disturbing findings in our study, Latter-day Saint youth generally are far less involved in immoral activities than their non-LDS peers, and faith and family will continue to be powerful influences for good.

References

Abma, J. C., Martinez, G. M., Mosher, W. D., & Dawson, B. S. (2004). *Teenagers in the United States: Sexual activity, contraceptive use, and childbearing, 2002.* National Center for Health Statistics, *Vital and Health Statistics, 23*(24).

Barber, B. K., Olsen, J. E., & Shagle, S. C. (1994). Associations between parental psychological and behavioral control and youth internalized and externalized behaviors. *Child Development, 65*(4), 1120–1136.

Beck, S. H., Cole, B. S., & Hammond, J. A. (1991). Religious heritage and pre-marital sex: Evidence from a national sample of young adults. *Journal for the Scientific Study of Religion, 30*(2), 173–180.

Benda, B. B., & DiBlasio, F. A. (1991). Comparison of four theories of adolescent sexual exploration. *Deviant Behavior, 12,* 235–257.

Brewster, K. L., Billy, J. O. G., & Grady, W. R. (1993). Social context and adolescent behavior: The impact of community on the transition to sexual activity. *Social Forces, 71*(3), 713–740.

Brewster, K. L., Cooksey, E. C., Guilkey, D. K., & Rindfuss, R. R. (1998). The changing impact of religion on the sexual and contraceptive behavior of ado-lescent women in the United States. *Journal of Marriage and Family, 60*(2), 493–504.

Capaldi, D. M., Crosby, L., & Stoolmiller, M. (1996). Predicting the timing of first sexual intercourse for at-risk adolescent males. *Child Development, 67*(2), 344–359.

Cochran, J. K., & Beeghley, L. (1991). The influence of religion on attitudes toward nonmarital sexuality: A preliminary assessment of reference group theory. *Journal for the Scientific Study of Religion, 30*(1), 45–62.

Cooksey, E. C., Rindfuss, R. R., & Guilkey, D. K. (1996). The initiation of ado-lescent sexual and contraceptive behavior during changing times. *Journal of Health and Social Behavior, 37* (1), 59–74.

Day, R. D. (1992). The transition to first intercourse among racially and culturally diverse youth. *Journal of Marriage and Family, 54*(4), 749–776.

Feldman, S. S., & Brown, N. L. (1993). Family influences on adolescent male sexu-ality: The mediational role of self-restraint. *Social Development, 2*(1), 15–35.

Flewelling, R. L., & Bauman, K. E. (1990). Family structure as a predictor of initial substance use and sexual intercourse in early adolescence. *Journal of Marriage and Family, 52*(1), 171–181.

Forste, R. T., & Heaton, T. B. (1988). Initiation of sexual activity among female adolescents. *Youth and Society, 19*(3), 250–268.

Harris, L., Oman, R. R., Vesely, S. K., Tolma, E. L., Aspy, C. B., Rodine, S., Mar-shall, L., & Fluhr, J. (2006). Associations between youth assets and sexual activity: Does adult supervision play a role? *Child: Care, Health and Develop-ment, 33*(4), 448–454.

Hayes, C. D. (1987). Adolescent pregnancy and childbearing: An emerging research focus. In C. Hayes (Ed.), *Risking the Future: Adolescent Sexuality, Pregnancy, and Childbearing, 2*, 1–6.

Hovell, M., Sipan, C., Blumberg, E., Atkins, C., Hofstetter, C. R., and Kreitner, S. (1994). Family influences on Latino and Anglo adolescents' sexual behavior. *Journal of Marriage and Family, 56*(4), 973–986.

Ku, L., Sonenstein, F. L., & Pleck, J. H. (1993). Neighborhood, family, and work: Influences on the premarital behaviors of adolescent males. *Social Forces, 72*(2), 479–503.

Levin, D. E., & Kilbourne, J. (2008). *So sexy, so soon: The new sexualized childhood.* New York: Ballantine Books.

McIlhaney, J. S., & Bush, F. M. (2008). *Hooked: New science on how casual sex is affecting our children.* Chicago: Northfield Publishing.

Miller, B. C., & Bingham, C. R. (1989). Family configuration in relation to the sexual behavior of female adolescents. *Journal of Marriage and Family, 51*(2), 499–506.

Miller, B. C., Monson, B. H., & Norton, M. C. (1995). The effects of forced sexual intercourse on white female adolescents. *Child Abuse and Neglect, 19*(10), 1289–1301.

Miller, B., & Moore, K. (1990). Adolescent sexual behavior, pregnancy, and parenting: Research through the 1980s. *Journal of Marriage and Family, 52*(4), 1025–1044.

Miller, K. S., Forehand, R., & Kotchick, B. A. (1999). Adolescent sexual behavior in two ethnic minority samples: The role of family variables. *Journal of Marriage and Family, 61*(1), 85–98.

Moore, K. A., Peterson, J. L., & Furstenberg, F. F. (1986). Parental attitudes and the occurrence of early sexual activity. *Journal of Marriage and Family, 48*(3), 777–782.

Newcomer, S. F., & Udry, J. R. (1984). Mothers' influence on the sexual behavior of their teenage children. *Journal of Marriage and Family, 46*(2), 477–485.

Petersen, L. R., & Donnenwerth, G. V. (1997). Secularization and the influence of religion on beliefs about premarital sex. *Social Forces, 75*(3), 1071–1088.

Perkins, D. F., Luster, T., Villarruel, F. A., & Small, S. (1998). An ecological, risk-factor examination of adolescents' sexual activity in three ethnic groups. *Journal of Marriage and Family, 60*(3), 660–673.

Pipher, M. (1994) *Reviving Ophelia: Saving the selves of adolescent girls*. New York: Ballantine Books.

Resnick, M. D., Bearman, P. S., Blum, R. W., Bauman, K. E., Harris, K. M., Jones, J., Tabor, J., Beuhring, T., Sieving, R. E., Shew, M., Ireland, M., Bearinger, L. H., & Udry, J. R. (1997). Protecting adolescents from harm: Findings from the National Longitudinal Study of Adolescent Health. *Journal of the American Medical Association, 278*, 823–832.

Rodgers, J. L. (1983). Family configuration and adolescent sexual behavior. *Population and Environment, 6*(2), 73–83.

Rodgers, K. B. (1999). Parental processes related to sexual risk-taking behaviors of adolescent males and females. *Journal of Marriage and Family, 61*, 99–109.

Schroeder, K. (1997). Parents pack power. *Education Digest, 63*(3), 73–74.

Sieving, R. E., Eisenberg, M. E., Pettingell, S., & Skay, C. (2006). Friends' influence on adolescents' first sexual intercourse. *Perspectives on Sexual and Reproductive Health, 38*(March), 13–19.

Small, S. A., & Kerns, D. (1993). Unwanted sexual activity among peers during early and middle adolescence: Incidence and risk factors. *Journal of Marriage and Family, 55*(4), 941–952.

Small, S. A., & Luster, T. (1994). Adolescent sexual activity: An ecologicial, risk-factor approach. *Journal of Marriage and Family, 56*(1), 181–192.

Smith, C., & Denton, M. L. (2005). *Soul searching: The religious and spiritual lives of American teenagers.* Oxford: Oxford University Press.

Studer, M., & Thornton, A. (1987). Adolescent religiosity and contraceptive usage. *Journal of Marriage and Family, 49*(1), 117–128.

Thornton, A., & Camburn, D. (1987). The influence of the family on premarital sexual attitudes and behaviors. *Demography, 24*(3), 323–340.

Thornton, A., & Camburn, D. (1989). Religious participation and adolescent sexual behavior and values. *Journal of Marriage and Family, 51*(3), 641–53.

Upchurch, D. M., Aneshensel, C. S., Sucoff, C. A., & Levy-Storms, L. (1999). Neighborhood and family contexts of adolescent sexual activity. *Journal of Marriage and Family, 61*(4), 920–933.

Weinstein, M., & Thornton, A. (1989). Mother-child relations and adolescent sexual attitudes and behavior. *Demography, 26*, 563–577.

Whitbeck, L. B., Conger, R. D., & Kao, M. (1993). The influence of parental support, depressed affect, and sexual experiences among adolescent girls. *Journal of Family Issues, 14(2)*, 261–278.

Whitbeck, L. B., Simons, R. L., & Goldberg, E. (1996). Adolescent sexual intercourse. In R. L. Simons and Associates (Eds.), *Understanding differences between divorced and intact families: Stress, interaction, and child outcome* (pp. 144–156). Thousand Oaks, CA: Sage.

Whitbeck, L. B., Yoder, K. A., Hoyt, D. R., & Conger, R. D. (1999). Early adolescent sexual activity: A developmental study. *Journal of Marriage and Family, 61*, 934–946.

Wu, L. L., & Martinson, B. C. (1993). Family structure and the risk of a premarital birth. *American Sociological Review, 58(2)*, 210–232.

Young, B. (1860). In *Journal of Discourses*. London: Latter-day Saints' Book Depot. 8:56.

Seven

DATING AND MARRIAGE

A 2001 study (Glenn & Marquardt) of 1,000 young women attending four-year colleges and universities across the United States found that "dating" has all but disappeared from American college campuses. Only half of the women reported they had been asked on six or more dates during their entire college career. In fact, one-third of the women had had two dates or fewer during the same four years.

Instead of dating, college students now "hang out" in mixed groups in a variety of settings, including apartments, dormitory rooms, student centers, pizza parlors, coffee shops, and bars. From these associations young people may pair off and "hook up" with a member of the opposite sex.

In Glenn and Marquardt's study, "hooking up" was defined as "when a girl and a guy get together for a physical encounter and don't necessarily expect anything further" (Glenn and Marquardt, 2001, p. 4). Forty percent of the women in the study had participated in a hookup, and over 90% indicated that hooking up is a regular activity on their campus.

However, the level of physical intimacy involved in a

hookup remains vague in student conversations, meaning any-thing from kissing to sexual intercourse. The vagueness of the term allows students to tell others that they have hooked up without completely compromising their reputation. Some col-lege students applaud the idea that hanging out and hooking up carry no commitment or responsibility, such as exclusivity or the designation of the relationship as "girlfriend and boyfriend."

The popularity of hanging out and hooking up has influ-enced many college students to shift their focus from seeking marriage to seeking casual sexual relationships. Phrases like "friends with benefits" and "sex without strings and relation-ships without rings" are tossed around on campus, and sexual intimacy has evolved into something casual and common.

This startling description of hooking up and the demise of dating on American campuses motivated us to conduct a study among BYU students to ascertain whether or not these trends have in any way invaded that campus as well. Upon enroll-ment, BYU students make a commitment to "live a chaste and virtuous life" (Honor Code). The Church of Jesus Christ of Latter-day Saints and BYU affirm that sexual relationships out-side the covenant of marriage are inappropriate.

President Gordon B. Hinckley (1988) told the BYU stu-dent body:

> This university will become increasingly unique among the universities of the nation and the world. We must never lose that uniqueness. We must hold tenaciously to it. With-out it there would be no justification whatever for sponsor-ship by the Church and the use of the tithing funds of the Church to support it. . . .
>
> The honor code to which you subscribe is also related to this. It is designed to insure the presence on this campus of a student body of young men and young women with standards above the cut of the world at large, ideals that are conducive to spiritual relationships and a social atmosphere of respectability.

Interestingly, Leon Kass (1997), a non-LDS researcher, suggested that in light of the disturbing findings about hooking-up activities on college campuses that American parents should steer their children "to religiously affiliated colleges that attract like-minded people" (p. 62). According to him, such a choice will assist their children in avoiding involvement in the hooking-up culture. The primary purpose of our study was to ascertain if BYU's unique culture offers the protection hoped for by Kass.

Over the past 40 years, young people have been marrying later and later in their lives. Parents, Church leaders, and public policy makers are seriously concerned about whether or not a substantial number of young Americans are merely delaying marriage or have rejected marriage and opted for singleness. The answer to this question has very significant implications for society. Unfortunately, a definitive answer will not be known for a generation or more. However, some clues about LDS young people are available now in this survey of unmarried BYU students.

THE BYU SURVEY

The survey was designed to learn about BYU students' goals and attitudes about marriage and dating: how important marriage is to them, how confident they are that they will find a mate, and how they go about the process of getting to know people of the opposite sex. We also asked what type of physical intimacy students thought appropriate for hanging-out and dating relationships and what intimate activity they had participated in. The methodology of the survey is given in Appendix A.

Life goals and attitudes about marriage. One indication of the relative importance of marriage was obtained by identifying how single BYU students ranked marriage in relation to several other important life goals, ranging from finishing college to helping the less fortunate. The highest-ranked goal for BYU students was a close personal relationship with God, closely followed by marriage in the temple, a goal which is both spiritual and marital (see Table 1). Ninety-seven percent of the BYU women and 93% of the BYU men answered that marrying in the temple is a "very important" goal.

We compared the attitudes of BYU students to those of a very large national sample of graduating high school seniors (eighteen years old) interviewed in the spring of 2000 in the Monitoring the Future Project (Bachman, Johnston, & O'Malley, 2001). These high school seniors are younger than typical BYU students, but they provide a reasonable picture of what young people are generally thinking about marriage. The goals ranked by the high school seniors, although not identical to those chosen by BYU students, were similar; marriage was an important goal for both groups. It seems that most young people in this country desire to marry.

Although aspirations for marriage and a happy family life were similar between BYU and the national sample, there is a striking difference concerning religious or spiritual goals.

We asked BYU students several other questions about their perceptions of and attitudes toward marriage (see Table 3).

Table 1. BYU Students' Life Goals

How important are the following goals to you? Percentage of single BYU students who responded "very important."		
Goal	Men (*n* = 327)	Women (*n* = 445)
A close personal relationship with God	93	98
Marrying in the temple	93	97
Finishing college	93	85
Having children	85	90
Marrying	87	88
Obtaining a job I like	89	53
Maintaining health/fitness	54	59
Helping people who are less fortunate	48	51
Having recreational and leisure activity	45	38
Earning considerable money	28	11

Ninety-six percent of the BYU students claimed that "being married is a very important goal" to them. In the Glenn and Marquardt study mentioned above, 83% of women agreed

Table 2. American High School Students' Life Goals

How important is each of the following to you in your life? Percentage who responded "very important."		
Goal	Men (n = 996)	Women (n = 992)
Having a good marriage and family life	73	83
Being able to find steady work	65	72
Finding purpose and meaning in my life	53	70
Having plenty of time for recreation and hobbies	41	27
Having lots of money	34	20
Working to correct social and economic inequalities	11	11

Bachman, J. G., Johnston, L. D., & O'Malley, P. M. (2001), *Monitoring the future: Questionnaire responses from the nation's high school seniors.* Ann Arbor, MI: Institute for Social Research, University of Michigan.

Table 3. BYU Students' Attitudes about Marriage, by Percentage

Percentage of single BYU students who responded "strongly agree" or "agree."		
Attitude	Men (n = 327)	Women (n = 445)
Being married is a very important goal to me.	96	97
I believe that when the time is right, I will find the right person to marry.	88	92
I would like to meet my future husband/wife at college.	68	57
When I look ahead five or ten years, it is hard to see how marriage fits in with my other plans.	7	5
Most people will have fuller and happier lives if they choose legal marriage rather than staying single or just living with someone.	93	87
I see so few good or happy marriages that I question it as a good way of life.	6	6

("strongly agree" or "somewhat agree") that marriage is a very important goal (see Table 4).

Interestingly, the women in the national study are more optimistic about finding a mate when the time is right than are BYU students. Nearly the entire national sample of women, 99%, is convinced the right spouse will appear in their lives at the appropriate time. The BYU women are a little less confident at 92%, followed by BYU men at 88%. The differences are small, but they do suggest that BYU students take seriously the task of finding a spouse who meets their high expectations. They are a little less sure that someone with the traits they desire will appear at the right time.

Table 4. American College Women's
Attitudes about Marriage, by Percentage

Being married is a very important goal for me.	
Strongly agree	85
Somewhat agree	14
I believe that when the time is right, I will find the right person to marry.	
Strongly agree	47
Somewhat agree	36
Somewhat disagree	12
Strongly disagree	6
I would like to meet my future husband at college.	
Strongly agree	19
Somewhat agree	44
Somewhat disagree	24
Strongly disagree	12
When I look ahead five or ten years, it is hard to see how marriage fits in with my other plans.	
Strongly or somewhat agree	29

Telephone survey of 1,000 women at four-year colleges and universities in the U.S. in winter 2000. In Glenn, N., & Marquardt, E. (2001), *Hooking up, hanging out, and hoping for Mr. Right: College women on dating and mating today.* New York: Institute for American Values, 42, 73, 74.

About two-thirds of the women in the national Glenn and Marquardt study and two-thirds of the BYU men in our study desired to meet their future husband or wife at college. We were a little surprised that only 57% of the BYU women hoped to meet their future husband at college. As we will discuss below, some BYU women planned on finishing their schooling before they marry. For whatever reason, nearly half of the young women at BYU reported not being very concerned about meeting their future spouse while attending BYU.

The vast majority of BYU students not only hope to marry but expect to be married within five to ten years. Only 5% of the men and 7% of the women do not see marriage in their future within that time frame. This is considerably less than the 29% of the national sample of women who feel that marriage is more distant than five to ten years in their future.

BYU students are convinced that marriage is a happier way of life than singleness or cohabitation. Approximately 90% of the BYU students feel marriage is the more fulfilling lifestyle, as compared to 39% of the female high school seniors and 28% of the male high school seniors (answering "agree" or "mostly agree" in Table 5). Clearly, the teaching of marriage as an important part of the "plan of happiness" in the doctrines and scriptures of the LDS Church influences the hopes of LDS youth and young adults.

While BYU students have likely seen family conflict and divorce in their own families or their friends' families, these experiences do not greatly discourage BYU students from seeking marriage. Only 6% of those attending BYU indicated that they questioned marriage as a way of life, as compared to 28% of the non-LDS high school seniors. However, this 6%, though a relatively low figure, may be cause for concern among parents and Church leaders. The Church gives marriage high priority because of its importance for happiness in this life and exaltation in the hereafter.

Although most studies among college students have discovered that to a large degree students feel marriage is important, have a desire to get married, and are confident they will eventually do so, these feelings and aspirations are significantly stronger among BYU students.

Hanging out. The hanging-out and hooking-up culture flourishes on college campuses across the country to such an extent that it has become the norm. In fact, few researchers bother to collect data on this phenomenon. They simply identify this culture as a way of life among modern college students (Milanese, 2002). As seen in Table 6, hanging out is also very popular among BYU students. One-fourth of the BYU students said they hang out in mixed groups six or more times a week. Hanging-out activities in some form have always been a staple of college social life. What seems to be different with the

Table 5. American High School Seniors'
Attitudes about Marriage, by Percentage

	Men	Women
Most people will have fuller and happier lives if they choose legal marriage rather than staying single or just living with someone.		
Agree	20	15
Mostly agree	19	13
Neither	36	31
Mostly disagree	11	13
Disagree	15	28
I see so few good or happy marriages that I question it as a way of life.		
Agree	11	12
Mostly agree	16	17
Neither	29	23
Mostly disagree	16	20
Disagree	27	29

Bachman, J. G., Johnston, L. D., & O'Malley, P. M. (2001). *Monitoring the future: Questionnaire responses from the nation's high school seniors.* Ann Arbor, MI: Institute for Social Research, University of Michigan, 167, 194.

current generation of college students is that men and women are hanging out together considerably more often than in generations past.

The most popular hanging-out activity among BYU students appears to be just sitting around a dorm or apartment and talking. Watching television or a video and going out to eat are also popular hanging-out activities. Ball games, concerts, plays, church meetings, or firesides were occasionally identified as things to do when hanging out.

Young women at BYU reported that they like hanging out because it allows them a more active role in initiating interaction with young men. Both men and women acknowledged that women often get a hanging-out session going, although hanging out is still more often initiated by men (see Table 7).

Table 6. Frequency of Hanging Out and Dating
among BYU Students, by Percentage

	Men (n = 324)	Women (n = 436)
How often each week did you hang out with members of the opposite sex last semester?		
0	3	2
1	15	18
2	17	22
3	15	14
4	13	12
5	9	11
6 or more	28	23
How often each month did you go on a date last semester?		
0	7	16
1	26	29
2	19	16
3	13	11
4	12	8
5	7	6
6 or more	16	13

Table 7. Initiation of Hanging Out and Dating among BYU Students, by Percentage

	Men (n = 321)	Women (n = 444)
Who initiated any hanging out you participated in last semester?		
Only men	6	16
Mostly men	36	53
Men and women equally	47	30
Mostly women	11	1
Only women	0	0
Who initiated any dates you went on last semester?		
Only men	27	26
Mostly men	44	36
Men and women equally	21	25
Mostly women	5	8
Only women	3	4

Young men at BYU reported that they often prefer hanging out to dating because it spares them having to ask for a date and risk rejection. Also, hanging out reduces a man's financial burden, since everyone pays his or her own way.

The only major regret BYU students have about hanging out is that they don't do as much of it as they would like. About 40% of both men and women indicated that they would like to hang out more often (see Table 8).

Dating. Dating involves one of the partners, usually the young man, extending an invitation to the other to participate together in a specified activity. Unlike dating at most American campuses, dating at BYU has not been replaced by hanging out. Twenty-three percent of the men and 19% of the women reported going on five or more dates per month (see Table 6). Thirty-five percent of the men and 27% of the women had at least one date a week. Only 7% of the young men and 16% of the women reported they had not been on a date during the previous month. Many BYU students have as many dates in

Table 8. Satisfaction with Frequency of Hanging Out and Dating among BYU Students, by Percentage

	Men (n = 325)	Women (n = 441)
How did you feel about the frequency of your hanging out with members of the opposite sex last semester?		
Too often	5	3
About right	59	57
Not often enough	25	31
Not nearly often enough	11	9
How do you feel about the frequency of your dating last semester?		
Too often	4	3
About right	45	34
Not often enough	35	36
Not nearly often enough	16	27

one month as the senior women in the national study had in nearly four years.

Dating practices at BYU today are not drastically different from those of previous generations. Men do most of the inviting (see Table 7). Our survey respondents said that the typical date involves dinner along with a concert, play, or similar activity. Most of the popular activities require the man to pay for dinner and tickets. BYU students listed less-expensive dates as well, such as watching a video, playing cards or board games, attending church activities, hiking, and going for a drive. What has changed is that a substantial number of BYU women have issued a date invitation, and hanging out takes the place of some of the dating. But hanging out has not replaced dating to the same extent it has at other universities.

Compared to men, BYU women were less happy with the frequency of their dating (see Table 8). A few BYU women said they have an active and satisfying dating life, while the others voiced a desire for more. Over half of the women felt they do not date often enough. A majority of the men, 51%, also felt they don't date often enough. When asked why they did not date more, BYU men identified the fear of rejection, financial constraints, and study demands as limiting factors.

Physical intimacy. As discussed earlier, hanging out on American campuses today is linked to hooking up, which usually involves some degree of physical intimacy. According to a study conducted by the Centers for Disease Control, 68% of college students in the United States had sexual intercourse during the three months previous to the survey (National College Health Risk Behavior Survey—United States, 1995). Among college senior women in Glenn and Marquardt's 2001 national study, only 31% reported they had never engaged in sex, and of the women who had sex, only 36% had not had sexual intercourse during the previous month (Glenn & Marquardt, 2001).

To determine the degree of physical intimacy that is part of the dating culture at BYU, we first asked the sample of students what they felt was acceptable and then the kinds of physical acts in which they had been involved. BYU students, not surprisingly, are quite conservative in their acceptance of physical intimacy in hanging out or in dating relationships. It is clear from the responses in Table 9 that they defined hanging out as largely platonic: around 70% feel that holding hands, hugging, and kissing are inappropriate in a hanging-out relationship. A small percentage of students said that "making out and intense kissing" are acceptable in a hanging-out relationship. Such activity is commonly known at BYU as a NCMO (nik-mo), a "noncommittal make-out," the BYU equivalent of the casual sexual behavior found on other American campuses.

Finally, an overwhelming majority of BYU students feel that premarital sexual intimacy is unacceptable. Given the Latter-day Saint doctrine and teachings on moral cleanliness, coupled with the BYU Honor Code, it is not surprising that casual sexual behavior is not nearly as prevalent at BYU as on other college campuses. BYU students are almost unanimous in feeling that physical expressions of affection like holding hands, hugging, and good-night kisses are appropriate and acceptable in a dating relationship. About half feel there is nothing wrong with more intense kissing while dating. But even among dating couples there is near-unanimous rejection of serious sexual involvement, mainly petting and intercourse.

Importantly, when it comes to actual behavior, the actions of BYU students closely reflect their ideals (see Table 9). The levels of holding hands, hugging, and kissing (including intense kissing) among those in a casual, hanging-out relationship are a little higher than we expected, but not much. Only 2% of the young men have engaged in oral sex or intercourse while in a hanging-out relationship with a young woman. Only 1% of the young women have done so.

Not surprisingly, intimacy is higher among dating couples. But the number who acknowledged having oral sex or intercourse is still remarkably low. Only 3 to 4% of single BYU students have had sex, as compared to 60 to 70% among their peers at other universities. Even if there is some underreporting among BYU students because of feelings of shame or a fear of being turned in to the Honor Code Office, the level is nowhere near the national average. At BYU, personal integrity and religiosity combine with the Honor Code and a religious environment including religion classes, campus congregations, and devotionals with Church authorities to produce a remarkably low rate of premarital sexual activity.

Shifting from hanging out to dating. Some confusion, conflict, disappointment, and pain have been observed among couples moving from a casual hanging-out relationship to dating (Kass, 1997). One person may define a relationship as intimate and long-term, while the other feels that it is strictly a casual association. Insights into how BYU students shift from a "just-friends" relationship to a dating relationship were ascertained from responses to our open-ended question: "How does someone try to shift a relationship from hanging out to dating?"

Table 9. Intimacy during Hanging Out and Dating among BYU Students, by Percentage

	Hanging Out		Dating	
	Men (n = 326)	Women (n = 445)	Men (n = 326)	Women (n = 445)
What role does physical intimacy such as holding hands, kissing, making out, petting, and sexual behavior play in hanging out and dating? (The following lists the percentage of single BYU students who said "appropriate" or "very appropriate.")				
Holding hands, hugging, and kissing	30	28	98	99
Making out and intense kissing	3	1	44	37
Petting	1	1	4	3
Sexual behavior	1	0	2	1
At college, which of these activities have you participated in while hanging out/while dating? (The following lists the percentage of single BYU students who said they have done the listed activities.)				
Holding hands, hugging, and kissing	47	49	86	81
Making out and intense kissing	13	10	54	46
Petting	3	2	12	12
Oral sex or intercourse	2	1	3	4

The ways and means of shifting hanging out into something more serious are presented in Table 10. The confusion noted on other campuses is also present at BYU, and there are no universally accepted ways of saying to one another, "We are now in a dating relationship."

Not surprisingly, the most frequently mentioned strategy was to spend time together outside the circle of friends. One student insightfully made this point: "Relationships are not formed in groups, so separate from the group and spend quality one-on-one time with the person. I think too many students are afraid of the transitional risk—the 'what will happen if I speak up and ask him or her for a date'—so they remain in the comfortable bubble of hanging out because there is no commitment or failure that way!"

Another said the shift comes when "they 'ask out' the other person, thus formally establishing interest." One young woman got right to the point: "Someone has to say the word *date*! This shift in formality sends the other person the message that another dimension of the relationship is desired."

An increase in physical intimacy is another important signal among BYU students. One student noted that "some sort

Table 10. *How BYU Students Shift from Hanging Out to Dating, by Percentage*

	Men (n = 476)	Women (n = 552)
How does someone try to shift a relationship from hanging out to dating?		
Spend more one-on-one time	45	44
Increase physical intimacy	19	21
Talking about creating a dating relationship	18	20
Happens naturally over time	6	5
I don't know	5	4
When man pays for activities	2	2
Other	5	6

of contact, like holding hands, cuddling, and kissing," defines the shift. Contact even as casual as holding hands sends the message that a couple has changed the type and intensity of the relationship. Kissing was cited by a large number as the most obvious sign that a relationship has grown serious.

Another described the shift in these words: "My friend turned into my boyfriend by asking me if it would ruin the friendship if he kissed me. He did, and I continued to think of him as a friend until a few more kisses. We realized that we were basically dating after we kissed. We hung out together more, talked more, and kissed more."

BYU students are similar in this regard to other college women in the national study, who reported that kissing signaled a dating relationship. Said one woman at Yale: "We didn't talk about it. We kissed. I guess that . . . at the end it sort of became clear [that we were together], and after that we just started to hang out all the time. And at that point I knew that we were dating. And later on, after a couple of weeks, like we actually became a couple, as in I would refer to him as my boyfriend" (Glenn and Marquardt, 2001, p. 28).

Only about 20% of the BYU students identified talking to each other as a way to confirm a dating relationship. This low level of using discussion as the definer is somewhat surprising, given that 85% of BYU students know about the concept of "defining the relationship," known popularly as "DTR." This type of discussion has different names but seems to be present on most campuses.

An illustrative comment from a BYU student is, "Verbally, you have to talk about it so both individuals know that now you are 'dating,' so there are not unmet expectations or misunderstanding."

Another student said, "DTRs—Defining the Relationship. In other words, you have to tell each other that you are only dating each other and no one else."

Student comments reveal a general loathing of the dreaded DTR. In spite of the distaste, nearly two-thirds had experienced at least one DTR during the previous semester. A few students, nearly 10%, had had four or more DTRs during the semester. Young men were a little more likely than women to initiate the "where are we going" talk. It seems that partners in dating relationships are moving at different speeds, and one generally feels the need for clarification before the other does.

Although the hanging-out culture is certainly prevalent at BYU, students here date more and hook up less than their national college-student peers. There is significantly less pre-marital sex among BYU students due to their strong religious values concerning chastity and their commitment to the Honor Code. BYU students, however, are like other college students in that they often experience uncertainty about shifting a casual relationship to a more serious one. Fortunately, most realize that one-on-one time, modest physical contact, and heart-to-heart talks are ways to communicate a desire to make the relationship more serious—to consciously move from the "just friends" to the "we are a couple" state.

The search for a spouse. Most BYU students reported they hoped to find someone to marry while at the university, so we asked them to identify the traits they were looking for in a spouse. We asked them to rate how important it is that the person they marry has certain traits (see Table 11).

We were pleasantly surprised that BYU students identified spirituality or religiosity as the most favored trait. Over 90% of the women and 87% of the men rated religiosity as "very important" in considering someone for marriage. They want to marry someone who is committed to The Church of Jesus Christ of Latter-day Saints and its doctrines, principles, and practices.

Most research on characteristics desired in a potential spouse has ignored religiosity. The few studies that have added religious orientation to the list have found college students rate it at or near the bottom (Buss, 1998; Stewart, Stinnett, &

Table 11. Traits BYU Students Desire in a
Spouse, by Percentage

How important are the following characteristics in the person you desire to marry? Remember, no one is perfect, so please don't mark "very important" for every trait. The following table lists answers marked "very important."	Men (n = 327)	Women (n = 445)
Spirituality, religious	87	91
Communicative, open	77	78
Wants children	69	80
Kind, considerate, understanding	67	78
Fun, sense of humor	59	61
Ambitious, hard worker	40	68
Educated	32	59
Intelligence/Smart	43	42
Healthy	35	26
Social, outgoing	26	28
Physically attractive	37	9
From a good family	12	16
Athletic	10	8
Earning capacity	1	12

Rosenfeld, 2000). This is another way in which BYU students are dramatically different from most other young adults.

Many studies have noted that both men and women desire pleasant, cooperative, and supportive personalities in those they consider for marriage (Buss, 1998; Stewart et al., 2000). Kindness, communicativeness, sense of humor, consideration for others, and empathy are strongly desired. These virtues were extolled by Elder Jeffrey R. Holland, a Church leader and former president of Brigham Young University, in counsel to BYU students: "There are many qualities you will want to look for in a friend or a serious date—to say nothing of a spouse and eternal companion—but surely among the very first and most basic of those qualities will be those of care and sensitivity towards others, a minimum of self-centeredness that allows compassion and courtesy to be evident" (Holland, 2000, p. 3).

Research reported prominently in national news has made much to-do about men's fixation on physical attractiveness in a potential wife. Such is not the case among BYU students, as only 37% of the men admitted that looks were "very important" to them.

An examination of these desired traits reveals that BYU students have a pretty good idea of the type of person they wish to marry. Fortunately, the desired traits are those that will most likely foster a fulfilling marriage. The most important traits in the eyes of BYU students are those of spirituality and a kind and open personality, both of which facilitate a strong marital relationship.

False starts. When students talk freely among themselves, it is common to hear stories of unrequited love and broken hearts, or what might be characterized as "false starts." Exactly half of the BYU students, both men and women, reported they had broken up a romantic relationship during the school year. One-third reported one broken relationship, 12% claimed two, and 4% of the men and 6% of the women reported three or more break-ups.

Not surprisingly, no single reason, event, or circumstance precipitated the demise of most courtships. The reasons these romantic relationships ended in failure are reported in Table 12. For about 20% of the students, as the couple spent more time together, feelings of attraction declined and the relationship lost its initial excitement.

As can be seen in Table 13, a study of 185 college students reported similar results: 27% of them cited being "tired of each other" as a factor in their decision to end a romantic relationship (Knox, Gibson, Zusman, & Gallmeier, 1997). One BYU woman's comment illustrates this process. "We didn't have very much in common—I fell out of love. I couldn't imagine marrying him."

Table 12. Reasons BYU Students Ended a Relationship,
by Percentage

Why did the last relationship end?	(*n* = 146)
Died out, boring, didn't feel right	19
Conflicts, possessive partner, unbalanced relationsip	19
Partner had someone else, cheating	11
Relationship became too physical	9
Physically separated, mission, moved	9
Not ready for marriage, too immature	8
Drifted apart, different goals	7
Relationship happened too fast	6
Met someone else, wanted to date others	6
Other	5

A young BYU man explained, "I stopped having feelings for her, so I ended it."

Another young BYU man noted, "I was not in love with her. We dated for ten months—she was in love with me—and I tried to fall in love with her. She is a great person, but I couldn't fall in love with her."

Besides just the gradual decline in romantic feelings, about 20% of the BYU student relationships fell apart due to serious conflicts when the students got to know each other better. In some cases, one partner became jealous and overly possessive, while in others the relationship became unbalanced, with one partner giving much more than the other.

As shown in Table 13, the study at a large southeastern university found that 43% of students terminated a relationship because of "too many differences/different values." This number is more than double the percentage at BYU. We suspect that a greater similarity of values and expectations has a positive effect on relationships among BYU students, since most are members of the LDS Church.

Table 13. Reasons American College Students Ended a Relationship, by Percentage

Reason for ending relationship	(*n* = 146)
Too many differences/different values	43
Got tired of each other	27
Cheating	18
Dishonesty	18
I met someone new	15
Separation	15
My partner met someone new	13
Parental disapproval	13
Violence/abuse	9
Alcohol/drugs	7
I went back to a previous lover	6
My partner went back to a previous lover	5

Survey of 185 undergraduates at a southeastern university.
Knox, D., et al. (1997). "Why college students end relationships," *College Student Journal* *31*(4), 451.

BYU students reported that they ended unbalanced relationships. "It was all one-sided," one young woman stated and went on to say, "He wanted to marry me, and I got swept off my feet at first, then I few days later realized I did not even like him, so I ended it."

A young man complained, "She started to get really annoying. We didn't get along anymore. I found myself caring about her less and less."

Several students noted religion was the source of their conflict. For example, "We ran out of things to talk about; we were just very different—different goals and levels of spiritual commitment."

One young woman ended a relationship "because he decided to leave the Church and began to question the principles that I believe in."

About 10% wanted out when they discovered their partner was "two-timing" them. Students made it clear that "cheating," even if it does not involve physical intimacy, is given zero tolerance at BYU. The anger of a young woman is obvious in her comment: "He had a girlfriend I did not know about!! I am not bitter, yeah right!"

Another said, "He strung several girls along without any of us knowing and then dumped all of us but one, got engaged in a month, and got married the next."

Another 10% of the students felt they were attracted only physically or became too physically involved; the resultant guilt caused them to flee the relationship and sometimes to resent their partner. One young man noted his mistaking lust for love: "It was all physical. I was deceiving myself about my love for her, which was actually only physical."

A young woman lamented, "I ended it because we were 'too physical' without having potential for marriage. We love each other, dated for two years, but it got too physical. We messed up and it ruined us! I'm glad it finally ended."

Physical separation, immaturity, and moving too quickly without really knowing each other were also mentioned by students as strong reasons for ending a relationship that seemed at one point in time to hold the promise of marriage.

The frequency of false starts and the variety of reasons for failed relationships suggest that finding a marriageable partner is not an easy task and often involves a certain amount of what some view as good luck or serendipity. It is clear that many events, experiences, and circumstances can doom a romantic relationship.

Contributing to the difficulty of the task is that both partners must be simultaneously motivated to pursue an enduring relationship. Unfortunately, if one of the partners loses interest, the other is left feeling rejected, hurt, and sometimes angry.

In spite of the long litany of things that go wrong in relationships, BYU institutional research shows that 63% of male students who graduate are married by graduation time, as are 55% of female students (Brigham Young University, 2003).

Deciding to marry. Making a decision to marry a person—which to most BYU students has eternal implications—can be a daunting challenge. Students were asked how they would know when they had found "the one" or "someone" to marry. The responses to this open-ended question revealed both considerable variation and some confusion among students about how to identify someone to marry (see Table 14). Most frequently mentioned was asking for some type of spiritual confirmation. 22% of the answers given by the men and nearly 30% by the women reported they focused primarily on spiritual feelings and answers to prayers. Looking to spiritual manifestations makes the BYU mate selection process considerably different from the process by which their national peers make the decision to marry.

Feelings that it is the right thing to do ranked next, followed by feelings of love. Compatibility in personality, goals, and hopes for the future accounted for 9 or 10%. Enjoyment of being together, bringing out the best in each other, friendship, open communication, physical attractiveness, and trust were mentioned in 1 to 7% of the answers. Interestingly, 7% of the young men and 4% of the young women admitted they were totally clueless about how they would make a decision whether or not to marry.

The rate of students' successful searches for an eternal companion is fairly high at BYU. Thirty-eight percent of the young women and 43% of the young men reported they were currently in a relationship with marriage potential. The percentage is somewhat higher for BYU seniors, at 48% for both men and women. This is the same proportion in the national sample, where 48% of senior women reported they currently had a boyfriend (Glenn & Marquardt, 2001).

Hesitation in the search. Even though BYU students engage in a lot of hanging out and dating, many do not seem to be

Table 14. How BYU Students Expect to Decide to Marry, by Percentage

How will you know when you have found a person or "the" person to marry?	Men (n = 486*)	Women (n = 767*)
Spiritual confirmation	22	29
Feels right	15	12
Feelings of love	10	10
Compatible, complement each other	10	9
Enjoy spending time together	7	7
Brings out the best in me	4	7
Friendship	3	5
Open communication	3	4
Physical attraction	3	1
Trust, confidence	2	1
I don't know	7	4
Other	15	11

* Some respondents gave more than one answer.

making much progress toward getting married. These unmarried students identified the factors that were influencing them to avoid marriage (see Table 15). Some of these students have experienced the divorces of their own parents. In addition, marriage is generally portrayed negatively in the media. A study of American young adults not attending college reported the same fear:

> Despite doubts and difficulties, young men and women have not given up on the ideal of finding a soul mate to marry. On the contrary, they are dedicated to the goal of finding a lifelong best friend and kindred spirit. However, their ideals of soul-mate marriage contrast sharply with personal experience—as well as the popular culture's portrait—of married people. Both media images and real-life models of marriage tend to be more negative than positive. Many in this study have grown up with unhappily married

or divorced parents. They know exactly what a bad marriage is, but they are less sure of what a good marriage looks like. Some can only describe a good marriage as "the opposite of my parents." (Popenoe & Whitefield, 2000, p. 16)

Sixty percent of BYU students indicated "fear of making a mistake" as a primary factor that discourages them in making decisions regarding marriage. Closely associated with this fear of selecting the wrong mate was a fear of the responsibilities of marriage, along with a fear of parenthood. About a third of the students identified both these fears as either "strong" or "moderate" influences to delay marriage.

Over half of the women and around one-third of the men claimed they had not yet had a viable opportunity to marry. Surprisingly, more young women than young men indicated they were delaying marriage to finish their schooling. Nearly half of the young women identified educational goals as a significant influence in their decision not to marry at that time.

About 10% of the students report that their family pressures them not to marry while in college. We feel this is unfortunate, because opportunities for meeting potential partners become much more limited after leaving BYU in most cases. Many BYU students are following the trend of the world to delay marriage and family for educational and professional reasons. Yet more undergraduates at BYU, 23%, are married than at other four-year institutions (Brigham Young University, 2003).

Conclusion

Leon Kass (1997) gave parents sound advice when he encouraged them to guide their children to religiously affiliated colleges and universities if they want their children to marry. This is particularly evident at BYU. Almost all students desire to marry and are confident that they will. They have been taught and recognize that marriage is "ordained of God" (D&C 49:15).

Table 15. Factors Influencing BYU Students
to Delay Marriage, by Percentage

Are any of the following factors influencing you to delay marriage? Choose "strong," "moderate," "weak," or "no influence." The following lists the percentage of single BYU students who responded "strong" or "moderate" influence.	Men (*n* = 327)	Women (*n* = 445)
Fear of making a mistake	59	58
Need more emotional maturity	44	59
No opportunity to marry	33	56
Desire to finish school	26	45
Fear of responsibility	33	34
Fear of responsibility of parenthood	29	33
Desire to establish career	29	22
Pressure from family not to marry	12	12
Pressure from friends not to marry	6	9
Unworthy to marry in the temple	9	5
Other	25	11

BYU students hang out in mixed groups, just like students at other universities, yet the casual sexual encounters associated with hooking up are mostly absent. Remarkably, relatively few single BYU students report sexual experience. Most are keeping their commitment to chastity. Even though the dating culture at BYU may have changed somewhat in recent years, it is still an environment conducive to finding a mate who shares fundamental beliefs and values.

The traits identified by BYU students as desirable in a spouse are in some ways similar to those identified by other college students. Most want to marry someone who has a pleasant personality and is motivated to complete his or her education and pursue a career. What is dramatically different is that BYU students place a much higher premium on spirituality and religiosity than other students do. The characteristics BYU students are seeking will generally foster a strong and satisfying marital relationship.

This is not to say that the process is easy. Students often struggle in the dating game. Most experience moments of fun and fulfillment but also times of despair when relationships are absent or fail.

BYU is a remarkable meeting place for LDS young people. Literally thousands of single members of the opposite sex, in the desired age range and with many of the desired traits, including shared religious values, are gathered there. The sheer number of potential partners may be bewildering and make it hard to decide whom to marry—77% of BYU's nearly 30,000 students are single—but most students appreciate the opportunity to meet and date in a religious atmosphere. It is encouraging to see that most BYU students eventually marry.

This chapter was coauthored with Lauren Smith, who at the time of this research was an undergraduate research assistant in sociology at BYU, and Mindy Judd, who was a graduate student in sociology at BYU.

REFERENCES

Bachman, J. G., Johnston, L. D., & O'Malley, P. M. (2001). *Monitoring the future: Questionnaire responses from the nation's high school seniors, 2000.* Ann Arbor, MI: Institute for Social Research, University of Michigan.

Brigham Young University (2005). *Honor Code* [Brochure]. Provo, UT.

Brigham Young University (2003). "Missions, marriage, and degree attainment at BYU—Summary, 2000," unpublished report prepared by Institutional Assessment and Analysis Division, 1.

Buss, D. M. (1998). The psychology of human mate selection: exploring the complexity of the strategic repertoire. In C. B. Crawford & D. L. Krebs (Eds.), *Handbook of evolutionary psychology: Ideas, issues and applications.* Mahwah, NJ: Erlbaum.

Centers for Disease Control and Prevention (1995). Youth risk behavior surveillance: National College Health Risk Behavior Survey—United States, 1995. *Morbidity and Mortality Weekly Report, 1997, 46*(SS-6), 1–56; http://www.cdc.gov/mmwR/preview/mmwrhtml/00049859.htm

Glenn, N., & Marquardt, E. (2001). *Hooking up, hanging out, and hoping for Mr. Right: College women on dating and mating today.* New York: Institute for American Values.

Hinckley, G. B. (1988). "A unique and wonderful university." Devotional speech given at Brigham Young University, Provo, Utah, on October 11, 1988, 2. Retreived from http://speeches.byu.edu

Holland, J. R. (2000). "How do I love thee?" Address given at Brigham Young University, Provo, Utah, February 15, 2000. Retreived from http://speeches.byu.edu

Kass, L. R. (1997). The end of courtship. *Public Interest, 126*, 39–63.

Knox, D., Gibson, L., Zusman, M., & Gallmeier, C. (1997). Why college students end relationships. *College Student Journal, 31*(4), 451.

Milanese, M. (2002, May/June). Hooking up, hanging out, making up, moving on. *Stanford Magazine*, 62–65.

Popenoe, D., & Whitehead, B. D. (2000). *The state of our unions: The social health of marriage in America.* New Brunswick, NJ: National Marriage Project Report, Rutgers University. Retrieved from http://marriage.rutgers.edu

Stewart, S., Stinnett, H., & Rosenfeld, L. B. (2000). Sex differences in desired characteristics of short-term and long-term relationship partners. *Journal of Social and Personal Relationships, 17*(6), 848.

Eight

FAMILY LIFE

Modern prophets and apostles have emphasized that social stability and individual happiness can only thrive within communities where marriage and family are a priority. Modern social science confirms the teachings of the prophets. In their widely acclaimed book *The Case for Marriage*, Linda Waite and Maggie Gallagher (2000) reviewed a large quantity of research literature and found compelling scientific evidence that married people have better health, finances, and happiness. Those who are married live longer, suffer less illness, recover faster when sick, have less depression and anxiety, and commit suicide less often. Married people have greater financial security. They also have children who grow up to be physically and emotionally healthier and who are less likely to be delinquent than children who are raised in single-parent homes. In spite of this positive evidence, marriage is on the decline in the United States. Some have suggested that factors such as modernization, changes in divorce laws, and increased educational opportunities for women have contributed to this shift (Gelles, 1995). Consequently, marital status in the United States over the past several decades has dramatically changed, so that not only are people marrying at a later age, but divorce, which peaked in 1979, continues to affect nearly half of all families (Stark, 2004). Recent data from the U.S. census indicates that the percentage of married-couple households with children under 18, normally referred to as the "traditional family," is at an all-time low of 24% compared to 45% in the 1960s (Schmitt, 2001).

President Gordon B. Hinckley observed in 1997:

> As I look to the future, I see little to feel enthusiastic about concerning the family in America and across the world. Drugs and alcohol are taking a terrible toll, which is not likely to decrease. Harsh language, one to another, indifference to the needs of one another—all seem to be increasing. There is so much of child abuse. There is so much of spouse abuse. There is growing abuse of the elderly. All of this will happen and get worse unless there is an underlying acknowledgment, yes, a strong and fervent conviction, concerning the fact that the family is an instrument of the Almighty. It is His creation. It is also the basic unit of society. (p. 69)

How are Latter-day Saint families doing? Are the trends of the world making their way into the families of the Church? In seeking to answer this, we investigated several familial factors among Latter-day Saints. First, we explored factors relating to marriage among members of the Church and their peers across the United States. Second, we compared data on divorce among Latter-day Saints and those not of our faith. Finally, we looked within Latter-day Saint families to learn more about their characteristics. Overall, we sought to clarify what we know and do not know about the familial health of Latter-day Saints at the dawn of the twenty-first century.

DATA ON FAMILIES

Data from three different random samples was used in this analysis. The first came from a survey in 1999 of 6,000 men and women from the United States who served missions for the Church. The sample was divided between those who had been back from their missions 2, 5, 10, and 17 years, respectively. The age of the respondents ranged from 21 to 45 years old. Sixty-seven percent of the men and 84% of the women responded to the survey, making a combined response rate of 73%. The second survey was conducted in 2000 and collected data from 6,000 LDS men and women in the United States who did *not* serve a mission. The survey was mailed to the same age groups as those of the returned-missionary survey. Only 12% of the men and 31% of the women responded, making a combined response rate of 20%. Further analysis showed that the extremely low response rate for non-returned-missionary men was mainly due to high rates of Church inactivity. Because of their alienation from the Church, they saw little reason to participate in the study. Therefore, any findings reported in this chapter on non-returned-missionary men may be generalized only for those who are more active in the Church. The full details of the methodology of these two studies are presented in Appendix A. The third sample represents the general population of men and women throughout the United States and comes from the 1998 and 2000 General Social Survey (GSS). The GSS is conducted by the National Opinion Research Center (NORC) at the University of Chicago. It collects interviews from a national sample of adult men and women. The response rates for 1998 and 2000 were 76% and 70%, respectively. We selected the men and women in the GSS survey between the ages of 24 to 41, which matches the age range of the LDS samples.

It is important to note that findings in this study often show that on average those who served missions for the Church tend to have greater marital success and happiness than those

Table 1. Marital Status among LDS and National Men and Women, by Percentage

	Men[1]				Women[2]			
	Returned Missionary (1999) n = 417	Non-Returned Missionary[3] (2000) n = 96	General Social Survey All[4] (1998/2000) n = 121	General Social Survey Whites Only[5] (1998/2000) n = 103	Returned Missionary (1999) n = 256	Non-Returned Missionary[6] (2000) n = 139	General Social Survey All[7] (1998/2000) n = 128	General Social Survey Whites Only[8] (1998/2000) n = 105
Single, never married	1	12	22	19	11	3	15	11
Married, first marriage	90	63	50	52	76	77	49	52
Remarried	7	18	11	10	7	14	15	15
Divorced/Separated	2	8	16	18	6	6	20	21
Widowed	1	0	3	1	0.4	0	1	1

1. Data is from specific age cohorts who are ages 38 and 39.
2. Data is from specific age cohorts who are ages 40 and 41.
3. Non-RM men's sample is significantly different at the .001 level when compared to the RM men.
4. GSS men's sample (all races) is significantly different at the .001 level when compared to RM men and at the .05 level when compared to non-RM men.
5. GSS men's sample (whites only) is significantly different at the .001 level when compared to RM men and is not significantly different compared to non-RM men.
6. Non-RM women's sample is significantly different at the .001 level when compared to the RM women.
7. GSS women's sample (all races) is significantly different at the .001 level when compared to either the RM women or non-RM women.
8. GSS women's sample (whites only) is significantly different at the .001 level when compared to either the RM women or non-RM women.

who did not serve. Recognizing this, we believe it would be a mistake to assume that missionary service alone is the sole cause of greater success in marriage and successful avoidance of divorce. Other stabilizing factors in the individual's adolescence likely led that person to choose to go on a mission in the first place. So, on the one hand, we in no way want to minimize the real changes that may result from missionary service, yet we must acknowledge that successful marriages may also be attributed to earlier adolescent factors that were not measured.

MARRIAGE

Over the past three decades, marital status in the United States has changed dramatically, and the divorce rate continues to remain relatively high. How do Latter-day Saint marriages compare to these national trends? Table 1 compares the current marital status of men and women by about age 40. Significantly more Latter-day Saint men, both returned missionaries and non-returned missionaries, are married, compared to men across the United States. Ninety percent of the returned-missionary men and 63% of the non-returned-missionary men are currently in their first marriage, with 7% and 18% who are remarried, respectively. Fifty percent of men nationally are in their first marriage and 11% are remarried.

Relatively few returned-missionary men are single (1%) or are currently divorced or separated (2%). Twelve percent of the non-returned-missionary men are single, and 8% are divorced or separated. By contrast, almost one-fourth (22%) of the men from the GSS sample have never married, 11% are remarried, and 16% are currently divorced.

By age 40, returned-missionary and non-returned-missionary women are also significantly different in their marital status than women across the nation. Seventy-six percent of returned-missionary women and 77% of non-returned-missionary women are in their first marriage. According to the GSS, 49% of the women in the national sample are in their first marriage.

Only about 11% of returned-missionary women and 3% of non-returned-missionary women are still single as compared to 15% of women nationally (11%—whites only). Twice as many non-returned-missionary women (14%) have remarried compared to returned-missionary women (7%). The rate of divorce for both groups is the same (6%). The data in Table 1 demonstrates that members of The Church of Jesus Christ of Latter-day Saints are significantly more likely to be in their first marriage and less likely to be single, remarried, or divorced.

Single-parent households. The increase of divorce since the 1970s has brought with it a rise in single-parent families. The U.S. Bureau of the Census (1990) reported that the percentage of children under age 18 living in a one-parent home in the United States (whites only) was around 19%. Most of these children are being raised by their mothers. This percentage is much smaller for Latter-day Saints. Heaton (1992) reported that the percentage of LDS children being raised in single-parent families in the United States was around 5%. These figures have probably increased by about 1% to 2% over the past 15 years.

Age at first marriage. A significant trend in marriage patterns in the United States, which also affects Latter-day Saints, is the age at which couples marry. The median age at first marriage in the United States has fluctuated during the past century. For example, in 1900, the median age at which a man married was about 26; a woman married around age 22. These ages steadily dropped until the 1950s, when the median age for men was 22 and for women, age 20. Since then, the median age at first marriage has dramatically increased. In 2003, the median age for men was almost 27 and for women, around 25 (U.S. Bureau of the Census, 2003).

Figure 1 shows the median age at first marriage for both LDS and non-LDS U.S. men and women from 1980 to 1995. Figures from 1995 show that the median age for first marriage among returned-missionary men is about 23, while

Figure 1. Median Age at First Marriage,
LDS and National Averages

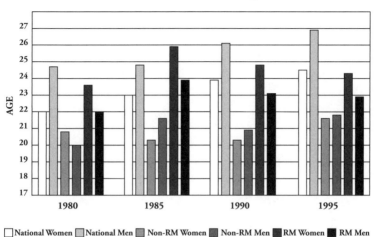

□ National Women ▨ National Men ▧ Non-RM Women ◼ Non-RM Men ◼ RM Women ◼ RM Men

non-returned-missionary men marry around age 22. The median age of first marriage for returned-missionary women is 24, and non-returned-missionary women are much younger, marrying between 21 and 22. Thus, on average, LDS men in 1995 married about 4.5 years younger than their male peers nationally, and LDS women married 1.5 years younger than their national peers.

LDS data since 1995 is unavailable. However, we do have information on men and women nationally. For example, the median age at marriage for men has not increased since 1995, but the age for women has increased almost a full year. So if a similar pattern is being followed by Latter-day Saints, we would assume that the age at first marriage for LDS women has increased, while age for LDS men has remained the same since 1995.

Marital happiness. Marital happiness in the United States has consistently been found to be extremely high. Since the GSS began surveying in 1973, the percentage of those who say they are either "very happy" or "pretty happy" in their marriages has hovered around 97% (General Social Survey, 2003).

Table 2. Marital Happiness,[1] by Percentage

	Men[2]				Women[3]			
	Returned Missionary (1999) n = 1376	Non-Returned Missionary (2000) n = 246	General Social Survey All (1998/2000) n = 154	General Social Survey Whites Only (1998/2000) n = 123	Returned Missionary (1999) n = 948	Non-Returned Missionary (2000) n = 522	General Social Survey All (1998/2000) n = 250	General Social Survey Whites Only (1998/2000) n = 213
1 = Not too happy	7	10	4	4	6	10	2	2
2 = Pretty happy	31	43	42	42	30	38	37	35
3 = Very happy	62	47	55	55	64	53	61	63
Mean	**2.54**[4]	**2.35**[5]	**2.51**	**2.50**	**2.57**[6]	**2.41**[7]	**2.59**	**2.62**

1. The RM and non-RM scales were collapsed to fit the same categories of the GSS scales. The question for the GSS sample was "All things considered, how happy is your marriage?" Categories are 1= Very Unhappy, 2 = Unhappy, 3 = Mixed, 4 = Happy, 5 = Very Happy. The question for GSS sample was "Taking things all together, how would you describe your marriage? Would you say that your marriage is very happy, pretty happy, or not too happy?
2. Data is from specific age cohorts who are between 24 and 40.
3. Data is from specific age cohorts who are between 25 and 41.
4. RM men's sample is significantly different at the .001 level when compared to the non-RM men but is not significantly different from each GSS men's sample (all and whites only).
5. Non-RM men's sample is significantly different at the .05 level when compared to each GSS men's sample (all and whites only).
6. RM women's sample is significantly different at the .001 level when compared to the non-RM men, but is not significantly different from each GSS women's sample (all and whites only).
7. Non-RM women's sample is significantly different at the .001 level when compared to each GSS women's sample (all and whites only).

Marital happiness among Latter-day Saints is also very high (see Table 2). Our analysis found that the happiness in returned-missionary marriages was not significantly different than that in the marriages of their U.S. peers. Marital happiness among non-returned-missionary marriages was also very high, although lower when compared to the other two groups for both men and women.

Given prophetic counsel concerning eternal marriage and the principles of the proclamation on the family, we are convinced that religious factors heighten marital happiness among Latter-day Saints. Our research confirmed this by showing that among three of the four LDS groups we studied, religiosity was clearly related to marital happiness. Those who regularly read scriptures; pray privately; and hold family scripture study, family prayer, and family home evening are happier in their marriages. Being temple worthy and holding strong personal religious beliefs are also related to happier marriages. We recognize that there may also be a number of other non-religious factors that lead to marital happiness, but for Latter-day Saints, religiosity appears to be salient.

LDS marital characteristics. Table 3 shows several marital characteristics of LDS couples. These ask if both spouses are members of the Church, if they were married in the temple, and under what circumstances the spouses met. When asked if his or her spouse was LDS, almost every married returned missionary said yes (men—99%; women—98%). Eighty-three percent of the non-returned-missionary men and 92% of the women had an LDS spouse. The vast majority of returned missionaries (97%—men; 96%—women) are currently sealed to their spouses, either through an original temple sealing or a sealing that took place later after a civil marriage. Just over half of the non-returned-missionary men (54%) have been sealed in the temple, as have around three-fourths of the non-returned-missionary women (78%).

Table 3. Marital Characteristics, by Percentage

	Men		Women	
	Returned Missionary $n = 1631$	Non-Returned Missionary $n = 257$	Returned Missionary $n = 1091$	Non-Returned Missionary $n = 529$
Is your spouse a member of the LDS Church?				
Yes	99	83	98	92
No	1	16	2	8
What type of ceremony did you have for your current marriage?				
Temple sealing	91	29	91	65
Civil marriage first, then temple sealing later	6	35	5	13
Civil marriage only	4	36	4	22
Where were you when you met your spouse?				
Church meeting or activity	41	18	40	32
Social event (not church related)	14	22	10	17
School event (e.g., in class, field trip)	11	20	7	12
Work-related activity	8	14	10	15
Other	26	26	33	24

One characteristic of mate selection that is unique in the LDS culture is where a person meets his or her spouse. We found that a church meeting or activity was the most popular place for returned-missionary men and women as well as for non-returned-missionary women to meet their future spouses. On the other hand, non-returned-missionary men generally found their spouses at a social or school event or some place other than a church meeting. This may be due in part to being less active in church attendance during their young adult years (Janson, 2002).

Divorce. Given the emphasis the LDS Church places on marriage, a significant and often-asked question is, What is the civil divorce rate among Latter-day Saints, especially for those with a temple marriage? Unfortunately, the information necessary to provide an exact answer to this question is not available. However, researchers have done their best to produce some type of estimate. For example, in the late 1970s, Albrecht, Bahr, and Goodman (1983) conducted a divorce study of individuals of various religious affiliations who lived in the Intermountain West. These researchers compared divorce rates by varying types of marriage settings (e.g., civil marriage, church marriage, temple marriage, other). Given the high rate of Mormons living in Utah, they included "temple marriage" as a category and assumed that only Mormons would select this response. In the end, they found that 7% of LDS members who had originally had a temple marriage were either now divorced or divorced and remarried. Thirty-five percent of the sample (includes all religious affiliations) who had originally married civilly were either currently divorced or remarried. Among those who were originally married in a church or synagogue, 15% were either divorced or remarried, and for those whose original marriage was classified in the "other" category, 21% had divorced.

Given the differences in these rates, divorce rates of temple marriages were about five times lower than civil marriages, two

Table 4. Marital Status among Ever Married LDS and National Men and Women, by Percentage

	Men[1]				Women[2]			
	Returned Missionary (1999) n = 411	Non-Returned Missionary[4] (2000) n = 85	General Social Survey All[5] (1998/2000) n = 101	General Social Survey Whites Only[6] (1998/2000) n = 88	Returned Missionary (1999) n = 229	Non-Returned Missionary[7] (2000) n = 135	General Social Survey All[8] (1998/2000) n = 122	General Social Survey Whites Only[9] (1998/2000) n = 101
First Marriage	91	71	59	61	85	79	52	55
Ever Divorced[3]	9	29	38	38	15	21	48	45
Widowed	1	0	3	1	0.4	0	1	1

1. Data is from specific age cohorts who are 38 and 39.
2. Data is from specific age cohorts who are 40 and 41.
3. Includes those who are divorced, separated, remarried, and widows who had ever been divorced.
4. Non-RM men's sample is significantly different at the .001 level when compared to the RM men.
5. GSS men's sample (all races) is significantly different at the .001 level when compared to the RM men and is not significantly different when compared to non-RM men.
6. GSS men's sample (whites only) is significantly different at the .001 level when compared to the RM men and is not significantly different when compared to the non-RM men.
7. Non-RM women's sample is not significantly different when compared to the RM women.
8. GSS women's sample (all races) is significantly different at the .001 level when compared to either the RM women or non-RM women.
9. GSS women's sample (whites only) is significantly different at the .001 level when compared to either the RM women or non-RM women.

times lower than church- or synagogue-type marriages, and three times lower than divorce rates of those who married in other settings.

In the 1980s, a study conducted by Heaton and Goodman (1985) compared divorce rates between Latter-day Saints and members of other religious denominations who were white and age 30 and older. They found that Latter-day Saints had the lowest rate of divorce compared to other religious denominations including Catholics, liberal and conservative Protestants, and those with no religious preference. They reported that around 14% of LDS men and 19% of LDS women had been divorced at the time of the study. Twenty percent of Catholic men had divorced, as had 23% of Catholic women. Other religions reported higher percentages than the Catholics, with the highest percentage of divorce found to be among those who claimed no religious preference. Nearly 40% of the men and 45% of the women from this category had divorced.

Heaton and Goodman also looked at the relationship between Church attendance and divorce. They found about 10% of active LDS men were divorced, while 22% of the LDS men who attended church less frequently were divorced. Fifteen percent of active LDS women were divorced as compared to 26% for those who did not go to church as often. Thus, LDS men and women who attended church regularly were about half as likely to be divorced as those who went to church only occasionally and about four times less than men and women nationally.

Finally, Heaton and Goodman showed the proportion of members who had divorced from a temple marriage as compared to a nontemple marriage. Of those who had originally married in the temple, about 5% of the men and 7% of the women had been divorced. Around 28% of non-temple-married men and 33% of non-temple-married women were divorced. Thus, temple marriages were about 5 times less likely to end in divorce than nontemple marriages.

Follow-up research by Heaton, Bahr, and Jacobson (2004) assessed data from the 1990s and suggested that the divorce rate gap between Latter-day Saints and their national peers is narrowing. Specifically, they estimated that the lifetime divorce rate for Latter-day Saints married in the temple may be two-thirds of the national average of divorce, around 30%.

We recently did our own assessment of divorce among Latter-day Saints from data collected between 1999 and 2001. Table 4 shows the marital status by about age 40 among ever-married LDS men and women and national men and women. Returned-missionary men rank lowest in divorce, at 9%. This is in comparison to 29% of non-returned-missionary men and 38% of men nationally. This shows that returned-missionary men are around three times less likely to divorce than non-returned-missionary men and a little over four times less likely than men nationally. Non-returned-missionary LDS men are about three-fourths as likely to divorce as men nationally. As for women, returned missionaries have a divorce rate of 15%, while non-returned missionaries are higher, at 21%, and U.S. women are the highest compared to all other categories, with 48% (45%—whites only) who have been divorced. Thus, returned-missionary women are about three-fourths less likely to divorce than non-returned-missionary women and slightly over three times less likely than women nationally. Marriages for LDS non-returned-missionary women are just over half as likely to end in divorce as their national peers of the same age.

If the above rates represent divorce by age 40, is it possible to calculate a lifetime divorce rate? Many scholars believe that the current lifetime divorce rate in the United States is now around 50%. We recognize that there continues to be an ongoing debate among scholars concerning the accuracy of reported divorce rates. Part of the problem is that there are a number of ways to calculate the rate, and each has its own strengths and weaknesses (Stark, 2004). We use the 50% estimate as a matter of convenience in comparing LDS to national rates. Assuming that the proportion of divorce between LDS members and their non-LDS U.S. peers is similar across the life span, we estimate that the current lifetime divorce rate for returned-missionary men is around 12% and 16% for women. The lifetime rate for non-returned-missionary men is around 38% and around 22% for non-returned-missionary women. These figures include both civil and temple marriages combined.

What, then, would be the divorce rate of temple marriages only? We, like previous researchers, must also estimate this figure. First of all, we know that returned missionaries represent a relatively active subgroup in the Church and, because almost all of them eventually attain a temple marriage (see Table 3), we believe that their lifetime divorce rate, which we reported earlier as 12% for the men and 16% for the women, would represent the lifetime divorce rate for temple marriages among typically active Latter-day Saints. Thus, our estimation of the lifetime divorce rate for those with temple marriages is somewhere in the teens and probably no higher than 20%.

LDS FAMILY CHARACTERISTICS

Family size. We found a relatively high fertility rate among the LDS men and women, which confirms the long-held notion that Latter-day Saint families are generally larger than others across the nation. Non-returned-missionary women have the highest number of children, with an average of 3.92 per household, followed by returned-missionary women at 3.83. Returned-missionary men had an average of 3.75 children per household, with non-returned-missionary men the lowest among the LDS groups at 3.31. Compare these to men and women across the United States, where men average 1.73 children and women 1.99 per household, respectively. With all LDS groups averaging more than three children by their early

Table 5. *LDS Family Religious Practices, by Percentage*

	Men		Women	
	Returned Missionary $n = 1678$	Non-Returned Missionary $n = 282$	Returned Missionary $n = 1129$	Non-Returned Missionary $n = 561$
During the past year, how often did you pray as a family?				
Every day/a few times a week	74	40	79	62
About once a week/2–3 times a week/About once a month	15	22	13	16
Less than once a month/not at all	10	38	7	22
During the past year, how often did you study the scriptures as a family?				
Every day/a few times a week	36	18	46	33
About once a week/2–3 times a week/About once a month	36	29	32	30
Less than once a month/not at all	27	53	21	37
During the past year, how often did you hold family home evening?				
About once a week/2–3 times a month	55	29	63	48
About once a month	15	12	12	15
Less than once a month/not at all	29	58	24	36

30s, this is almost twice the rate of their peers across the United States.

Family religious behavior. Family religious behavior such as family scripture study, family prayer, and family home evening are shown in Table 5. As can be seen, 74% of the men and 79% of the women who served missions hold regular family prayer. Around 40% of the non-returned-missionary men hold regular family prayer, as do 62% of the non-returned-missionary women. Family scripture study occurs less often than family prayer. Nearly half (46%) of the returned-missionary women say they hold family scripture study at least a few times a week. Returned-missionary men are next at just over one-third (36%). Non-returned-missionary women are at 33%, and only about 18% of the non-returned-missionary men have family scripture study several times a week. Finally, more than half of the families of returned-missionary men (55%) and women (63%) hold regular family home evening. For families of women who did not serve a mission, the rate is around 48%. Twenty-nine percent of the men in this category say they are having regular home evenings with their families.

CONCLUSION

Our findings suggest that most members of The Church of Jesus Christ of Latter-day Saints are earnestly striving to live the principles found in the proclamation on the family. Research shows significant differences in several marital factors of Latter-day Saints as compared to their peers throughout the United States. A higher percentage of Latter-day Saints are married, fewer are divorced or single, they have more children per family, they marry earlier in life, and they have comparable marital happiness to those across the nation.

Such an enduring social structure within the Church is encouraging, given the antifamily sentiments that seem to be sweeping across the country through various media and political platforms. If families are to receive the help and healing they need, they must continue to follow the prophetic counsel of both past and present prophets—that the family is the fundamental institution of society, and that love and respect within marriage will create lasting happiness for families and stability in society.

REFERENCES

Albrecht, S. L., Bahr, H. M., & Goodman, K. L. (1983). *Divorce and remarriage: Problems, adaptations, and adjustments.* Westport, CT: Greenwood Press.

Gelles, R. J. (1995). *Contemporary families: A sociological view.* Thousand Oaks, CA: Sage Publishing.

Heaton, T. B. (1992). Vital statistics. In D. H. Ludlow (Ed.), *Encyclopedia of Mormonism.* New York: Macmillan, 4:1533.

Heaton, T. B., Bahr, S. J., & Jacobson, C. K. (2004). *A statistical profile of Mormons: Health, wealth, and social life.* Lewiston, NY: Edwin Mellen Press.

Heaton, T. B., & Goodman, K. L. (1985). Religion and family formation. *Review of Religious Research, 26*(4), 349–352.

Hinckley, G. B. (1997, November). Look to the future. *Ensign, 27*(11), 67–69.

Janson, D. A. (2002). *Religious socialization and LDS young adults.* Doctoral dissertation. Brigham Young University, Provo, UT.

Schmitt, E. (2005, May 15). For the first time, nuclear family drops below 25% of households. *New York Times*, A1, A20.

Stark, R. (2004). *Sociology.* Belmont, CA: Wadsworth Publishing.

Waite, L. J., & Gallagher, M. (2000). *The case for marriage: Why married people are happier, healthier, and better off financially.* New York: Doubleday.

Nine

MISSIONARY SERVICE

E ach year, nearly 30,000 Latter-day Saint young adults leave their homes to serve missions in various countries throughout the world for the purpose of converting others to the tenets of the Church. Once these young adults return home from their missionary service, many go on to further their education, begin a career, marry, and establish a family.

Returned missionaries are a unique group in the Church and are often a point of interest in family, Church, and other social settings. Parents, for example, note the challenges their returned missionaries face as they make the transition from the mission field to the home. Parents sometimes observe a raised level of stress that occurs as their sons or daughters shift from the focus of the mission to the focus of school, work, and dating.

Ward and stake leaders also have an interest in returned missionaries, often giving them counsel and encouragement as well as assigning them the most suitable Church callings during the transitional time. President Gordon B. Hinckley (2001, March) emphasized the importance of this duty to Church leaders when he said: "I am satisfied that if every returning missionary had a meaningful responsibility the day he or she came home, we'd have fewer of them grow cold in their faith. I wish that you would make an effort to see that every returned missionary receives a meaningful assignment. Activity is the nurturing process of faithfulness" (p. 65).

Missionary service and returned missionaries are also a point of discussion in the day-to-day conversations among Latter-day Saints. Statements or questions such as "He's a returned missionary," or "She went on a mission," or "Did you serve a mission?" can often be heard wherever Church members are gathered.

Why are Latter-day Saints interested in knowing if someone is a returned missionary? One reason may be that when Church members learn that someone has served a mission, they naturally see that person differently. People somehow expect more of returned missionaries—that they should be more spiritually grounded, that they should be leaders in the Church, that their homes and families should be stable, that they should be successful in their schooling and careers.

These assumptions, although commonly and culturally accepted, unfortunately may not always be the case. One bishop in a BYU singles ward observed a number of returned missionaries who regretted the "loss of the Spirit" since returning from the mission field, including some whose Church attendance gradually dropped off until they eventually disappeared from the landscape. Others had dropped out of school; were working in low-paying, dead-end jobs; were waiting longer to marry; and were alienated from their families. Some had experienced severe depression during their first two years home, while others had committed rather serious sins, including involvement with drugs, alcohol, pornography, and sexual transgressions.

Are these behaviors isolated cases or part of an emerging pattern of secularization among returned missionaries in the United States? We set out to further investigate this and other questions by surveying 5,000 returned missionaries scattered across the United States, hoping to gain a more accurate view about how they are doing—both in the early stages of their return home and the later stages as they settle into adulthood.

Three general questions were assessed in this study. First, how are returned missionaries doing in their current spiritual, family, and educational pursuits? We answered this question by looking at a number of demographic factors of returned missionaries. These include the educational attainment, socio-economic status, family life, and religious experiences of those who had been back from their missions 2, 5, 10, and 17 years, respectively. The original strategy was to look at those who had returned from their mission 15 years before our study, rather than 17 years. However, a two-year adjustment was made because missionaries who returned 15 years before our study served for only 18 months. We thus selected the 17-year group who served for 24 months, the same length of time as the 2-, 5-, and 10-year groups.

Assessing these areas in the lives of returned missionaries provided a barometer on how successful they are as they venture out in the various roles of life. Part of this assessment was to also identify similarities and differences between the demographic traits of men and women. Duke and Johnson (1998) surmise that for Latter-day Saints, "The experiences of men and women are quite different and have a significant impact on the way they feel and worship" (p. 317). Thus, we sought to understand the unique differences and similarities in life outcomes of returned-missionary men and women.

A second question we set out to answer is whether or not more recently returned missionaries are as committed to gospel values and Church activity as those who returned from their missions decades ago. Unlike most recent research on returned missionaries, which has mainly looked at the impact of the mission experience itself, our objective here was to examine if social change in the United States over the past several decades has influenced returned missionaries' religiosity in some way (Thomas, 1992; Roghaar, 1991).

Three decades ago, Madsen (1977) found that returned missionaries were doing very well in their religious activity. He summarized his findings by saying that "the vast majority of returned missionaries attend Church meetings regularly, possess a current temple recommend, serve in Church callings, pay tithing, and observe the Word of Wisdom" (abstract). We used Madsen's study as a baseline to compare the religious behavior and marital status of returned missionaries in our sample, thus allowing us to observe any changes over the past 30 years.

One of the theoretical foundations for hypothesizing whether returned missionaries of today should be any more or less religious than those studied back in the 1970s comes from the secularization thesis, a commonly discussed theme in industrial society. Scholars who accept this thesis propose that religious commitment in American society has been in a decline over the past several decades (Lechner, 1991). They believe that as modernization and science have increased in the United States, people are replacing faith in God with belief in science. Taking this view, we might predict that the religiosity of returned missionaries is also in decline and that our sample of returned missionaries would have lower religiosity than those who returned 30 years ago.

On the other hand, those who reject the secularization thesis argue that despite science's increasing influence, a religious revival is occurring and religious devotion in the United States is as high as it has ever been (Caplow, Bahr, & Chadwick, 1983; Stark & Iannaccone, 1992; Warner, 1993). If this is true, we would anticipate that religiosity among LDS returned missionaries has actually increased over the past three decades or at least has remained steady.

Finally, a third question we desired to answer was, What things will help returned missionaries stay active and committed to the gospel after they return home? We assessed this with two approaches. First, we asked those in our sample to report their own insights about post-mission adjustment challenges as well as what they and the Church can do to help with that adjustment. Second, because private religiosity is a significant part of a Latter-day Saint life, we applied statistical modeling procedures to identify the most important factors that lead to private religiosity in adulthood among returned missionaries. Private religiosity involves such things as reading scriptures, personal prayer, and thinking about religion. The data collection procedures are described in detail in Appendix A.

RETURNED MISSIONARIES: SOCIOECONOMIC STATUS, FAMILY LIFE, AND RELIGIOSITY

It is commonly believed that missionary service produces not only a strong testimony but also a foundation for success in a number of other areas of their lives. Based on our findings, there is solid evidence supporting this claim.

Socioeconomic status. Church leaders have consistently stressed the value of preparing for life's work through a proper education. President Hinckley (2001, January) counseled youth and young adults of the Church: "You are moving into the most competitive age the world has ever known. All around you is competition. You need all the education you can get. . . . You belong to a church that teaches the importance of education. You have a mandate from the Lord to educate your minds and your hearts and your hands" (p. 4).

How are returned missionaries doing in this endeavor? We found 95% of them had at least some college or skill training (see Table 1). Among those who had been back from their missions the longest (17 years), 37% of the men and 45% of the women had completed an undergraduate degree. Another 33% of the men and 14% of the women had earned an advanced degree. The rate for both men and women combined in these two categories is 40% with an undergraduate degree and 25% with an advanced degree. These rates are considerably higher

Table 1. Educational Attainment and Socioeconomic Status of LDS Returned Missionaries and National Rates, by Percentage (Ages 35–44)

	Returned Missionary			United States[1]
	Men (*n* = 456)	Women (*n* = 308)	Combined (*n* = 761)	Combined (*n* = 44,462)
Education Level (1999)				
Did not finish high school	0	0	0	12
High school	4	3	4	34
Some college/skill training	26	38	31	18
College	37	45	40	18
Graduate/professional school	33	14	25	8

	Returned Missionary		United States[2]	
	Men (*n* = 451)	Women (*n* = 306)	Men (*n* = n/a)	Women (*n* = n/a)
Employment Status (1999)				
Employed	98	57	93	77
Unemployed	1	44	7	23

	Returned Missionary	United States[3]	
	Combined (*n* = 749)	Combined (*n* = 18,823)	
Family Income (1998)			
Under $19,999	3	9	Under $14,999
$20,000 to $29,999	7	9	$15,000 to $24,999
$30,000 to $39,999	12	11	$25,000 to $34,999
$40,000 to $49,999	17	18	$35,000 to $49,999
$50,000 to $74,999	30	24	$50,000 to $74,999
$75,000 and over	31	28	$75,000 and over

1. U.S. Bureau of the Census, *Statistical Abstract of the United States: 1999*, no. 265.
2. U.S. Bureau of the Census, *Statistical Abstract of the United States: 1999*, no. 650.
3. U.S. Bureau of the Census, *Statistical Abstract of the United States: 2000*, no. 746.
Note: This scale is not exactly the same as the returned missionary scale but is close enough to see the relative differences between the two groups.

than the national average. For example, among those in the United States of about the same age (35 to 44) in 1998, only 18% of men and women combined had a college degree, and an additional 8% had an advanced degree (U.S. Bureau of the Census, 1999, no. 265).

Two other important indices of socioeconomic status are employment and income. Returned missionaries rank relatively high in both. We found that 95% of the men and 63% of the women were gainfully employed at the time of this study. Employment among the 17-year group was at 98% of the men and 57% of the women (see Table 1), while the national rate for men of the same age group was at 93% and 77% for the women (U.S. Bureau of the Census, 1999, no. 650). The lower employment rate among returned-missionary women when compared to other women in the United States is not surprising given the Church's view that the primary role of mothers should be centered on more domestic responsibilities.

The higher levels of education found among returned missionaries is evident in family income, which was a little above the national average. Eighty-five percent of the men in the 17-year group and 67% of the women (78% combined) made $40,000 or more in 1998 (see Table 1). By comparison, 70% of families in the United States made $35,000 or more in 1998 (U.S. Bureau of the Census, 2000, no. 746).

Family life. The LDS Church is known for its strong family values. Accordingly, we looked at a number of family indicators to ascertain the family life of returned missionaries. Table 2 shows the marital status of returned missionaries. Among the male 17-year group, about 90% were in their first marriage, while 6% had been divorced or remarried. Only 1% were currently divorced, and 2% were still single.

Among men in the national sample in 1998, around 69% were married (first marriage or remarriage), 12% were divorced, and almost 19% had never married (U.S. Bureau of the Census, 1999, no. 63). Thus, returned-missionary men were more

Table 2. Family Characteristics of LDS Returned Missionaries and National Rates, by Percentage (Ages 35-44)

	Returned Missionary		United States[1]	
	Men (n = 454)	Women (n = 312)	Men (n = 22,055)	Women (n = 22,407)
Marital Status				
Single, never married	2	13	19	12
Cohabiting	0	2	*	*
Married, first marriage	89	76	69	72
Remarried	6	5	*	*
Divorced	1	3	12	14
Widowed	1	0	0	1

	Returned Missionary		
	Men (n = 438)	Women (n = 260)	Combined (n = 698)
Marriage Ceremony Type			
Temple ceremony	91	87	90
Civil ceremony	3	7	4
Civil ceremony, then temple ceremony	6	7	6
LDS Spouse			
Yes	99	95	98
No	1	5	2
	Men (n = 426)	Women (n = 297)	Combined (n = 723)
Number of Children			
None	4	15	9
One	3	5	4
Two	12	14	13
Three	25	20	23
Four	30	20	26
Five	14	16	15
Six or more	12	10	11

1. U.S. Bureau of the Census, *Statistical Abstract of the United States*, 1999, no. 63.
* No data.

likely to get married and less likely to divorce than other men across the United States.

Among women returned missionaries, 75% of those in the 17-year group were married (first marriage), 5% were remarried, about 4% were separated or divorced, and 13% had never married. For women of comparable age on a national scale (1998), about 72% were married (first marriage or remarried), around 14% were divorced, and 12% had never married (U.S. Bureau of the Census, 1999, no. 63). Like the men, these figures show that the divorce rate among returned-missionary women is much lower than the national rate. The percentage who had not yet married was nearly identical.

We also found that nearly all returned missionaries who were married had a spouse who is a member of the Church, and 96% either had married in the temple or had been sealed later. In addition, a relatively high fertility rate was discovered. Latter-day Saints have been known for having larger families than the national average, and this study verifies this pattern. The average number of children among returned-missionary families for the 17-year group was 3.7 for the men and 3.2 for the women. In contrast, the average number of children ever born to women between the ages of 35 and 44 in the United States in 1995 was around 1.9 (Chadwick & Heaton, 1999).

Religious activity. Full-time missionary service provides young adults with an opportunity unlike any other to develop personal spiritual habits. Results from our research suggest that these habits are not abandoned once the missionaries return home. For example, 87% of all returned missionaries attend sacrament meeting almost every week (see Tables 3 and 4). Sunday School and priesthood/Relief Society attendance are slightly lower, with 81 and 82% weekly attendance reported respectively. Forty-eight percent of returned missionaries read their scriptures at least a few times a week, 79% pray at least a few times a week, 87% hold a current temple recommend, 90% are full-tithe payers, and 97% keep the Word of Wisdom.

A comparison between men and women reveals women are consistently higher in their religiosity than men. This fits the same pattern found nationally, as women are often much higher in their religious beliefs, commitments, and behavior than men (Stark, 2004).

The relatively high rates of religiosity for returned missionaries is notable. This is especially significant given that our sample included not only recently returned missionaries but also those who have been home for a considerable length of time. These findings, when added to results from previous research on returned missionaries, provides consistently strong evidence that the vast majority of returned missionaries stay strongly committed to gospel values not only immediately upon their return but also later in their lives.

Family religious activities are at the core of a Latter-day Saint home. Recently, Elder Russell M. Nelson (1999) counseled, "Happiness at home is most likely to be achieved when practices there are founded upon the teachings of Jesus Christ. Ours is the responsibility to ensure that we have family prayer, scripture study, and family home evening" (pp. 39–40). We assessed these three religious activities among returned-missionary families. As Table 4 illustrates, we found that 73% have family prayer at least a few times a week, 39% hold family scripture study that often, and 55% hold family home evening at least two or three times a month. Given the complexities and demands on the modern family, these figures indicate a relatively sound commitment to family religious practices in the homes of returned missionaries.

COMPARING RECENTLY RETURNED MISSIONARIES TO THOSE OF A GENERATION AGO

Research on secularization of Latter-day Saints shows they may show resistance to the acceptance of "worldly values." Stark (1984; 1996) found little evidence to support the idea that the LDS Church was in any kind of religious decline. He

Table 3. Family Religious Activity of LDS Returned Missionaries, by Percentage (All Age-Groups, Married and Divorced Only)

	Men (*n* = 1,657)	Women (*n* = 1,084)	Combined (*n* = 2,741)
Family scripture study			
Not at all	14	14	14
Less than once a month	16	11	14
About once a month	10	8	9
2–3 times a month	12	10	11
About once a week	12	13	12
A few times a week	23	23	23
Every day	13	22	17

	Men (*n* = 1,659)	Women (*n* = 1,091)	Combined (*n* = 2,750)
Family prayer			
Not at all	7	7	7
Less than once a month	6	5	6
About once a month	5	3	4
2–3 times a month	5	4	5
About once a week	7	6	7
A few times a week	21	18	20
Every day	50	58	53

	Men (*n* = 1,589)	Women (*n* = 1,068)	Combined (*n* = 2,657)
Family scripture study			
Not at all	16	17	16
Less than once a month	16	11	14
About once a month	15	12	14
2–3 times a month	21	21	21
About once a week	31	38	34

explained that the "secularization thesis would hold that religious movements such as Mormonism will do best in places where modernization has had the least impact. . . . These assumptions about secularization are refuted by research. . . .

Table 4. Private Religious Behavior of LDS Returned Missionaries in 1977 as Compared to Those in 1999, by Percentage (Collapsed Scales)

Madsen's Study (1977) (n = 1,122)			Current Study (1999) (n = 2,600)
Personal Scripture Study			
Seldom or never	4	4	Not at all
Infrequently	21	18	Infrequently
Weekly	20	30	Weekly
Few times per week	35	33	Few times per week
Daily	20	16	Daily
Mean = 3.473 SD = 1.141		t-value = 2.18[1]	Mean = 3.386 SD = 1.065

Madsen's Study (1977) (n = 1,118)			Current Study (1999) (n = 2,594)
Personal Prayer			
Specific occasions or rarely	3	2	Not at all
Infrequently	8	20	Infrequently
Few times per week	18	24	Few times per week
Daily	71	54	Daily
Mean = 3.570 SD = 0.773		t-value = 9.46[2]	Mean = 3.305 SD = 0.847

Madsen's Study (1977) (n = 1,123)			Current Study (1999) (n = 2,613)
Tithing Status			
Non-tithe payer	3	4	Non-tithe payer
Partial-tithe payer	5	7	Partial-tithe payer
Full-tithe payer	92	90	Full-tithe payer
	$\chi^2 = 4.95$		

Madsen's Study (1977) (n = 1,128)[3]			Current Study (1999) (n = 2,611)
Temple Recommend			
Yes	85	85	Yes
No	15	15	No
	$\chi^2 = 0.013$		

1. Statistically significant at p ≤ 0.05.
2. Statistically significant at p ≤ 0.01.
3. Madsen (1977) did not provide the n for this category, so 1128 (n for his total response rate) was included as the n in order to calculate the χ^2 value.

Mormons thrive in the most, not the least, secularized nations" (1984, p. 25).

In 1984, Albrecht and Heaton found that among many religious groups in the United States, "educational achievement impacts negatively on religious commitment and that increased levels of education often lead to apostasy as individuals encounter views that deemphasize spiritual growth and elevate scientific and intellectual achievement" (1998, p. 298)

For Latter-day Saints, however, they found a positive relationship between education and religiosity and concluded that there was very little evidence to support the secularization thesis. Chapter 4 in this book provides powerful evidence refuting the notion that education is resulting in the secularization of LDS young adults. Others have found similar results (Stott, 1984; Merrill, Lyon, & Jensen, 2003; Top & Chadwick, 2001).

To test the secularization notion among returned missionaries, we examined the religiosity between returned missionaries of the 1960s and 1970s to those of the 1980s and 1990s. In 1977, Madsen conducted a survey of nearly 1,800 returned missionaries from the United States who had been home from their missions up to 10 years. This information provided a baseline against which we compared our sample in both private and public religiosity as well as marital status. Private religious behavior includes such things as personal scripture study, personal prayer, holding a current temple recommend, and paying tithing. Areas of public religious behavior include attendance at sacrament meeting and other church meetings.

Private religious behavior. We found that returned missionaries in our sample read their scriptures and prayed somewhat less than those in Madsen's study. As illustrated in Table 5, 49% of current returned missionaries had personal scripture study at least a few times a week or daily, compared to 55% of those 30 years earlier. In addition, 54% had daily prayer, compared to Madsen's sample, which was at around 71%. About 85% in each group held a current temple recommend, and both groups were between 90 and 92% full-tithe payers.

Why returned missionaries are praying and reading their scriptures less today than they did 30 years ago is not clear. Certainly secularization could account for this decline. Modernization has set up a more competitive world, requiring greater time demands on the family. More fathers are working longer, more mothers are entering the workplace, and more children are competing and specializing at school than they were 30 years ago. For returned missionaries, as with the rest of society, this tide of busyness may be sweeping them up, perhaps leaving them less time for private religious observances.

Another possibility is that given the added emphasis the Church has placed on the family during the past several decades, private religious practices are shifting to family religious practices. In other words, married couples, although recognizing the value of private religiosity, may end up substituting family prayer and scripture study for personal prayer and scripture study in order to keep up with the demands of other responsibilities.

Public religious behavior. As for public religiosity, 86% of the returned missionaries we studied attended sacrament meeting on a weekly basis. This is higher than the 78% reported by returned missionaries 30 years ago. Both groups of returned missionaries ranged between 75 and 79% weekly attendance at Sunday School and priesthood/Relief Society. Adherence to the Word of Wisdom for both groups was extremely high, with 99% of the current sample indicating that they do so, and 97% of the earlier group of returned missionaries indicated the same.

Even though sacrament meeting attendance is significantly higher now than it was 30 years ago, a second look at where the shift occurs (see Table 5) explains that most of the movement is between those who attended "two to three times a month" and "almost every week." In other words, the difference is found among those who were already very active and then became even more active.

Table 5. Public Religious Behavior of LDS Returned Missionaries in 1977 as Compared to Those in 1999, by Percentage (Collapsed Scales)

Madsen's Study (1977) (n = 1,120)			Current Study (1999) (n = 2,604)
Sacrament Meeting Attendance			
Seldom or never	1	1	Not at all
Infrequently	2	2	Infrequently
Weekly	1	2	Weekly
Few times per week	18	10	Few times per week
Daily	78	86	Daily
Mean = 4.686 SD = 0.710		t-value = −3.64[1]	Mean = 4.777 SD = 0.650

Madsen's Study (1977) (n = 1,117)			Current Study (1999) (n = 2,602)
Sunday School Attendance			
Never	1	2	Never
Infrequently	3	3	Infrequently
One time per month	2	4	Once a month
2–3 times a month	19	12	2–3 times a month
Every week	75	79	Almost every week
Mean = 4.638 SD = 0.773		t-value = 0.07	Mean = 4.636 SD = 0.849

Madsen's Study (1977) (n = 1,121)			Current Study (1999) (n = 2,601)
Priesthood/Relief Society Attendance			
Never	2	3	Never
Infrequently	3	3	Infrequently
One time per month	1	4	Once a month
2–3 times a month	20	12	2–3 times a month
Every week	74	78	Almost every week
Mean = 4.616 SD = 0.807		t-value = 0.40	Mean = 4.603 SD = 0.898

Madsen's Study (1977) (n = 1,128)[2]			Current Study (1999) (n = 2,613)
Word of Wisdom Status			
Yes	97	99	Yes
No	3	1	No

1. Statistically significant at p ≤ 0.01.
2. Madsen (1977) did not provide the n for this category, so 1,128 (n for his total response rate) was used in order to calculate the χ^2.

The increase of public religiosity during the past 30 years can certainly be attributed to an increase in personal faith. There may be, however, a couple of structural explanations as well. One is that the Church has continued to build buildings closer to the people, making it easier to attend Church than in the past. A second possibility is because of the establishment in the early 1980s of the three-hour block of Church meetings. Prior to that time, members attended Sunday morning meetings comprised of priesthood and Sunday School, and later in the evening they would return for sacrament meeting. Unlike returned missionaries of the 1960s and 1970s, the establishment of the more time- and travel-efficient three-hour meetings may have played a part in higher Church attendance among returned missionaries of the 1980s and 1990s. Whatever the reasons, in the end, returned missionaries continue to remain extremely active in the public aspects of their religiosity in spite of so-called secularization.

When looking at the overall trend in religiosity among returned missionaries during the past several decades, we can see that some measures in the private realm have declined, while others have held steady. In the public sector, some indicators have increased, and others have remained the same. It would be premature, then, to suggest that secularization is found among returned missionaries. Other than private prayer, it is our feeling that as a whole, the religious behavior of returned missionaries today is generally similar to those studied in 1977.

Marital status and temple marriage. Another indicator of religious conviction among Latter-day Saints is temple marriage. We found that 63% of those in our sample had a current temple marriage, as compared to 67% of Madsen's sample (see Table 6). This marks a decrease of 4 percentage points over a 30-year period. However, the number of those remaining single has increased by 6 percentage points from 28% in Madsen's sample to 34% in our sample.

*Table 6. Marital Status of LDS Returned Missionaries in 1977 as
Compared to Those in 1999, by Percentage
(Collapsed Scales)*

Madsen's Study (1977) (n = 1,114)			Current Study (1999) (n = 2,618)
Marital Status			
Current temple marriage	67	63	Current temple marriage
Current civil marriage	4	2	Current civil marriage
Single, never married	28	34	Single, never married
Single, divorced	1	1	Single, divorced
	χ^2 = 19.15[1]		

1. Statistically significant at p ≤ 0.01.

It appears that the decrease in temple marriages is attributed to the higher numbers of those not yet married, rather than an increase in civil marriages. This tendency for returned missionaries to wait longer to marry follows the pattern in the United States over the same period of time. In the 1970s men and women in the United States married around the age of 24 and 21, respectively. The average age in 1990 was 26 for men and 24 for women. Increased opportunities for both education and work are some of the reasons attributed to the postponement of marriage among Americans (Gelles, 1995).

HELPING RETURNED MISSIONARIES STAY
COMMITTED TO GOSPEL VALUES

As mentioned earlier, Church leaders have encouraged returned missionaries to continue living the same standards after their missions as they did while serving. Elder Dallin H. Oaks (1997) said: "I say to our returned missionaries—men and women who have made covenants to serve the Lord and who have already served Him in the great work proclaiming the gospel and perfecting the Saints—are you being true to the faith? Do you have the faith and continuing commitment to demonstrate the principles of the gospel in your own lives, consistently? You have served well, but do you, like the pioneers, have the courage and the consistency to be true to the faith and to endure to the end?" (p. 73).

We found that the large majority of returned missionaries in our study were doing well in their early postmission adjustments. For example, when asked how difficult it was for them to adjust to postmission life, only about 20% indicated that it was either "quite difficult" or "very difficult." The vast majority (80%) indicated that this adjustment was either "somewhat difficult," "a little difficult," or "not at all difficult."

We further examined adjustment issues by asking returned missionaries to respond to three open-ended questions about the specific difficulties they encountered as they returned home, and what things the returned missionaries themselves, as well as family and Church leaders, could do to help ease the stress of this transition.

Adjustment concerns. The major concerns among returned-missionary men are how to handle dating and the marriage question, adjusting to family and friends, and dealing with culture shock (see Table 7). One man wrote, "Dating was a challenge, as relationships with young women had been carefully monitored by myself for two years. Also, dating leads to marriage, and with my parents' marriage ending in divorce, this activity was scary."

Another man reported the most difficult adjustment he faced was how "to make so many critical decisions about my schooling, career, employment, and social adjustment in such a short time."

Women rated adjusting to family and friends and culture shock as the top two problems they faced. One young woman explained that because she saw her family in a new light, "[I] was very critical of them. This caused big problems with [my] mother."

Table 7. *Adjustment Problems and Concerns*[1]
Response Rate among LDS Returned Missionaries (1999)

Top Adjustment Problems[2]	Men (n = 1,639)	Women (n = 1,245)
Dating, courtship, and marriage	22	20
Adjusting to family and friends	21	28
Social adjustment—culture shock	14	19
Maintaining spirituality	13	15
Lack of routine, rules, structure, goals, and effective use of time	13	13
Finding employment	13	10
Schooling	12	8
Psychological adjustments: feelings of loneliness, selfishness	9	15
Identity crisis—not being needed	7	14
Longing for companionship, associations, and activities of the mission field	7	11

1. Question: "Upon arriving home from your mission, what were the most difficult adjustments or problems you faced?"
2. Because this was an open-ended question, some returned missionaries gave several suggestions. Up to the first three suggestions were included in the response rates. Thus, the total response rate for each group may exceed 100%.

Other women found that old friends had changed. "My friends were all married," one woman wrote, "so the friends I had were all in the mission field. I was very lonely."

Another commented, "All of my closest friends were either married or currently serving a mission, so I felt the adjustment of making new friends. Also, I had a boyfriend who had waited for me, and we went through an adjustment phase and the stresses of deciding whether to get married, etc." As this statement suggests, a concern about dating, courtship, and marriage was also ranked as a difficult problem for women. Although this "social life" adjustment does not appear to be as critical for the women as it is for the men, it is still a major concern for returned-missionary women.

Women ranked psychological adjustments higher on the list than men did. One woman explained that the most difficult adjustment she faced was "having a focus on *myself!* I felt so guilty. . . . Finding a new social group seemed so daunting and impossible. I felt so 'nerdish' and that was a new feeling and made me feel guilty that I cared about all that." It appears that some young women may be more prone to experience a sense of guilt or frustration than men do as they make the transition from the mission field to home.

Although our focus here is on returned missionaries, it should be pointed out that these types of feelings and adjustments are certainly not unique to returned missionaries. All LDS young adults experience similar challenges, and they must navigate their way through what is termed "the transition into adulthood."

How the Church could help. When asked how the Church could help returned missionaries successfully cope with adjustments upon their return home, the most frequent suggestion was for them to receive a call to a responsible position as soon as possible (see Table 8). This is important in light of the statement by President Hinckley mentioned earlier that if every returning missionary had a "meaningful responsibility" once they returned home, they would have a greater chance at remaining strong and active in the Church. Confirming President Hinckley's invitation, one young man stated, "Put the RMs to work right away, meaning a calling. Don't let them drift for weeks or months with no responsibility. Challenge them. Most missionaries enjoyed the challenge of knocking on stranger's doors, etc. Don't feel like they need 'time off.'"

This sentiment was also expressed among the women in the study. For example, one woman declared, "I think that missionaries need to be involved immediately in Church positions so they stay active in serving and teaching." She concluded, "They need to feel that their experiences and service to the Lord are valued and appreciated. The best way to do that is use them."

Another women advised, "Give them a calling, or keep them busy. Be their friend. Talk with them on an individual basis. Really care about them."

Other insightful suggestions from both men and women included involvement in service, providing strong young single adult programs, holding interviews at regular intervals with a Church leader, and holding special classes or seminars for returned missionaries. Counsel, support, and encouragement from Church leaders concerning educational pursuits, the launching of careers, and dating would perhaps ease the difficult decisions following mission service.

How returned missionaries could help themselves. The most frequent suggestion on how returned missionaries could help themselves was for them to request a church assignment, keep busy, and get involved in church activity and service (see Table 9). In other words, newly returned missionaries should be proactive in finding ways to serve. Setting goals, getting involved in school and work, having a regular gospel study program, and continuing to hold personal prayer were also important activities suggested by returned missionaries.

One young man said, "Continue to keep mission grooming standards and scripture study and prayer schedules. Don't 'take a break' from serving in the Church (go on splits, home teach, attend firesides and socials, etc.)." Other suggestions were getting involved in dating, maintaining mission standards, seeking spiritual associations, attending all church meetings, and accepting personal responsibility for adjustment.

Staying committed to private religiosity in adulthood. Another way in which we probed the dynamics of the postmission experience was by assessing what factors in returned missionaries' high school and mission years are related to helping them stay strong in their private religiosity after they return home. In other words, we wanted to know what things a person can do before, during, and soon after a mission that will help them to

286 Shield of Faith

Table 8. How the Church Could Help Returned Missionaries,[1]
Percentage Rates among LDS Returned Missionaries (1999)

Top Responses, Church Help[2]	Men (n = 1,397)	Women (n = 1,146)
Call to responsible position	38	52
Involve in service	18	18
Involvement in YSA programs	11	10
Interview at regular intervals	9	7
Special classes/firesides for RMs	7	7
Provide educational and career counseling and job placement	5	3
Less emphasis on marriage immediately after release	5	5
Special programs through elders quorum/RS/Sunday School	4	3
Call as stake or ward missionaries	4	6
RM gatherings/support/reunions	3	6

1. Question: "What could the Church (stakes and/or wards) do to help returned missionaries successfully cope with the adjustments or problems they face upon returning home?"
2. Because this was an open-ended question, some returned missionaries gave several suggestions. Up to the first three suggestions were included in the response rates. Thus, the total response rate for each group may exceed 100%.

maintain a strong commitment to reading scriptures, praying, and thinking about religion.

Figure 1 shows a conceptual model of the various dimensions that we hypothesized would influence private religiosity in adulthood. Private, public, and family religious practices at various times in life; parent and peer influences during adolescence; mission experiences; religious education; and church social involvement after a mission were all included in the model.

Results from our assessment concluded that private religiosity when the future missionaries were young was by far the most powerful predictor of private religiosity in adulthood. For example, the strongest correlation in the model was between early postmission private religiosity and adult private religiosity for both the men and the women. The relationship between

Table 9. How Returned Missionaries Could Help Themselves,[1]
Percentage Rates among LDS Returned Missionaries (1999)

Top Responses, Self Help[2]	Men (n = 1,397)	Women (n = 1,146)
Request Church assignment, keep busy, get involved in Church activity and service	23	36
Get involved in school/work	18	20
Regular gospel study (scriptures)	17	22
Personal prayer	16	22
Date/get involved socially	13	12
Set goals; priorities	13	14
General involvement (social and community)	10	11
Maintain mission standards	10	11
Stay close to Spirit, God, Christ, build testimony	5	8
Attend all church meetings	3	5
Seek spiritual associations	3	8

1. Question: "What could missionaries do to help themselves with the adjustments of returning home from the mission field?"
2. Because this was an open-ended question, some returned missionaries gave several suggestions. Up to the first three suggestions were included in the response rates. Thus, the total response rate for each group may exceed 100%.

premission private religiosity and early postmission private religiosity was also significant. Thus, if returned missionaries had a strong commitment to reading scriptures, praying, and thinking about religion during their high school years, they were more likely to continue these practices during the first year home from a mission, which leads to higher commitment later in life.

Another essential factor that led to strong private religiosity in adulthood, at least for the men, was the avoidance of R-rated movies and videos after their missions. We used R-rated media as an indicator of exposure to things such as profanity, violence, and pornography in the media. A strong relationship between avoiding R-rated movies and videos before a mission and staying away from them immediately after was also found. In other

Figure 1. Conceptual Model for Predicting Early
Postmission, Mission, and Premission Factors on
Private Adult Religiosity

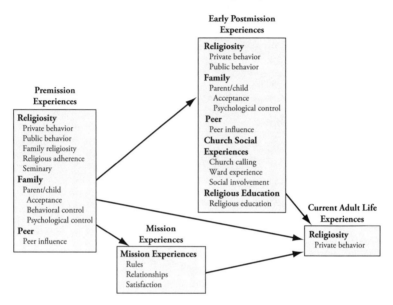

words, if youth disciplined themselves not to see R-rated movies (and for that matter, any media, regardless of rating, that offers exposure to inappropriate behavior) while in their high school years, they were less likely to view this material during the first year home from their missions, as well as later.

Private religiosity in adulthood was influenced by the type of mission experience as well, albeit indirectly. Findings vary between men and women. However, in general, missionaries who kept the mission rules, got along well with their companions, and had a satisfying mission experience were more likely to continue to read their scriptures, pray, and think about religion right after their missions, which is strongly linked to private religiosity in adulthood. In addition, men who kept mission rules and were more satisfied with their missions were more likely to avoid R-rated media immediately after their missions, thus leading them to higher religiosity in later life.

Figure 2. Model of Significant Estimates for Predicting Premission, Mission, and Early Postmission Factors on Private Adult Religiosity (Men)

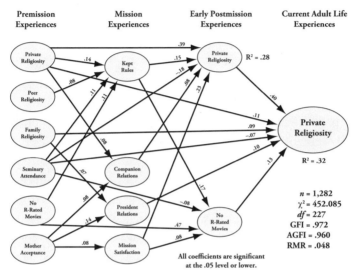

Figure 3. Model of Significant Estimates for Predicting Premission, Mission, and Early Postmission Factors on Private Adult Religiosity (Women)

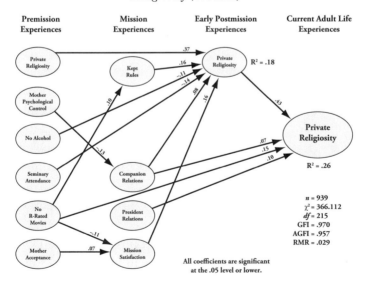

So the mission experience seems to matter when it comes to religious commitment later in life. However, we are a little more cautious when it comes to interpreting these correlations, because we are unsure if they represent a causal relationship or are the outcome of selection bias. In other words, certain missionaries bring with them into the mission field traits that help them keep mission rules or get along with a companion. Thus, the indicators we used to measure the mission experience may actually be measuring premission characteristics.

In addition, we found that family experiences, including family religious practices and the parent-child relationship, had a significant influence on private religiosity in adulthood. Specifically, men who were raised in homes where family home evening, family prayer, and family scripture study were practiced had higher adult private religiosity.

Notably, this direct relationship was not found for the women. They seemed to be more resilient to any neutral or negative experiences in their families than the men in terms of premission family religious practices. Perhaps the influence of Church advisors and/or friends during adolescence helped to moderate these effects in some way. It may also be that their husband's religiosity had a greater effect on their current religiosity than did any of their premission factors.

We also found that the parent-child relationship during high school is indirectly related to adult private religiosity through the mission experiences. For both men and women, their mother's acceptance influenced their experiences in the mission field. Women, however, were also influenced by their mother's psychological control, directly influencing how these women got along with their mission companions.

CONCLUSION

Many feel that the postmission experience is a pivotal time for LDS young adults, where maintaining the religious identity they developed in the mission field is tested. Latter-day

Saints tend to attach higher spiritual and social expectations to returned missionaries given their unique "life-transforming" experiences in the mission field. Results from this study indicate that such high expectations may be warranted. Returned missionaries are doing very well not only in the religious aspects of their lives but in a number of other areas as well.

Of significance is the finding that the socioeconomic status among returned missionaries exceeds that of the national average. Family characteristics were also different than those nationally, with returned missionaries showing a much lower average of divorce and also more children than their peers across the United States.

High religiosity across a number of indicators was also found among returned missionaries. Although it is unfortunate that any returned missionary falls into inactivity, the fact that almost nine out of ten returned missionaries continue to regularly attend church for up to 17 years after their missions is remarkable. A comparison of returned missionaries' private religiosity over the past 30 years shows a modest decline in their scripture study and prayer, yet these levels still remain relatively high. On the other hand, an increase in church attendance was also found. A number of other factors remained the same. All of this underscores the point that the vast majority of returned missionaries continue to hold strong to their religious convictions and refutes any notion that there is an emerging pattern of inactivity or secularization among them.

The study shows that if returned missionaries had a strong commitment to private religiosity during their high school years, they were more likely to continue that practice during the first year home from their missions, which in turn continued into adulthood. Thus it is important for parents and Church leaders to help young men and young women to begin a habit of personal prayer and scripture study during these impressionable high school years.

Other notable factors that were associated with private religiosity in adulthood were the avoidance of viewing R-rated movies; having positive mission experiences and attitudes; being involved in family home evening, family prayer, family scripture study while a youth; and having a positive relationship with parents.

Finally, the majority of returned missionaries are adjusting to regular life after a mission very well. As suggested by the returned missionaries themselves, the most important thing they can do to help themselves during this stage is to continue to maintain good spiritual habits such as daily prayer and scripture study, to attend church, and to serve in significant callings in their wards. Many of them recognize that such spiritual maintenance will help them have the spiritual resources to draw upon when they are challenged by other areas in their life, including dating, family, culture shock, school, and work.

In 1997, President Hinckley counseled Church leaders that the most important things they can do to help retain new converts is to provide them with "a friend, a responsibility, and nurturing with 'the good word of God'" (p. 47). Certainly this counsel can pertain to all members of the Church, and based on the findings in this study, it can especially be applied to "retaining" newly returned missionaries. Once home, if returned missionaries are provided with the responsibility of a church calling, involve themselves in church social activities where they can develop good friendships, and continue to be nurtured through personal prayer and scripture study, they will find the strength to successfully navigate their way through their postmission pursuits and continue to contribute as members of their families, society, and the Church.

REFERENCES

Albrecht, S. L., & Heaton, T. B. (1998). Secularization, higher education, and religiosity. In J. T. Duke (Ed.), Latter-day Saint social life (pp. 293–314). Provo,

UT: Religious Studies Center, Brigham Young University. (Reprinted from *Review of Religious Research, 26*[1], 43–58)

Caplow, T., Bahr, H. M., & Chadwick, B. A. (1983). *All faithful people: Change and continuity in Middletown's religion.* Minneapolis: University of Minnesota Press.

Chadwick, B. A., & Heaton, T. B. (1999). *Statistical handbook on the American family* (2nd ed.). Phoenix: Oryx Press.

Clawson, R. (1936, October). The returned missionary: A statistical survey. *Improvement Era, 39*(10), 590–594.

Duke, J. T., & Johnson, B. L. (1998). The religiosity of Mormon men and women through the life cycle. In J. T. Duke (Ed.), *Latter-day Saint social life: Social research on the LDS Church and its members* (pp. 315-343). Provo, UT: Religious Studies Center, Brigham Young University.

The First Presidency and Council of the Twelve Apostles of The Church of Jesus Christ of Latter-day Saints (1995). The family: A proclamation to the world. *Ensign, 25*(11), 102.

Gelles, R. J. (1995). *Contemporary families: A sociological view.* Thousand Oaks, CA: Sage Publications.

Groberg, L. B. (1936). *A preliminary study of certain activities, the religious attitudes, and financial status of seventy-four returned missionaries residing within Wayne Stake, Wayne County, Utah* (Master's thesis). Brigham Young University, Provo, UT.

Hinckley, G. B. (1997). Converts and young men. *Ensign, 27*(5), 47–50.

Hinckley, G. B. (2001, January). A prophet's counsel and prayer for youth. *Ensign, 31*(1), 2–11.

Hinckley, G. B. (2001, March). Selections from addresses by President Gordon B. Hinckley. *Ensign, 31*(3), 64–65.

Hoglund, W. J. (1971). *A comparative study of the relative levels of physical fitness of male L.D.S. missionaries who are commencing and those just concluding their missionary service* (Master's thesis). Brigham Young University, Provo, UT.

King, A. W. (1936). *A survey of the religious, social, and economic activities and practices of returned missionaries* (Master's thesis). Brigham Young University, Provo, UT.

Lechner, F. J. (1991). The case against secularization: A rebuttal. *Social Forces, 69*(4), 1103–1119.

Madsen, J. M. (1977). *Church activity of LDS returned missionaries* (Doctoral dissertation). Brigham Young University, Provo, UT.

McClendon, R. J., & Chadwick, B. A. (2004). LDS returned missionaries in the United States: Religious activity and post-mission adjustment. *BYU Studies, 43*(2), 131–156.

Merrill, R. M., Lyan, J. L., & Jensen, W. J. (2003). Lack of secularizing influence of education on religious activity and parity among Mormons. *Journal for the Scientific Study of Religion, 42*(1), 113–124.

Nelson, R. M. (1999). Our sacred duty to honor women. *Ensign, 29*(5), 38.

Oaks, D. H. (1997). Following the pioneers. *Ensign, 27*(11), 72–74.

Probst, R. G. (1936). *A study of fifty-seven return missionaries of The Church of Jesus Christ of Latter-day Saints in Idaho Stake of Bannock County, Idaho, 1935–36* (Master's thesis). Brigham Young University, Provo, UT.

Roghaar, H. B. (1991). *The influence of primary social institutions and adolescent religiosity on young adult male religious observance* (Doctoral dissertation). Brigham Young University, Provo, UT.

Stark, R. (1984). The rise of a new world faith. *Review of Religious Research, 26*(1), 18–27.

Stark, R. (1996). So far, so good: A brief assessment of Mormon membership projections. *Review of Religious Research, 38*(2), 175–178.

Stark, R. (2004). *Sociology* (9th ed.). Belmont, CA: Wadsworth Publishing Company.

Stark, R., & Iannaccone, L. R. (1992). Sociology of religion. In E. F. Borgatta & M. L. Borgotta (Eds.), *Encyclopedia of Sociology* (Vol. 4, pp. 2029–2037). New York: Macmillan.

Stott, G. (1984). Effects of college education on the religious involvement of Latter-day Saints. *BYU Studies, 24*(1), 43–52.

Thomas, D. L. (1992). Reflections on adolescent and young adult development: Religious, familial, and educational identities. *Family Perspective, 26*(4), 383–404.

Top, B. L., & Chadwick, B.A. (2001). "Seek learning, even by study and also by faith": The relationship between personal religiosity and academic achievement among Latter-day Saint high-school students. *Religious Educator, 2*(2), 121–137.

U.S. Bureau of the Census (1999). *Statistical abstract of the United States: 1999* (119th Ed.). Washington DC.

U.S. Bureau of the Census (2000). *Statistical abstract of the United States: 2000* (120th Ed.). Washington DC.

Warner, S. R. (1993). Work in progress toward a new paradigm for the sociological study of religion in the United States. *American Journal of Sociology*, 98(5), 1044–1093.

Yamane, D. (1997). Secularization on trial: In defense of neosecularization paradigm. *Journal for the Scientific Study of Religion, 36*(1), 109–122.

Ten

MENTAL HEALTH

In June 2001 and again in February 2007, newspapers headlined the findings of a nationwide study by Express Scripts that ranked Utah first in the nation for the use of antidepressant drugs such as Prozac, Zoloft, and Paxil (Express Scripts, 2001; Express Scripts, 2008; Goodman, 2001; Thalman, 2001). Another study, published by Mental Health America, found Utah to have the highest occurrence of depression in the United States (Mental Health America, 2008).

These studies have led many observers to wonder why Utah leads the nation in mental health illnesses such as depression and anxiety as well as in antidepressant use. Unfortunately, these studies examined only the rates of incidence and not the reasons why Utah is the leader in these areas.

Previous to these studies, there had already been some suspicion that Utah had a higher rate of Prozac use than the national average (Jensen & Jensen, 1999). Discussions surrounding this issue pointed to what some consider to be the overburdened lifestyle of members of The Church of Jesus Christ of Latter-day Saints, Utah's dominant religion. Some speculated that Utah's high rate of antidepressant use was connected to Latter-day Saint women specifically, claiming the LDS ideology creates a culture of perfectionism that leads to higher levels of stress, depression, and anxiety disorders (Goldman, 2008).

The large majority of scientific research on mental health among Latter-day Saints, however, clearly shows that LDS women are no more likely to have mental illnesses than members of other religions (Judd, 1999). So it seems strange that Utah, with the majority (at least 60%) of its population comprising members of the LDS Church, would rank number one in the nation in depressive symptoms and antidepressant use.

The purpose of this chapter is twofold: first, to further investigate depression levels among Latter-day Saints across the United States and compare them to national data to see if there are significant differences, and second, to identify factors that are significantly related to depression among Latter-day Saints.

MENTAL HEALTH AND RELIGION: THE LATTER-DAY SAINT CASE

The relationship between religion and mental health has been discussed among social scientists and lay people alike for some time. Though the religious life has generally been held in high regard for thousands of years, during the past two hundred years some social theorists and therapists have questioned the benefits of religion in the lives of individuals, families, communities, and nations. The opinions of social scientists and mental health professionals are mixed concerning the impact of religion on mental health. Sigmund Freud (1989) described religion as "the universal obsessional neurosis of humanity" (p. 55). More recently, Albert Ellis (1980), creator of Rational Emotive Theory and Therapy, stated: "Religiosity is in many respects equivalent to irrational thinking and emotional disturbance. . . . The elegant therapeutic solution to emotional disturbance is quite unreligious. . . . The less religious they are, the more emotionally healthy they will be" (Ellis as cited in Bergin, 1983, p. 170).

On the other hand, the American philosopher and psychologist William James defended humankind's relationship with God when he stated: "We and God have business with each other; and in opening ourselves to His influence our deepest destiny is fulfilled. The Universe, and those parts of it which our personal being constitutes, takes a turn for the worse or for the better in proportion as each one of us fulfills or evades God's commands" (1902, pp. 516–17).

Although history provides examples of religious belief and practice that have led to ill health and even destructive behavior, the great majority of recent research studies have reported the relationship of religion and mental health to be positive (Larson et al., 1992). This relationship holds true for most measures of religious affiliation, belief, and practice in relation to a variety of measures of mental health.

Various measures of mental health among Latter-day Saints have been studied in detail. Daniel K Judd edited a book entitled *Religion, Mental Health, and the Latter-day Saints*, wherein the affiliation, beliefs, and practices of various samples of Latter-day Saints were examined with respect to measures of mental health, including depression, suicide, drug use, perfectionism, and family affection. Although many anecdotal descriptions argue otherwise, the research indicates that Latter-day Saints report either the same or lower incidences of mental illness as those of other religious faiths and those who claim to not believe in God or who do not practice any form of religion (Jensen, Jensen, & Wiederhold, 1993; Judd, 1999).

With this background in mind, our first objective was to probe how depression rates among LDS men and women living in the United States compared to the national average. This objective was accomplished by comparing depression levels between Latter-day Saint men and women and women from the National Study of Families and Households (NSFH). As an additional assessment, we compared the LDS rates of depression to those estimated by the American Psychiatric Association and the National Mental Health Association for the nation as a whole.

PREDICTING DEPRESSION AMONG LATTER-DAY SAINTS

Our second objective was to develop and test a multivariate model predicting depression among Latter-day Saints. Figure 1 presents the conceptual model of the hypothesized factors, taken from the literature that are believed to influence depression. For example, previous research has revealed that adult religious experiences, including affiliation, church attendance, and private religious experience, are relevant when assessing mental health (Schnittker, 2001; Cadwallader, 1991; Murphy et al., 2000; Ellison, 1995; Mirola, 1999; Doxey, Jensen, & Jensen, 1997; Genia & Shaw, 1991; Watson et al., 1988; Jensen et al., 1993).

Although previous studies are not unanimous, the majority have found that higher religiosity is associated with lower frequency of depression. Given the focus of this paper, as well as earlier research, we included several measures of religiosity in the model. We also added religiosity during the respondent's adolescence to the model, because feelings of religious

Figure 1. Conceptual Model Predicting Depression among Members of the LDS Church

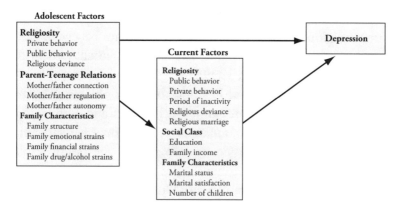

inadequacy or limited self-worth created in youth may persist into adulthood.

Socioeconomic factors, including educational attainment and family income, provide some understanding of psychological well-being (Reading & Reynolds, 2001; Miech & Shanahan, 2000; Miech et al., 1999; Lloyd & Turner, 1999). People with higher education are more likely to recognize the symptoms of depression and to seek treatment. Higher family income is often obtained from employment that provides medical insurance covering treatment for mental illness, and if not, provides the means to pay for treatment. Because of this previous research support, both of these factors were included in the model predicting depression.

Marital status and marital satisfaction have also been linked to depression. Married men and women have been reported to have lower rates of depression (Waite & Gallagher, 2000). Among the married, those experiencing higher marital satisfaction tend to have less depression.

One area that has been specifically tied to marital satisfaction and depression is that of marital roles. Whisman and Jacobson (1989) found that "husbands and wives in relationships in which the wife was depressed showed greater inequality in decision making and dissatisfaction with the distribution of decision making and household tasks; wives additionally indicated greater dissatisfaction with the distribution of childrearing responsibilities" (p. 177).

Assh and Byers (1996) suggested that the quality of the "marital exchange" is also important to happiness in marriage. Women who experienced greater rates of displeasing marital exchanges ranked higher in their daily dysphoric mood, higher in marital dissatisfaction, and higher in global depression (p. 549).

Others have also found a salient relationship between marital satisfaction and depression (Gotlib & Whiffen, 1989;

Earle et al., 1998;). We therefore included measures of both marital status and marital satisfaction in our model.

In addition, we added the factor of family size, because fertility among LDS families tends to be significantly higher than the national average (3.4 children as compared to 2.1). Hypothetically, supporting and caring for a large family adds to a parent's stress and subsequent depression. We also added whether or not the person had been married in an LDS temple, because a temple marriage is an indicator of high religiosity among LDS members.

Research has also shown that family structure during adolescence is related to depression later in life. Children of divorced parents or children who grow up without both parents in the home are more at risk for adult depression (Amato, 1991; Ross, 2000). In addition, parenting practices such as connection, regulation, and psychological autonomy have both direct and indirect effects on child and young adult depression (Barber, 1997; Barber, 2002; Gray & Steinberg, 1999). Adults who grew up closely connected to their parents and had parents who set rules, monitored their behavior, dispensed discipline when appropriate, and encouraged them to develop their own beliefs, values, and principles have been found to experience less depression. Therefore, family structure and parental connection, regulation, and psychological autonomy were included in our model predicting depression.

Family emotional and financial strains in childhood and teenage years are also connected to mental health outcomes in adulthood. Adults who were raised in homes with family violence, excessive criticism, or shaming were prone to higher levels of depression as adults (Kessler & Magee, 1994; Robertson & Simons, 1989; Mizell, 1999). Thus, we included whether or not the young adult recalled his or her family being stressed over financial problems, family members' emotional problems, or family members' alcohol or drug addictions while the young adult was growing up.

In summary, Figure 1 shows the various measures of religiosity, family structure, parenting practices, and family stresses in adolescence that were included in the model predicting depression among members of the LDS Church.

Data from three studies were used to complete the two objectives. The first set of data came from a study of men and women who served missions for the LDS Church. The second set of data was collected in the year 2000 from a sample of 4,000 LDS men and 2,000 LDS women who did not serve a mission. The details of the data collection for these two studies are reported in Appendix A.

The third data set came from the second wave of the National Study of Families and Households (NSFH2) collected in 1992–1994 (Sweet & Bumpass, 1996). This was a five-year follow-up survey that included personal interviews with 10,007 of the original 13,007 primary respondents who were surveyed in Wave 1 (1987–88). Data for Wave 1 (NSFH1) were collected from a sample of 13,007 who were drawn from a noninstitutionalized U.S. population. It included adults from a main cross-section of 9,637 households.

The Center for Epidemiological Studies Depression Scale (Radloff, 1977) was used to measure depression. This widely used scale consists of 12 questions that reflect symptomatic manifestations of depression. These questions include: "On how many days during the past week did you (1) feel bothered by things that usually don't bother you? (2) feel that you could not shake off the blues, even with help from your family or friends? (3) have trouble keeping your mind on what you were doing? (4) feel depressed? (5) feel that everything you did was an effort? (6) feel you could not get going? (7) feel fearful? (8) sleep restlessly? (9) feel lonely? (10) feel sad? (11) not feel like eating; your appetite was poor? (12) talk less than usual?" The answers ranged from 0 to 7 (days per week), with higher numbers indicating a greater level of depression.

Religiosity was conceptualized as having four dimensions: private religiosity, public religiosity, religious deviance, and history of church activity. These dimensions were measured for the adolescent and young adult years.

Private religiosity, an indicator that measures intrinsically motivated religious behavior, was determined by responses to the question, "During the past year, how often did you do the following: (1) read the scriptures by yourself, (2) pray privately, (3) think seriously about religion." The possible responses for ranged from (1) not at all to (7) every day.

Public religiosity, which measures extrinsically motivated religious behavior, was ascertained from responses to the question, "How often in the past year did you attend (1) sacrament meeting, (2) Sunday School, (3) priesthood/Relief Society meeting." Responses were ranked from (1) never to (6) almost every week.

Religious deviance comprised six items. Each respondent was asked, "During the last year, how often have you done the following: (1) taken things that did not belong to you, (2) smoked or used chewing tobacco, (3) watched R-rated movies, (4) viewed pornography in books or magazines or on the Internet, (5) drunk alcohol (beer, wine, etc.), (6) used drugs like marijuana, heroin, cocaine, etc." Response categories ranged from (1) never to (5) ten or more times. All six items were combined to measure religious deviance during the adult years, while items 3, 4, and 5 were combined to measure deviance during the adolescent years.

Finally, history of church activity was measured by the following question: "Have there ever been periods of one year or more since your baptism (which generally occurs at age eight) when you did not attend church at least once a month?" Respondents indicated yes or no.

Family structure while the respondent was growing up was determined by asking, "During your high school years, which parent(s) did you mostly live with?" Potential responses included: both a mother and father in the same household, only a mother, a mother and stepfather, only a father, a father and stepmother, or other. We recoded these responses into two dummy variables: those who grew up with both parents versus those in the other five categories.

Marital status was determined by asking, "Which best describes your marital status?" Response categories were (1) never married, (2) cohabiting (living with a partner in an intimate relationship), (3) married, first marriage, (4) married but separated, (5) divorced, (6) remarried, and (7) widowed. These categories were combined into three dummy variables: married, single, and divorced/separated.

Marital satisfaction was ascertained from asking married respondents the following question: "Compared with other couples you know, how satisfied are you with your marriage?" The range of responses for both questions was (1) very dissatisfied to (5) very satisfied.

Family size was assessed by asking, "How many children do you have?"

Type of marriage was measured with the question, "What type of ceremony did you have for your current marriage?" Response categories were (1) temple ceremony, (2) civil ceremony, and (3) civil ceremony followed by a temple sealing. These three response categories were coded into dummy variables.

Three scales were used to assess the parent-child relationship during adolescence. These scales were adapted from widely used adolescent inventories and measure the degree to which parents supported and controlled their child. Parental connection was determined by responses to four of ten questions originally developed by Shaefer (1965) and tested by Barber, Olsen, and Shagle (1994).

Parental regulation identified the level of behavioral control that each parent gave to his or her child. It was determined by responses to questions about parental awareness in five areas

Table 1. Scores on the Center for Disease Control's Depression Scale, by Sex and Religious Affiliation

"On how many days during the past week did you . . ."	Men			Women		
	National	LDS		National	LDS	
		Served Mission	No Mission		Served Mission	No Mission
	(n = 2,170)	(n = 1,893)	(n = 332)	(n = 2,915)	(n = 1,400)	(n = 570)
Feel bothered by things that usually don't bother you?	1.29	0.81	1.00	1.73	1.12	1.16
Feel that you could not shake off the blues, even with help from family and friends?	0.79	0.45	0.82	1.25	0.63	0.75
Have trouble keeping your mind on what you were doing?	1.08	1.27	1.28	1.46	1.26	1.33
Feel depressed?	1.05	0.63	0.97	1.51	0.84	1.11
Feel everything that that you did was an effort?	1.22	1.48	1.82	1.49	1.48	1.53
Feel you could not get going?	1.10	1.02	1.30	4.55	1.33	1.44
Feel fearful?	0.58	0.47	0.57	0.88	0.54	0.65
Sleep restlessly?	1.49	1.37	1.77	1.79	1.61	1.73
Feel lonely?	0.93	0.73	1.22	1.29	4.05	1.12
Feel sad?	1.04	0.77	1.21	1.53	1.12	1.30
Not like eating; your appetite was poor?	0.74	0.41	0.65	1.19	0.47	0.63
Talk less than usual?	0.82	0.59	0.76	0.99	0.54	0.57
Scale mean	**1.01**	**0.83**	**1.12**	**1.39**	**1.00**	**1.11**

of their children's lives (Dornbusch et al., 1987; Barber et al., 1994).

Psychological control focuses on parents' encouragement of their teenagers to trust the teens' own thoughts, ideas, and feelings. It was measured by four of the eight questions originally used by Barber et al. (1994) in their study of parental use of psychological controlling behavior. Three questions were used to assess the level of family emotional, financial, and addictive strains in adolescence. The items used to calculate these factors are presented in Appendix B.

Educational attainment was measured by asking, "Circle the highest grade or year of school that you have completed." Response categories ranged from (1) none to (6) graduate/professional school.

Family income information was obtained by the question: "What was your total family income from all sources for 1998 (before taxes)?" Response categories ranged from (1) under $10,000 to (8) over $100,000.

LDS AND NATIONAL RATES OF DEPRESSION

Looking at Table 1, we see that the returned-missionary men have significantly less depression than their non-returned-missionary counterparts. The returned-missionary men are also lower than men in the national sample. Men in the national sample reported an average of just over one day per week with one or more symptoms (1.01) as compared to 0.83 for the returned-missionary men.

Similar findings appeared for the women in the three samples. Because young women in the LDS Church are not generally encouraged to serve a mission like the young men are, the non-returned-missionary women more accurately represent the majority of LDS women. However, like the men, LDS women who do serve missions have significantly higher religiosity levels than the average LDS woman (see Chapter 2). These returned-missionary women also revealed the lowest rate

Table 2. Covariance/Correlation Matrix (Returned-Missionary Men)

Indicator	1	2	3	4	5	6	7	8	9	10	11	12	13	14	15	16	17	18	19	20	21
Current factors																					
Depression		-.171	.152	-.019	-.109	.053	.084	.016	-.354	.005	-.033	.092	-.093	-.050	-.050	-.025	.073	.060	.208	.173	.012
Private religiosity	.139		.555	.157	.069	-.079	.026	-.022	-.193	.457	-.059	-.372	.103	.058	.029	.012	-.006	.003	.057	-.000	.168
Public religiosity	-.181	.457		-.017	.054	-.137	-.025	-.024	-.061	.112	.072	-.122	.052	.029	.028	.025	-.044	-.028	-.082	-.065	-.020
Religious deviance	-.022	.126	-.019		-.046	.089	-.018	-.007	.137	-.590	-.312	.958	-.085	-.083	-.178	-.190	.095	.114	.132	.068	.391
Educational attainment	-.142	.061	.070	-.059		-.029	-.069	-.004	.536	.109	.046	-.023	-.005	.003	.012	.029	-.030	-.026	-.020	-.046	-.023
Periods of inactivity	.136	-.140	-.355	.222	-.081		-.002	.008	.059	-.141	-.114	.019	-.045	-.029	-.047	-.040	.032	.024	.067	.071	.075
Single	.244	.052	-.074	-.051	-.219	-.013		-.003	-.317	.004	.006	-.010	-.000	-.001	-.000	-.002	.004	.002	.017	.010	-.001
Divorced/Separated	.123	-.118	-.185	-.055	-.036	.138	-.029		-.004	-.004	-.008	.023	-.005	-.002	-.001	.000	.003	-.001	.008	.002	-.003
Family income	-.191	-.071	-.033	.072	.315	.069	-.417	-.015		-.278	-.036	.046	.048	-.062	-.016	-.016	-.032	.007	-.121	-.168	-.059
Adolescent factors																					
Private religiosity	.004	.230	.082	-.420	.087	-.222	.008	-.019	-.092		.641	-.139	.193	.140	.197	.205	-.079	-.087	-.013	.009	-.189
Public religiosity	-.037	-.045	.081	-.340	.056	-.275	.015	-.056	-.018	.440		.018	.120	.080	.135	.129	-.073	-.058	-.156	-.113	-.283
Religious deviance	.090	-.251	-.120	.917	-.025	.041	-.025	.145	.020	-.084	.017		.015	.039	.025	.024	-.040	-.053	-.015	.001	-.213
Father's connection	-.154	.118	.087	-.138	-.008	-.161	-.002	-.057	-.036	.197	.188	.020		.128	.190	.097	-.137	-.068	-.165	-.117	-.156
Mother's connection	-.103	.082	.061	-.167	.006	-.127	-.004	-.020	-.057	.177	.155	.067	.368		.093	.117	-.038	-.117	-.115	-.076	-.075
Father's regulation	-.092	.037	.053	-.322	.025	-.188	-.002	-.007	-.013	.224	.235	.038	.492	.297		-.075	-.080	-.066	-.166	-.140	-.205
Mother's regulation	-.053	.018	.053	-.387	.067	-.180	-.010	.000	-.015	.24	.253	.041	.284	.423	.715		-.048	-.062	-.121	-.088	-.152
Father's psych. control	.165	-.010	-.100	.208	-.075	.156	.022	.046	-.033	-.110	-.156	-.074	-.432	-.147	-.280	-.190		.089	.131	.106	.122
Mother's psych. control	.141	.004	-.067	.260	-.067	.119	.009	-.019	.008	-.124	-.128	-.103	-.222	-.471	-.241	-.256	.397		.113	.083	.100
Family emotional strains	.202	.038	-.080	.125	-.021	.140	.040	.047	-.053	-.008	-.142	-.012	-.224	-.193	-.251	-.207	.242	.216		.417	.397
Family financial strains	.162	-.000	-.061	.062	-.047	.144	.023	.010	-.071	.005	-.099	.001	-.153	-.123	-.203	-.146	.188	.152	.318		.267
Family drug/alcohol strains	.011	.110	-.019	.362	-.024	.154	-.001	-.020	.026	-.110	-.252	-.167	-.207	-.124	-.303	-.255	.221	.187	.308	.200	

of depression symptoms among the three women's samples, with an average of one day per week (see Table 1). The LDS women who had not served a mission reported a higher rate of depression than the returned-missionary women, with 1.11 days per week, but they had a lower rate of depression than the same age of women in the national NSFH study (1.39).

Another way we assessed depression rates among Latter-day Saints and others in the United States was by comparing our data to estimates taken from various mental health agencies. In 1990 Robins and Regier estimated that 19 million adults suffered from clinical depression. The American Psychiatric Association (1998) estimated that 17 million adults were affected by depression. The National Mental Health Association (1999) also estimated that 17 million adults had clinical depression. These estimates suggest that one in ten American adults suffers from depression.

Using the standard scoring of four of the twelve symptoms occurring most days of the week from the depression scale in our study (the Center for Epidemiological Studies Depression Scale), we found that over 9% of the adults in the NSFH sample were depressed (which is close to the estimates from the mental health associations) and about 8% of the LDS men and women with lower religiosity experienced depression as compared to only 4% of the male returned missionaries and 6% of the female returned missionaries.

PREDICTING DEPRESSION AMONG LDS MEN AND WOMEN

Our second objective was to identify factors related to depression among members of the LDS Church. We accomplished this objective by testing the multivariate model presented in Figure 1. We estimated the model for eight separate groups in order to isolate the effects of sex, marital status, and religiosity on depression. This also allowed us to add marital satisfaction, number of children, and type of marriage ceremony to the model for those who were married.[1]

Table 3. Structural Model Fit Indicators, by Sex, Marital Status, and Missionary Service

Fit Indicators	Men				Women			
	All		Married		All		Married	
	Mission	No	Mission	No	Mission	No	Mission	No
Sample size	1683	277	1285	167	1218	476	813	352
Chi-square	554	218	532	214	432	368	403	406
Degrees of freedom	106	106	132	132	106	106	132	132
S^2/df ratio	5.2	2.1	4.0	1.6	4.1	3.5	3.1	3.1
Goodness of fit index	.972	.938	.968	.914	.970	.941	.960	.922
Adjusted goodness of fit index	.933	.853	.927	.805	.929	.859	.915	.804
Standardized root mean squared	.045	.073	.043	.068	.031	.076	.036	.100

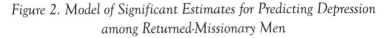

Figure 2. Model of Significant Estimates for Predicting Depression
among Returned-Missionary Men

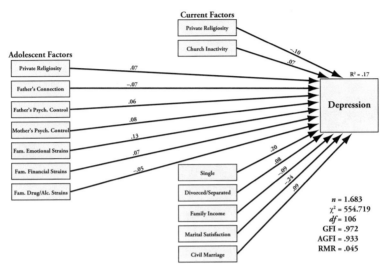

Across all models, the most consistent finding is the strong
link between family emotional strains experienced as a teenager and adult depression. These results illustrate the long-
term effect of family stress on teenagers. Those LDS men and
women who had a family member with severe emotional problems reported greater depression as an adult. This effect was
observed in all eight samples.

These results confirm previous studies about the long-term
effects of family emotional trauma on children. In addition,
family emotional stress and financial stress caused by the addiction of a family member to alcohol or drugs also made a contribution to explaining depression in three of the eight samples.
It appears that family stress, regardless of the cause, fosters
depression when a teenager becomes an adult.

A second finding specific to the married samples was the
association of marital satisfaction to depression. Married people
who reported higher levels of satisfaction in their marriages

Table 4. Beta Coefficients from the Structural Models, by Sex, Marital Status, and Missionary Service

Independent Variables	Men				Women			
	All		Married		All		Married	
	Mission	No	Mission	No	Mission	No	Mission	No
Adolescent Factors								
Private religiosity	.07	*	.10	.24	*	*	*	*
Public religiosity	*	*	*	*	−.07	.11	*	.15
Religious deviance	*	*	*	.24	*	*	*	.25
Father's connection	−.07	*	*	*	*	*	*	*
Mother's regulation	*	*	*	−.17	*	*	*	*
Father's granting of psychological autonomy	.06	*	*	*	.13	.12	.12	*
Mother's granting of psychological autonomy	.08	*	*	*	*	*	*	*
Family emotional strain	.13	.17	.09	.16	.07	.20	.10	.23
Family financial strain	.07	*	*	*	*	.15	*	.12
Family addiction strain	−.05	*	*	*	*	*	*	*
Current Factors								
Single	.30	.21	—	—	.07	*	—	—
Divorced/separated	.08	.31	—	—	*	*	—	—
Education	*	−.10	*	*	*	−.09	*	−.12
Family income	−.09	−.16	−.12	*	−.15	*	−.12	*
Private religiosity	−.10	*	−.07	*	−.18	*	−.08	*
Public religiosity	*	−.18	*	−.23	*	*	*	*
Inactivity	.07	*	.08	*	.08	*	.09	*
Civil marriage	—	—	.09	*	—	—	−.12	*
Civil/temple marriage	—	—	*	.19	—	—	*	*
Marital satisfaction	—	—	−.24	−.12	—	—	−.31	−.32
R^2	.17	.31	.17	.18	.12	.18	.20	.29

* Not statistically significant.

scored significantly lower on the depression scale. The effect appears to be stronger for women than men.

Obviously, a fulfilling marriage provides a sense of contentment that mediates against depression, even though there may be strains in other areas of a person's life. In addition, most LDS people have a rather positive attitude towards marriage and see a successful marriage as part of the Church's spiritual charge to its members. Thus, it is not surprising that high marital satisfaction is related to lower depression.

In the four models that included both married and single respondents, marital status was a significant factor predicting depression. Those men and women who had never married or who were divorced or separated scored higher on the depression scale than did those who were married. This was especially true for men (see Table 4). The comparison of divorced or separated men to married men produced similar results. Marriage provides various benefits for both men and women. However, men seem to benefit more and usually report higher marital satisfaction than women (Waite & Gallagher, 2000). These results suggest that the emotional support received from marriage somewhat protects the couple from depression.

Religiosity was significant in the structural equation models predicting depression for the men and women who served missions. Specifically, those with higher private religious behavior were less likely to experience depression. Similar results appeared for having a period of at least one year of inactivity in the Church among the returned-missionary men and women. If highly religious men and women neglect their religious responsibilities for a period of time, then depression is a little more likely. Interestingly, other than the public religiosity of the men, religiosity had no effect on depression among those who had not served missions. Perhaps men who did not serve a mission value public religiosity in much the same way that returned-missionary men and women value private religiosity.

Consistent with previous research, socioeconomic factors of education and income were significant predictors in about half of the models predicting depression. Higher education and income reduce some of life's stresses, which results in lower depression scores.

Finally, a significant contribution to predicting depression as an adult was the psychological autonomy that fathers granted LDS female teenagers. Based on Barber's (2002) review of the literature, as well as his own research, the link between fathers' psychological control and the emotional health of their children, especially their daughters, is well established. Barber's review of the research shows that a lack of psychological autonomy from fathers is related to a variety of mental health conditions and related behaviors among young women, including depression, low self-esteem, suicide ideation, eating disorders, and sexual promiscuity. The relationship we found between how the fathers treated the women when they were teens and the onset of depression in young adulthood is modest but should be noted.

CONCLUSION

The findings of this study found no evidence that members of The Church of Jesus Christ of Latter-day Saints experience depression more often than others across the nation. In fact, we discovered that, on the whole, LDS men and women with higher rates of religiosity had significantly lower levels of depression than the average American. Apparently, the religious LDS lifestyle acts as a buffer against depression rather than heightening it, as some have previously assumed.

In all the different analyses, we found no evidence linking membership in the LDS Church to a greater risk of depression. This finding is consistent with previous research noting a negative relationship between religiosity and depression among members of the LDS Church (Judd, 1999; Hilton, 2002; Jensen & Jensen, 1993; Spendlove, 1984).

So how does all of this connect back to why Utah has the highest ranking in both depression symptoms and antidepressant drug use? Perhaps Utah Latter-day Saints are an anomaly in comparison to LDS members in other parts of the United States, or perhaps they are more apt to report their symptoms and prescription drug use compared to those nationally.

On the other hand, maybe the other 25% of Utah's population, the non-LDS group, have higher level of depression levels, thus boosting Utah's percentages up a few points. Unfortunately, our data are not able to test these questions.

In terms of antidepressant use and sales, perhaps the most plausible explanation is that those in other states are more likely to self-medicate with alcohol or illegal drugs. The literature provides evidence that drinking alcohol or taking illegal drugs is a very common way people cope with symptoms of depression (Weiss, Griffin, & Mirin, 1992; Schinka, Curtiss, & Mulloy, 1994; Miller, Miller, Verhegge, Linville, & Pumariega, 2002; Moore, 1998; Hendrie, Sairally, & Starkey, 1998). Although some Utahns may follow this practice, most of those who are LDS are less likely to turn to alcohol or drugs because of the LDS Church's strong stance against the consumption of alcohol and illegal drugs for any reason. Thus, instead of self-medicating with alcohol or drugs, LDS Utahns may be more likely to seek medical assistance from their doctor, who may then prescribe an antidepressant.

Another possiblity is that since Utahns are generally more educated and aware of the symptoms and treatments of depression, they are more likely than residents of some other states to seek medical treatment. Prescription practices in Utah point this out, as physicians in Utah have high prescription rates not only for antidepressants, but for other medications as well (Lamb, 2002). In fact, the study that reported Utah's high use of antidepression prescriptions also found the state to be the highest in the nation prescribing antibiotics, analgesics (painkillers), and antiinflammatory drugs (Express Scripts, 2001).

Our second objective was to identify the determinants of depression among LDS populations. Several important findings emerged. First, marital status has a strong relationship to depression among LDS men and women. Single or divorced members of the LDS Church, especially men, were significantly more depressed than their married counterparts. Waite and Gallagher (2000) recently synthesized the latest research on the effects of marriage. Although their review found some inconsistency among studies, the overall pattern discovered was that higher levels of depression are found among the single or divorced than those who are married.

Among those married, marital satisfaction was a powerful predictor of lower depression. Those reporting lower levels of marital satisfaction were much more likely to report higher levels of depressed symptoms. Although this makes sense when considering the high emotional value that Latter-day Saints put on marriage, they as a group are not unique when it comes to this outcome. A number of studies consisting of couples with varying backgrounds have found this same association (Assh & Byers, 1996).

Our results add to the literature previously cited that finds a salient link between religiosity and depression. We found that a person's private religious behavior, including scripture study or private prayer, as well as their public behavior, such as church attendance, are negatively associated with depression. These effects, however, vary according to the level of religiosity. Private religiosity influenced depression for returned-missionary men and women, and public religiosity only for non-returned-missionary men.

The significant inverse link between private religiosity and depression unique among returned missionaries may be explained by the relatively high religious standards returned missionaries set for themselves as compared to non-returned missionaries. While serving as missionaries, these men and women developed consistent habits of daily scripture study, private prayer, and religious observance. Once home, varying from these habits may lead to strong feelings of guilt and thus a greater strain on emotional health.

Most non-missionary LDS men and women, not experiencing these elevated levels of private religious commitment in the first place, would therefore not experience the same level of guilt or self-incrimination. However, for them, at least for the men, a similar pattern occurs in public religiosity. When they see themselves falling below a previous standard in Church attendance, feelings of inadequacy and guilt may set in, eventually leading to depression.

A final significant finding in the study is the link between childhood experiences and adult depression. Those members of the LDS Church who experienced greater family emotional strains during adolescence experienced greater depression in adulthood. A father's psychological control over a teenager is related to adult depression. This finding corroborates the literature summarized by Barber and Harmon (2002) on parental psychological control and its association with depression and other mental health problems among teenagers when they become adults.

Depression is one of the fastest-growing mental health problems in the United States. It is a growing concern among Latter-day Saints. We believe the findings in this study will provide valuable information to help social scientists and mental health experts further understand its extensiveness among Latter-day Saints and its relationship to their religiosity.

This chapter was coauthored with Daniel K Judd and Sherrie Mills Johnson. Dr. Judd is a professor of ancient scripture at Brigham Young University. He has a PhD in counseling psychology from Brigham Young University and is the author of several books and articles on mental health and family issues. Dr. Johnson holds a PhD in sociology from Brigham Young University.

NOTES

1. Structural Equation Modeling (SEM) techniques were used to perform confirmatory factor analysis for each of the latent variables. The factor loadings and squared multiple correlations for the latent variables in each model were acceptable. We also calculated the bivariate correlations between the different

indicators to identify any possible multicolinearity problems. Kline (1998) suggests that any bivariate correlation that exceeds .85 indicates a possible problem. The covariance/correlation matrix used to estimate the structural model for the returned-missionary men is shown in Table 2.

An inspection of the correlations from this model, as well as the other seven models, revealed no multicolinearity concerns. However, while estimating each model, we did find a problem with the indicator that measured family structure. Because of the low variance in this indicator, as well as a possible suppression effect while interacting with the other variables in the model, we dropped this variable from our analysis.

Table 3 shows the structural model fit indicators for all eight models. The chi-squares (χ^2), degrees of freedom (df), ratio between χ^2 and df, Goodness of Fit Index (GFI), Adjusted Goodness of Fit Index (AGFI) and Standardized Root Mean Square Residual (RMR) for each of the models is presented there. The χ^2/df ratio should be less than 5.0, the GFI and AGFI should exceed .90 and the SRMR should be less than .10. Only a few of the many indicators fell below the recommended levels. The χ^2/df ratio is 5.2 for men who served a mission and the AGFI dipped into the .80s for the four samples who had not served missions. Overall, these measures indicate that the model fits the data reasonably well for each of the eight samples.

References

Amato, P. R. (1991). Parental absence during childhood and depression in later life. *Sociological Quarterly, 32*(4), 543–556.

American Psychiatric Association (1998). *Depression.* Retrieved from http://www .psych.org/public_info/depression.cfm.

Assh, S. D., & Byers, E. S. (1996). Understanding the co-occurrence of marital distress and depression in women. *Journal of Social and Personal Relationships, 13*(4), 537–552.

Barber, B. K. (1997). Adolescent socialization in context: The role of connection, regulation, and autonomy in the family. *Journal of Adolescent Research, 12*(1), 5–11.

Barber, B. K. (Ed.), (2002). *Intrusive parenting: How psychological control affects children and adolescents.* Washington, DC: American Psychological Association.

Barber, B. K., & Harmon, E. L. (2002) Reintroducing parental psychological control. In B. K. Barber (Ed.), *Intrusive parenting: How psychological control affects children and adolescents* (pp. 15–52). Washington DC: American Psychological Association.

Barber, B. K., Olsen, J. E., & Shagle, S. C. (1994). Associations between parental psychological and behavioral control and youth internalized and externalized behaviors. *Child Development, 65*(4), 1120–1136.

Bergin, A. E. (1983). Religiosity and mental health: A critical reevaluation and meta-analysis. *Professional Psychology: Research and Practice, 14*(2), 170–184.

Buchta, C. (1998, January 5). Living in Utah: What's fact, fiction? *Daily Herald.*

Cadwallader, E. (1991). Depression and religion: Realities, perspectives, and directions. *Counseling and Values, 35*(2), 83–92.

Department of Health and Human Services. Public Health Service. National Institute of Health (2000). Depression. Retrieved from http://www.nimh.nih.gov/publicat/depression.pdf.

Dornbusch, S. M., Ritter, P. L., Leiderman, P. H., Roberts, D. E., & Fraleigh, M. J. (1987). The relation of parenting style to adolescent school performance. *Child Development, 58*(5), 1244–1257.

Doxey, C., Jensen, L., & Jensen, J. (1997). The influence of religion on victims of childhood sexual abuse. *International Journal for the Psychology of Religion, 7*(3), 179–186.

Earle, J. R., Smith, M. H., Harris, C. T., & Longino, C. F., Jr. (1998). Women, marital status, and symptoms of depression in a midlife national sample. *Journal of Women and Aging, 10*(1), 41–57.

Ehrmin, J. T. (2002). "That feeling of not feeling": Numbing the pain for substance-dependent African American women. *Qualitative Health Research, 12*(16), 780–791.

Ellis, A. (1980). Psychotherapy and atheistic values: A response to A. E. Bergin's "Psychotherapy and religious values." *Journal of Consulting and Clinical Psychology, 48*(5), 635–639.

Ellison, C. G. (1995). Race, religious involvement and depressive symptomatology in a southeastern U.S. community. *Social Science and Medicine, 40*, 1561–1572.

Express Scripts (2001). Retrieved from http://www.corporate-ir.net/ireye/ir_site.zhtml?ticker=ESRX&script=410&layout=-6&item_id=184178.

Express Scripts (2008). Retrieved from http://phx.corporate-ir.net/phoenix.zhtml?c=69641&p=irol-newsArticle&ID=1107721&highlight=.

Freud, S. (1989). *The future of an illusion.* New York: W. W. Norton.

Genia, V., & Shaw, D. G. (1991). Religion, intrinsic-extrinsic orientation, and depression. *Review of Religious Research, 32*(3), 274–283.

Goldsmith, R. J. (1993). An integrated psychology for the addictions: Beyond the self medication hypothesis. *Journal of Addictive Diseases, 12*(3), 139–154.

Goldman, R. (2008, March 7). Two studies find depression widespread in Utah: Study calling Utah most depressed, renews debate on root causes. ABC News. Retrieved from http://abcnews.go.com/Health/MindMoodNews/Story?id=4403731&page=1.

Goodman, T. (2001, June 21). Utahns no. 1 in use of antidepressants: Factors for high usage undetermined. *Salt Lake Tribune*.

Gotlib, I., & Whiffen, V. (1989). Stress, coping, and marital satisfaction in couples with a depressed wife. *Canadian Journal of Behavioural Science, 21*(4), 401–418.

Gray, M. R., & Steinberg, L. (1999). Unpacking authoritative parenting: Reassessing a multidimensional construct. *Journal of Marriage and Family, 61*(3), 574–587.

Hendrie, C. A., Sairally, J., & Starkey, N. (1998). Self-medication with alcohol appears not to be an effective treatment for the control of depression. *Journal of Psychopharmacology, 12*(1), 108.

Hilton, S. C., Fellingham, G. W., & Lyon, J. L. (2002). Suicide rates and religious commitment in young adult males in Utah. *American Journal of Epidemiology, 155*(5), 413–419.

James, W. (1902). *The varieties of religious experience: A study in human nature*. New York: The Modern Library.

Jarvik, E. (1989, November 12). Prozac: Survival pill many Utahns pay antidepressant's price for happiness. *Deseret News*.

Jensen, J., & Jensen, L. (1999, August 26). Utah women use no more antidepressants than the rest of nation. *Deseret News*.

Jensen, L. C., Jensen J., & Wiederhold, T. (1993). Religiosity, denomination, and mental health among young men and women. *Psychological Reports, 72*(3), 1157–1158.

Judd, D. K. (Ed.). (1999). Religion, mental health, and the Latter-day Saints. Provo, UT: Religious Studies Center, Brigham Young University.

Kartchner, C. (2002, March 25). Higher Utah suicide rates are not due to stresses within the church. *Daily Universe*.

Kessler, R. C., & Magee, W. J. (1994). Childhood family violence and adult recurrent depression. *Journal of Health and Social Behavior, 35*(1), 13–27.

Lamb, S. (2002, September 6). Women suffer depression more often than men. *Deseret News*, C5.

Larson, D. B., Sherill, K. A., Lyons, J. S., Craigie, F. C., Jr., Thielman, S. B., Greenwold, M. A., & Larson, S. S. (1992). Associations between dimensions of religious commitment and mental health reported in the *American Journal of Psychiatry* and *Archives of General Psychiatry*: 1978–1989. *American Journal of Psychiatry, 149*(4), 557–559.

Lawrence, L. (1998, June). Making a world of difference. *PT Magazine*, 43–51.

Marks, N. F., & Lambert, J. D. (1998). Marital status continuity and change among young midlife adults: Longitudinal effects on psychological well-being. *Journal of Family Issues, 19*(6), 652–686.

Mental Health America (2008). Ranking America's mental health: An analysis of depression across the States. Retrieved from http://www.mentalhealthamerica. net/go/state-ranking.

Miech, R. A., Caspi, A., Moffitt, T. E., Wright, B. R. E., & Silva, P. A. (1999). Low socioeconomic status and mental disorders: A longitudinal study of selection and causation during young adulthood. *American Journal of Sociology, 104*, 1096–1131.

Miech, R. A., & Shanahan, M. J. (2000). Socioeconomic status and depression over the life course. *Journal of Health and Social Behavior, 41*(2), 162–176.

Miller, B. E., Miller, M. N., Verhegge, R., Linville, H. H., & Pumariega, A. J. (2002). Alcohol misuse among college athletes: Self-medication for psychiatric symptoms? *Journal of Drug Education, 32*(1), 41–52.

Mirola, W. A. (1999). A refuge for some: Gender differences in the relationship between religious involvement and depression. *Sociology of Religion, 60*(4), 419–437.

Mizell, C. A. (1999). Life course influences on African American men's depression: Adolescent parental composition, self-concept, and adult earnings. *Journal of Black Studies, 29*(4), 467–490.

Moore, A. (1998). Why people drink: Alcohol dependence from an interpersonal perspective. *Dissertation Abstracts International, 59*, 2426.

Moore, C. (2002, August 11). Statistics offer good and bad news for LDS. *Deseret News.*

Murphy, P. E., Ciarrocchi, J. W., Piedmont, R. L., Cheston, S., Peyrot, M., & Fitchett, G. (2000). The relation of religious belief and practices, depression, and hopelessness in persons with clinical depression. *Journal of Consulting and Clinical Psychology, 68*, 1102–1106.

National Mental Health Association (1999). *Depression: What you need to know.* Retrieved from http://www.nmha.org/infoctr/factsheets/21.cfm.

Radloff, L. S. (1977). The CES-D Scale: A self-report depression scale for research in the general population. *Applied Psychological Measurement, 1*(3), 385-401.

Reading, R., & Reynolds, S. (2001). Debt, social disadvantage and maternal depression. *Social Science & Medicine, 53*(4), 441–453.

Rich, A. R., & Scovel, M. (1987). Causes of depression in college students: A cross-lagged correlational analysis. *Psychological Reports, 60*(1), 27–30.

Robertson, J., & Simons, R. (1989). Family factors, self-esteem, and adolescent depression. *Journal of Marriage and Family, 51*(1), 125–138.

Robins, L. N., & Regier, D. A. (1990). Psychiatric disorders in America: The Epidemologic Catchment Area Study. New York: The Free Press.

Ross, C. (2000). Neighborhood disadvantage and adult depression. *Journal of Health and Social Behavior, 41*(2), 177–187.

Ross, C. E., & Mirowsky, J. (1999). Parental divorce, life-course disruption, and adult depression. *Journal of Marriage and Family, 61*(4), 1034–1045.

Ross, E. (2002, October 5). Study questions feminist belief. *Salt Lake Tribune.*

Schaefer, E. (1965). Children's reports of parental behavior: An inventory. *Child Development, 36*(2), 413-424.

Scheff, T. J. (2001). Shame and community: Social components in depression. *Psychiatry: Interpersonal and Biological Processes, 64*(3), 212–224.

Schinka, J. A., Curtiss, G., & Mulloy, J. M. (1994). Personality variables and self-medication in substance abuse. *Journal of Personality Assessment, 63*(3), 413–422.

Schnittker, J. (2001). When is faith enough? The effects of religious involvement on depression. *Journal for the Scientific Study of Religion, 40*(3), 393–411.

Scott, R. L., & Cordova, J. V. (2002). The influence of adult attachment styles on the association between marital adjustment and depressive symptoms. *Journal of Family Psychology, 16*(2), 199–208.

Spendlove, D. C., West, D. W., & Stanish, W. M. (1984) Risk factors and the prevalence of depression in Mormon women. *Social Science and Medicine, 18*(6), 491–495.

Stack, P. F. (2002, October 15). How do LDS women in U.S. live their lives? *Salt Lake Tribune*, C1.

Sweet, J. A., & Bumpass, L. L. (1996). The National Survey of Families and Households—waves 1 and 2: Data description and documentation. Center for Demography and Ecology, University of Wisconsin-Madison. Retrieved from http://www.ssc.wisc.edu/nsfh/home.htm.

Thalman, J. (2001, June 21). Utahns among top prescription-pill poppers. *Deseret News.*

Turner, R. J., & Lloyd, D. A. (1999). The stress process and the social distribution of depression. *Journal of Health and Social Behavior, 40*(4), 374–404.

Watson, P. J., Hood, R. W., Foster, S. G., & Morris, R. J. (1988). Sin, depression, and narcissism. *Review of Religious Research, 29*(3), 295–305.

Waite, L. J., & Gallagher, M. (2000). *The case for marriage: Why married people are happier, healthier, and better off financially.* New York: Broadway Books.

Weiss, R. D., Griffin, M. L., & Mirin, S. M. (1992). Drug abuse as self-medication for depression: An empirical study. *American Journal of Drug and Alcohol Abuse, 18*(2), 121–129.

Whisman, M. A., & Jacobson, N. S. (1989). Depression, marital satisfaction, and marital personality measures of sex roles. *Journal of Marital and Family Therapy, 15*(2), 177–186.

Willson, W., Parsons, R. J., & Funk, C. (1995). UCHP: A case study of access for the medically uninsured. *Health Marketing Quarterly, 13*(1), 3–18.

Afterword

RELIGION MATTERS

The first chapter of this book—"Does Religion Matter?"—introduced readers to the ongoing debate among social scientists about whether religion is relevant in modern society. During the early 1990s, most social scientists were convinced that secularization, a major decline in the influence of religion, had occurred in American society. In addition, they boldly predicted that the decline would continue until religion had no place in American society, and some vociferously declared that religion not only does not matter but actually harms youth and adults alike.

From our own experiences and from observing the lives of family and friends, we were convinced that religion does matter a great deal. However, personal experience, observation, and "gut feelings" would not impress or influence serious scholars. They would need empirical evidence. Our research agenda generally and this book specifically emerged out of our efforts to provide scientific evidence that religion is indeed a significant force in the lives of members of The Church of Jesus Christ of Latter-day Saints.

Before we even commenced the research, we were confident that religion matters, but now, 15 years later, we are convinced. We have the empirical evidence to prove it. The chapters in this book give resounding evidence that religion matters to society generally and continues to be a vital force in the lives of teenage and college-age Latter-day Saints specifically.

CONNECTION, NOT COMPARTMENTALIZATION

The word *religion* is believed to share the same linguistic root as the word *ligament*—the Latin word *ligare*. It means to "bind" or "hold together." In many previously published studies on the impact of religion on behavior, researchers defined "religiosity" only in terms of affiliation with a denomination and/ or attendance at meetings. These researchers have often ignored family, social, academic, emotional, and other dimensions of their subjects' lives. This has sometimes created a perception that a person's life can be compartmentalized into categories, like boxes. One box is labeled "family life," another "social life," another "school," and so on. Religion is thus sometimes seen as just another box and was not studied in connection to the others.

In our studies, the terms "religion" and "religiosity" have much more comprehensive definitions. We are convinced that the terms should involve much more than just church attendance or affiliation. For Latter-day Saints, "religion" is synonymous with "gospel"—the gospel of Jesus Christ as manifest in the totality of one's life. This includes not only all professed beliefs, but also public and private worship, behavior, feelings, and social interactions. Consequently, we sought to examine the deeper dimensions of religiosity. As detailed in Chapter 2, those dimensions include such things as religious beliefs, private religious behaviors, family religious practices, spiritual experiences, and acceptance within the faith community. When those factors were studied, a clearer picture of religion's relevance in life emerged.

As our research attests, religiosity—learning, living, and loving the gospel of Jesus Christ—connects, like a ligament, the various aspects of the lives of Latter-day Saints. Although our research was conducted exclusively among Latter-day Saints, we are convinced that other denominations and faiths also enjoy the beneficial effects of religion, the clear and positive connection between belief and behavior. When one's faith is deep seated—internalized and pervasive—it will inevitably be reflected in one's entire life. It will have profound effects. Religion matters.

With several thousand LDS teens and young adults participating in our studies, the research presented in this book comes from one of the largest samples of Latter-day Saints ever studied. Because of this, our results take on an even greater significance, giving a more accurate picture of how religion affects LDS adolescents and young adults. In each of the chapters of this book, we have presented strong statistical evidence that the more religious LDS teens and young adults are, the less likely they are to be delinquent or to be involved in substance abuse and promiscuity.

The results also indicate that religiosity is a strong predictor of academic achievement, high levels of self-esteem, and low rates of depression. In addition, we have shown how a deep belief in the gospel of Jesus Christ as taught by The Church of Jesus Christ of Latter-day Saints, when coupled with living its principles, guides youth and young adults in some of life's most important decisions. The empirical evidence strongly suggests that religion matters to these young people; it deeply affects their lives and influences their choices.

The statistical results we have presented in this book speak loudly and clearly. But perhaps more eloquent than empirical evidence are the words and testimonies of the many young Latter-day Saints who participated in our studies. One young woman said, "Because of the training I have received in the Church, I have a testimony of the gospel that has come to

me by my own study and prayer and by living gospel standards. This has been the leading force in encouraging me and
strengthening my desires to do what is right and true. This has
been the most powerful influence in my life. It touches every
part of me."

These values are much more likely to protect youth and
young adults when taught in both home and Church settings,
as President Boyd K. Packer taught: "In the Church we can
teach about the materials from which a shield of faith is made:
reverence, courage, chastity, repentance, forgiveness, compassion. In church we can learn how to assemble and fit them
together. But the actual making of and fitting on of the shield
of faith belongs in the family circle" ("The Shield of Faith,"
Ensign, May 1995, 8). We hope this book underscores the vital
role of parents and Church leaders in forming and fitting this
shield of faith.

Appendix A

RESEARCH METHODOLOGY

T he research findings reported in this book came from a number of different studies. Each was conducted with great attention to the principles of scientific research. We endeavored to collect data utilizing research techniques that yield findings that are not only statistically valid but also generalizable to populations of LDS youth. The procedures we followed in each study are reported below.

HIGH SCHOOL SURVEYS

Data were collected from the various samples of high school students via mail questionnaire surveys. The same data collection procedures, with some slight local variations, were employed in each of the survey samples. In addition, the same 12-page questionnaire was administered in each of the studies. The questionnaire included questions measuring several different dimensions of religiosity, personality traits such as self-esteem and risk taking, measures of family life, attitudes about school and academic performance, delinquent activities including drug use and premarital sex, and peer pressures to participate in various activities. Most of the questions were close-ended, meaning the youth selected the appropriate answer such as "strongly agree" or "strongly disagree." A few open-ended questions were included so the youth could speak about the influence of the gospel in their own words.

The scales measuring family life that were used in the East Coast study were replaced by the family characteristics of connection, regulation, and psychological autonomy in the later surveys. New research indicated that these three traits provided greater insight into the influence of family in the lives of teens. We added them to the questionnaire for the subsequent studies. This is why the data from the students living along the East Coast were excluded from some of the models that included these three family characteristics.

East Coast sample. The mail questionnaire survey was conducted in the spring of 1990 with a random sample of 2,143 LDS high school students between the ages of 14 and 19 in Delaware, New York, North Carolina, Pennsylvania, Virginia, Washington DC, and West Virginia. The sampling frame was the list of ninth- through twelfth-graders who were eligible to attend early morning seminary. This list of potential seminary students is drawn from membership records of the Church and includes all youth of the appropriate age, regardless of their level of church activity.

A packet was sent to the parents of the young people in the sample with a letter explaining the study and asking their permission for their son or daughter to participate. All of the mailings were sent first-class postage so that undeliverable packets were returned to us. Parents were informed that the questionnaire asked about sensitive topics such as drug use and sexual activity. If parents did not want their child to be in the study, they were asked to return the mailing labels in the business reply envelope. Those families that returned their mailing label were not bothered with any follow-up requests. Surprisingly, we did not receive a single refusal from parents by this means.

Parents were instructed to give the explanation letter, the questionnaire, and business reply envelope to their child. This letter was addressed to the teenagers and requested their honest replies to the questions. The confidentiality of the responses of the youth was strongly emphasized. We also stressed to both parents and teens that if meaningful data were to be collected, the teens had to answer the questionnaire in complete privacy. In order to encourage the youth to participate and to honestly answer the sensitive questions, it was promised that parents and Church leaders would never have access to their responses. Finally, the youth were asked to return the completed questionnaire in the enclosed business reply envelope. Using a business reply envelope allowed the research project to pay the postage for the return of the completed questionnaire.

The cover letters to both parents and youth listed a toll-free phone number and those with questions about the study were encouraged to call. A few parents did so with questions about who was sponsoring the study and how the findings would be utilized. The cover letters also pointed out that a number was printed on the business reply envelope for tracking purposes. It was explained that this number would be marked out with black pen before the questionnaire was removed from the envelope. This maintained the anonymity of the information provided by each teenager. This number allowed us to track those who had responded and to limit follow-up mailings to those who had not.

A postcard reminder was mailed to the families who had not responded approximately three weeks later. One month after the postcard, a new packet was sent to those who had not returned the questionnaire. A final appeal for participation was made one month later with another full packet to hold-outs. The postcard and letters were modified for each subsequent contact.

One hundred twenty packets were undeliverable. Most of these packets were undeliverable because the family had moved and had not left a forwarding address with the post office.

The youth in these families were removed from the sample, which reduced its size to 2,123. The four appeals obtained 1,398 completed questionnaires for a 69% response rate. An 80% response rate is the gold standard extolled in textbooks on research methods. Unfortunately, social scientists rarely achieve this high of a response rate. Most studies end up with a response rate in the 60s. We wish we had obtained a higher level of participation from the youth, but the 69% response rate is very good for this kind of study.

The data were entered into an SPSS data file for statistical analysis. A software program was utilized that required the data to be entered twice so that errors in entry were identified. This reduced data entry errors to very near zero. Finally, the responses to the open-ended questions were transcribed so they could be used as illustrations of the youths' feelings and also for content analysis.

Pacific Northwest survey. The Pacific Northwest survey was conducted in the spring of 1995. This region was selected because sociologists have determined that it is the most secular part of the country. LDS youth received little social pressure to live the commandments in these communities, so it was likely that adherence to gospel principles would result from internalized religious values. We obtained permission from the Church and from the respective Area President to survey youth living in the Seattle and Portland areas. The potential seminary student lists were again utilized as sampling frames in those areas.

The data collection procedures used in the East Coast study were employed. Parents were sent a packet via first-class mail which included a letter addressed to them, a letter to their teen, a questionnaire, and a business reply envelope. Only three parents returned their mailing labels in order to remove their youth from the study. As in the earlier study, both parents and youth were informed that it was imperative that the youth be allowed to complete the questionnaire in complete privacy and that parents should not have access to the youths' responses.

The sample was reduced by 81 youth because the packets were undeliverable by the postal service. We obtained 658 completed questionnaires from the 997 potential respondents for an acceptable response rate of 66%.

Utah County survey. The Utah County survey was conducted in the spring of 1995 concurrently with the Pacific Northwest survey. The potential seminary student lists from towns in Utah County, ranging from Lehi in the north to Provo in the south, were used as a sampling frame. We selected a random sample of 1,849 teenagers from these lists. An interesting note is that the youth in Utah County attended release-time seminary during the school day as compared to the youth in the other surveys who primarily attended early morning seminary.

We employed the same procedure of sending via first-class mail a packet addressed to the parents of the teen selected in the sample and asking permission for their child to participate. Only four parents overtly refused by returning the mailing label.

Only 39 potential youth were removed from the sample because of incorrect addresses. This number is low because staff members who live in Utah County were able to track down some families who had moved. Over 1,000 young people (1,122) completed questionnaires from the 1,810 potential respondents, which produced a 62% response rate.

Great Britain survey. We collected data from LDS youth living in Great Britain in 1999 because it is an English speaking country with a very low religious ecology. For example, in 1987 only 12% of the adult population in the United Kingdom reported they were affiliated with a religion or church. This compares to over 60% of adults affiliated with a church in the United States. Less than 8% of the British adult population indicated that they attended church on any given Sunday during 1999. In the United States, over 40% of adults attend some type of religious service each week. LDS youth trying to keep the commandments of the gospel in Great Britain find themselves going against the grain. Not only do they fail to receive social support for their beliefs and practices, but they are often ridiculed.

Data collection procedures used in the surveys in the United States were modified somewhat to fit the British Isles. First, potential seminary lists were not used as a sampling frame since most youth in Great Britain do not attend seminary. Instead we selected a representative sample of ten stakes scattered across Great Britain. Because of problems with postage, the Irish stake was dropped from the study. The membership rosters of families in the wards in the remaining nine stakes were used as sampling frames. In families with more than one teenager, we selected the oldest youth for the sample. This turned out to be a mistake, as will be explained later. These procedures produced a sample of 1,490 LDS teenagers.

The data collection was supervised by Renata Forste and Cory Harmon, who were teaching at the BYU London Center at this time. They hired and supervised research assistants who prepared the packets and recorded the returned questionnaires.

The questionnaire was modified slightly to conform to British society. For example, questions dealing with money were changed from dollars to pounds. Also, questions about school attendance were altered to match public schools in England.

As in the United States, a packet containing a cover letter asking parents' permission for their son or daughter to participate was sent via the British equivalent of first-class mail. The packet also included a letter relevant to LDS youth in Great Britain, a questionnaire, and a business reply envelope. The parents were requested to permit their teen to complete the questionnaire in privacy.

The cover letter to both parents and youth called attention to the number printed on the business reply envelope. It was explained that this number allowed the researchers to identify those who had responded and to spare them follow-up contacts. It was emphasized that the number was marked out before the questionnaire was removed from the envelope to preserve anonymity. In addition, a toll-free number to the BYU campus in Provo, Utah, was listed. Parents and teens were encouraged to call with questions. A few called asking about who was conducting the study and what its purpose was. A senior member of the research team answered these calls.

Two weeks after the initial mailing we sent a postcard reminding those who had not returned the questionnaire to please do so. About five weeks after the first contact another packet with cover letters, questionnaire, and return envelope was sent those that had not responded. Finally, two months after the initial mailing, we sent a third packet of the research material to those who had failed to return the questionnaire.

The sample of 1,490 was reduced to 1,286 because 214 packets were returned by the postal service due to inadequate addresses. In addition, 31 parents either wrote or called refusing to allow their teen to participate. This parental resistance is stronger than we encountered in the United States. The parents who thus refused appeared to not be of the LDS faith and did not wish for their son or daughter to be involved in any way with the Church, including participating in a Church-related survey.

Despite four contacts with the family, we received only 475 completed questionnaires from the 1,286 potential youth. This response rate of 38% is considerably lower than what we obtained in the United States survey samples. Some families or individual youth had joined the Church at an earlier time but had subsequently fallen away and no longer considered themselves members. They refused to participate because they wanted to distance themselves from the Church and also because they felt the survey did not pertain to them.

A second reason was the selection into the sample of the oldest child in a family. We did not realize that after age 16 youth in the British Isles can leave their equivalent of high school. Some go on to additional education, while others enter the labor force. Parents were reluctant to forward the questionnaire to "adult" children who had left the home. And when parents did forward the materials, they often came back to us undeliverable. Finally, the British are more hesitant about participating in social research, especially a mail survey conducted by a university in the United States.

To identify who had refused to participate in the study, we telephoned a sample of 50 bishops and asked them about the level of church activity of the 179 youth in their wards. Bishops were given the name of the teens in the sample residing in their ward and were asked to describe them as "active," "semiactive," or "inactive." "Active" denoted a high degree of participation in Sunday worship and church activities. "Semiactive" referred to youth who occasionally came to church and church-related activities. "Inactive" identified teens who rarely or never attended church functions. Youth whose names were not recognized by the bishop were assumed to be inactive.

The information from the bishops revealed considerable bias in participation in the study. For example, 64% of those identified as "active" returned their questionnaire compared to only 18% of the "inactive" who did so. This 64% response is comparable to what we obtained in the United States among active LDS youth. Obviously, most of the bias was a consequence of those having little, if anything, to do with the Church not returning the questionnaire.

This bias does prevent us from generalizing about the activities of *all* LDS youth in Great Britain because inactive teens are underrepresented. But the sample is appropriate for testing the model predicting the behavior of LDS youth. The fact that the sample contains youth with a broad range of religious activity demonstrates religiosity's relationship to delinquency and other behaviors.

Mexico survey. Our 2001 survey of Mexican LDS teenagers offered us the opportunity to test the influence of the gospel in the lives of youth from a different culture who also speak a different language. Data were collected from the students attending the LDS-sponsored boarding school Benemerito de las Americas, located a short distance from Mexico City. In addition, a sample of youth in several stakes in the Mexico City area was selected for participation.

The questionnaire was translated into Spanish using the back-translation method. A small team of bilingual individuals translated the English questions into Spanish. A different team translated the Spanish questions back into English. The two English versions were compared and any differences were corrected in the Spanish version.

The questionnaires were administered by Church Educational System personnel, primarily teachers at Benemerito and seminary teachers in Mexico City. Teachers in the school simply passed out the packets, which included a cover letter, a Spanish version of the questionnaire, and an envelope in which to place the completed questionnaire. Parental consent laws are not as rigorous in Mexico as in the United States, and since the youth were attending a boarding school, parental permission to participate in a school-sponsored survey was implicit. For the teens not attending Benemerito, parental consent was obtained. Seminary teachers in the Mexico City stakes passed the questionnaires out in class and asked the students to take them home. The parents were asked in a cover letter which the students took home to allow their son or daughter to participate in the study.

We marked a set of questionnaires for use in Benemerito so we could differentiate them from those filled out by youth living at home. Unfortunately, those collecting the questionnaires mixed the questionnaires together before administration so that it was impossible to identify from which population a given questionnaire came.

We obtained 1,303 completed questionnaires from the Mexican students. CES employees assure us that nearly all the students attending Benemerito participated and that the response rate is probably around 95%. The response rate for the students living at home was estimated by CES employees to exceed 80%.

Castle Dale survey. The study in Castle Dale, Utah, was conducted in 2003 at the request of educational and Church leaders in the community. We were pleased to accommodate their request, because it provided us an opportunity to sample another religious ecology. Castle Dale and surrounding communities have a large LDS population that is nonetheless different from Utah Valley's, which had been surveyed earlier. In contrast with the youth surveyed in the earlier Utah study, high school students in Emery county generally had many non–Latter-day Saint peers. As a result, the study in Castle Dale provided us with a different snapshot of LDS youth in Utah. The area is not only different as a religious ecology, but is also considerably different in socioeconomic ways. This sample is predominantly rural, whereas the previous Utah sample was primarily suburban.

The data were collected by the seminary staff. The research packets were passed out in class and the students were asked to take them home to their parents. If parents were agreeable to their son or daughter participating, then they gave them the questionnaire and business reply envelope. The completed questionnaires were returned to the seminary teachers, who collected the sealed envelopes and delivered them to us. With this process, the study was completed much quicker than usual as we did not have to wait for four time-consuming mailings.

As was done in the other studies, a cover letter listed a toll-free number at BYU and parents and students were invited to call if they had questions. Very few did so. The seminary teachers made several appeals to the students but we did not do any systematic follow-ups. Completed questionnaires were obtained from 354 youth, or about 70%. The data were analyzed in detail and a lengthy presentation was made to Church leaders and parents.

Utah County Unwed Mothers Survey

We were surprised to discover in our surveys of LDS high school students that a larger percentage of young women were sexually active than young men. This was an anomaly in adolescent research because young men in American society had a much higher rate of early sexual experience than girls. We were puzzled as to the difference between LDS youth and youth in society at large. To shed some light on the sexual initiation of LDS young women, we conducted an exploratory interview study of young women in Utah County who were 19 or younger and had a baby born out of marriage. The study was conducted during the summer of 1998.

One of the major methodological problems in the study of premarital sexual activity is the validity of self-reported sexual behavior. Some teens are afraid of the consequences of such behavior and deny their involvement. On the other hand, others brag about exploits that never happened. We conducted this survey among women with a baby born outside of marriage because they obviously had been sexually active.

Data were collected through a lengthy, in-depth, face-to-face interview. The interviewer asked a leading question about a particular aspect of the teens' life and then let them talk. An example is "Tell me about school and how you did." If insufficient detail was given, the interviewer asked a probing question to stimulate discussion. An example is "Which was your favorite class? Which was your worst?" The basic areas asked about were family life, school activity, friends, dating, sexual activity, religion, how they dealt with their pregnancy, and their plans and hopes for the future. The interviews generally lasted an hour and a half, but some ran well over two hours. The interviews were tape-recorded with the girls' permission.

The interviews were conducted by a young woman graduate student. She was only three or four years older than the girls she interviewed. This similarity in age helped her establish good rapport with these teenagers. Also, she dressed up a little to match the role of interviewer, but not so formally as to inhibit the girls from telling their stories.

This exploratory study did not select a sample because this is a very difficult population to identify. Rather, we located young unwed mothers from a variety of sources. A poster was placed in a doctor's office whose practice included unwed mothers. An advertisement seeking unwed mothers to be interviewed was placed in the local newspaper. We also placed a poster in the alternative high school where many unwed mothers finish their high school careers. The girls were paid a $100 honorarium for their time. Once the study commenced, a few girls who heard about the study by word of mouth called to volunteer so they could earn the honorarium.

Fifty girls were interviewed. Unfortunately, the tape recorder malfunctioned and some interviews were lost. The interviewer transcribed the interviews. Since she had conducted the interview, she usually could remember any nuances in the girls' answers as she listened to the tapes. The interviews averaged 12 double-spaced pages and contained a wealth of qualitative information.

A team of three research assistants independently conducted content analysis of the written comments. They first worked together to develop a series of quantitative categories for important topics in the interview such as the reason(s) for the girls' initial sexual experience or the quality of their relationship with their father. Once the categories were established, each research assistant independently coded the comments into them. The three independent codings were then compared and disagreements resolved. These procedures produced quantitative values from these subjective comments with at least 85% agreement among three research assistants. These data were then entered into a SPSS file, which allowed statistical analysis.

DATING SURVEYS

BYU–Provo survey. A 2001 study of 1,000 young women attending four-year colleges and universities across the United States found that "dating" has all but disappeared from

American college campuses. Only half of the women reported they had been asked on six or more dates during their entire college career. In fact, one-third of the women had two or fewer dates during the same four years. Instead of dating, college students now "hang out" in mixed groups. From these associations young people pair off and "hook up" with a member of the opposite sex.

To ascertain whether this shift in dating culture had spread to the BYU campus we conducted a mail survey of BYU students during winter semester 2002. We developed a 14-page questionnaire that asked the students about their hanging-out and dating activities, their attitudes about marriage and family, personality traits including self-esteem and a scale of depression, traits they were seeking in a mate, traits they felt they would bring to marriage, reasons for delaying marriage, school performance, and religiosity. The questionnaire was pretested, then revised and pretested a second time. The pretests were conducted with seniors who graduated before we started data collection so they did not contaminate the study.

We selected a 5% sample of the 35,000-plus students listed in the electronic student directory. The sample of 1,893 students was sent packets with a cover letter explaining the study, a questionnaire, and a business reply envelope. The cover letter explained the intent of the study and asked the students to participate by completing the questionnaire. We asked those that had married during the previous semester to answer about their behavior during the semester before they did so.

Attention was called to a number printed on the business reply envelope. It was explained this number would be marked out before the envelope was opened so that the student's responses remained anonymous. In addition, a toll-free number was listed and students were encouraged to call if they had questions about the study.

Two weeks later a postcard reminder was sent asking the students to return the questionnaire sent earlier. If it had been misplaced, they were invited to call a toll-free number and request another. Five weeks after the initial mailing, another complete packet was mailed to those who had not responded. Two months after the first contact, another complete packet was sent pleading for their participation in this important study.

One hundred fifty-five packets had incorrect addresses. We attempted to find forwarding addresses from school records but we were not very successful. We were surprised that 176 potential respondents either telephoned or wrote to explain that they were older married students who were taking correspondence courses. Because their dating experience had occurred many years earlier, they removed themselves from the study. We obtained completed questionnaires from 1,124 students for a 72% response rate. This is a rather high response rate for a mail survey but was probably influenced by the topic and by the study being conducted by BYU faculty. We are confident that if we could have removed all of the Independent Study students who were not living on campus that the response rate would have perhaps exceeded 80%.

A little over 70% of the respondents were single, and the responses from these 784 students are reported in this book.

BYU–Idaho survey. In 2003 we replicated the study among a random sample of students attending BYU–Idaho. The same procedures were followed and 1,187 completed questionnaires were obtained. The response rate was 73%, which is similar to that obtained at BYU–Provo. The findings of the BYU–Idaho students were nearly identical to those of BYU–Provo. In order to not slow down the production of this book and because the results were so similar, we chose not to redo the analysis for the dating chapter with the BYU–Idaho data.

BYU–Hawaii survey. The following year, 2004, we repeated the study among students attending BYU–Hawaii. Given that only approximately 2,000 students attend this campus, we surveyed the entire student body rather than a random sample.

We were surprised with the high percentage of students attending the Hawaii campus who hail from Taiwan, Japan, China, Polynesia, and other Pacific Rim countries. If students returned home before completing the survey, it was difficult to follow up with them. This influenced the response rate which was 67%, which is only slightly lower than in Provo and Rexburg.

We anticipated that the students attending the Hawaii campus would be somewhat different than those in Provo or Rexburg because of the variety of cultures and the social environment of the island. We expected them to be a little more liberal in attitudes about drinking and sex and to engage in more deviant behavior. Such was not the case, and their responses were very similar to the other two campuses. Again, we opted not to redo the analysis for the dating chapter with the Hawaii sample.

RETURNED-MISSIONARY STUDY

When Bruce Chadwick served as a bishop on the BYU campus, he was frequently asked how the returned missionaries in his ward in particular and in the Church in general were doing. He regretted that he did not have a reasonable answer to these questions. This was the major motivation behind this survey of returned missionaries.

At the time of this study, Richard McClendon was a graduate student in the BYU Department of Sociology. He was also a seminary teacher on leave from the Church Educational System. This study was part of his doctoral dissertation.

During the winter of 1999, four random samples were generated of 1,000 men and 500 women who had been back from their missions approximately 2, 5, 10, and 17 years. Originally, the older cohort included men who had been home 15 years, but we discovered that these missionaries had served during the brief era of 18-month missions. The shorter mission would have made analysis much more complex, so we opted instead for missionaries who had been home for 17 years.

The random samples included returned missionaries who came from both the United States and Canada. As we prepared to print the business reply envelopes, we encountered some serious problems with business reply mail from Canada. Thus we decided to delete the returned missionaries from Canada. The loss was modest with only 71 men and three women being dropped from the samples.

A rather exhaustive questionnaire was developed and pre-tested on returned missionaries who had been home for a length of time that excluded them from being selected in the samples. The questionnaire went through at least six revisions. Questions were asked about the missionaries' high school experiences and what they did during the time after graduating high school and before receiving their mission calls. Another set of questions focused on their mission experiences. A third set of questions asked about what the young man or woman did during the first year they were home from the mission field. The final set of questions focused on their current lives. We asked about religious beliefs and behaviors before, during, and immediately after their missions, and their current activity. Questions focused on school and academic performance. Others asked about dating, marriage, and family life. Finally, a number of demographic items were assessed such as marital status, number of children, educational attainment, employment, income, and church positions held.

During the first two weeks of March 1999, a packet was sent via first-class mail to the sample of men. The packet included a cover letter explaining the study and asking for their participation, a questionnaire, and a business reply envelope. The women's sample was surveyed two weeks later during early April.

A toll-free number was listed in the cover letter and post-card, and those with questions about the study were invited to call. A number of men and women telephoned and asked who was sponsoring it, why was it being done, how the results were going to be used, and how the results would be made available to the membership of the Church. Senior members of the research team fielded these phone calls.

The cover letter explained that the number on the business reply envelope would be blacked out before the envelope was opened. This protected their anonymity while also allowing us to identify those who had not returned their questionnaire. A postcard was sent to those who had not responded approximately three weeks after the initial mailing encouraging them to do so.

Approximately six weeks after the first mailing, another complete packet including a modified cover letter, questionnaire, and business reply envelope was sent to nonrespondents. A fourth and final packet was sent to the holdouts approximately three months after the initial contact asking one last time for their participation in the study.

The postal service was unable to deliver 332 of the packets sent to men, which reduced the sample to 3,081. Completed questionnaires were obtained from 2,078 men for a 67% response rate.

The nondeliverable packets numbered 194 for the women, which reduced their sample to 1,802 potential respondents. Among the women, 1,535 participated in the study, producing an 85% response rate. We do not know why the women were more willing than the men to participate in the study.

The responses to the open-ended questions were transcribed so they could be used as illustrations of the returned missionaries' feelings. In addition, important content analyses was conducted on questions such as "What could Church leaders have done to ease your transition after your mission?"

NON-MISSIONARY SURVEY

This study was prompted by the discovery that only 30% of the young men of the Church who live in the United States currently serve full-time missions. This observation elicited questions about why 70% of the young men in the Church choose not to serve a mission. Also we were interested in what happens with these men in later years. This study was conducted in 2000 and was a follow-up to the previous study of returned missionaries. This study was the doctoral dissertation of Darrell Janson, a graduate student in the BYU Department of Marriage, Family, and Human Development and a seminary teacher.

We attempted to match the men who did not serve missions with the samples from the returned missionaries. Since missionary service is not emphasized for young women, we excluded women from this study. We drew samples of four cohorts of men who were 23, 26, 31, and 38 years old who had not served a mission. The sampling procedures produced a sample of 3,796 men who had not served.

In September 2000, packets containing a cover letter, a questionnaire, and a business reply envelope were sent through first-class mail to the men in the samples. The cover letter explained that the study was being conducted by the Family Studies Center at BYU and was interested in LDS young adults who had not served missions for the Church. They were encouraged to participate regardless of their present Church activity. The number on the business reply envelope was explained as a means to note who had responded so as to spare them any follow-up contacts. They were assured that the number would be blacked out before the envelope was opened so their responses would be anonymous. Those who did not wish to participate were encouraged to return the empty envelope. Those that did so were removed from the sample.

About two months later, postcards were sent to encourage the nonrespondents to participate. Approximately four months after the initial mailing, a new packet containing a revised cover letter, questionnaire, and business reply envelope was sent. Because of the very negative response of the men in the sample to the study, the usual fourth mailing was not sent.

The cover letters and postcard listed a toll-free telephone number, and those with questions about the study were invited to call. Some people called to complain. They were upset at being contacted by BYU, an affiliate of the LDS Church. For the most part these were men who had dropped out of the Church years earlier and wanted nothing to do with it. We attempted to soothe their concerns but promptly removed them from the samples.

The sample was reduced by 28 men who had actually served missions. Another 466 were dropped because we could not find a correct address. The packet sent to them via first-class mail came back undeliverable. Thus the sample was reduced to 3,302 men including 697 23-year-olds, 737 26-year-olds, 926 31-year-olds, and 942 38-year-olds. Only 380 completed questionnaires were returned for a 12% response rate. We had anticipated a low response rate given the population; we certainly were not prepared for 12%.

In an effort to acquire some information about the church activity of the nonrespondents, we selected a sample of 230 of the nonrespondents. The current bishops of these 230 men were telephoned. To maximize contact with the bishops, calls were made at different times of the day and during different days of the week, including weekends. One hundred seventy-five of the 230 bishops were contacted. Twenty-seven (15%) of the bishops had never heard of the person. They were confident that the potential respondent was not on their ward roll. One hundred fifteen of the bishops, 66%, reported that the man we asked about was totally inactive. The bishops were confident there had been no contact with the man by home teachers. The other 33 bishops, 19%, reported that the man asked about occasionally came to church. Very few of these relatively active men attended more than once a month.

It is very obvious that the 12% who responded was heavily biased with an overrepresentation of somewhat active men. Those who had physically and emotionally withdrawn from the Church are vastly underrepresented. Perhaps the most significant finding to emerge from this study was the loss of so many young men. It was extremely disconcerting to see how many men had completely dissociated themselves from the Church. We had originally anticipated that many of the men who had not served missions later met a young woman who wanted to be married in the temple. We had hoped they many had become worthy to enter the temple and then continued to live the gospel. Such was not the case. Once these young men dropped out, many while still in Primary, they became alienated from the Church with little prospect of return.

Appendix B

MEASUREMENT SCALES

Delinquency

Offenses against Others
Have you ever…?
If yes, how many times?
- Physically beat up other kids.
- Hurt someone badly enough that they had to go to a doctor.
- Threatened or attacked someone with a knife, gun, or other weapon.
- Been in a gang fight.
- Taken money or other things from someone else by using force or threats.
- Picked a fight with other kids.
- Openly defied a teacher or official at school.
- Openly defied a teacher or leader at church.
- Pushed, shoved, or hit one of your parents.
- Been suspended or expelled from school.
- Cursed or sworn at one of your parents.

Offenses against Property
Have you ever . . . ?
If yes, how many times?
- Stolen anything worth between $5 and $50.
- Stolen anything worth less than $5.
- Purposely ruined or damaged someone else's property or possessions.
- Taken something from a store without paying for it.
- Stolen something from someone else's locker, desk, purse, etc.
- Purposely damaged or destroyed things at school, the store, etc.
- Thrown things (rocks, bottles, eggs, garbage, etc.) at cars, people, or buildings.
- Gone on someone's property when you weren't supposed to be there.
- Stolen anything worth more than $50.
- Taken a car or other motor vehicle without the owner's permission.
- Broken into a building, car, house, etc.

Status Offenses
Have you ever . . . ?
If yes, how many times?
- Drank alcoholic beverages (beer, wine, liquor).
- Used marijuana ("grass," "pot").
- Been drunk or high on drugs.
- Smoked cigarettes.
- Used other drugs (heroine, LSD, amphetamines, etc.)
- Used "smokeless" or chewing tobacco.
- Been involved in heavy petting.
- Used cocaine ("crack," "coke").
- Had sexual intercourse.

Peer Pressure for Delinquent Behavior

Offenses against Others
Has anyone pressured you to . . . ?
If yes, how many times?
- Physically beat up other kids.
- Purposely pick on other kids, make fun of them, or call them names.
- Make obscene phone calls.
- Take money or other things from someone by using force or threats.
- Curse or swear at one of your parents.
- Join in a gang fight.
- Shove or hit one of your parents.

Offenses Against Property
Has anyone pressured you to . . . ?
If yes, how many times?
- Take something from the store without paying for it.
- Steal anything worth less than $20.
- Throw things (rocks, bottles, eggs, etc.) at cars, people, or buildings.
- Break into a building, car, house, etc.
- Take a car or other motor vehicle without the owner's permission.

Status Offenses
Has anyone pressured you to . . . ?
If yes, how many times?
- Drink alcoholic beverages (beer, wine, liquor).
- Use marijuana ("grass," "pot").
- Smoke cigarettes.
- Use "smokeless" or chewing tobacco.
- Use other drugs (heroin, LSD, amphetamines, etc.).

- Be involved in heavy petting.
- Watch sexually explicit or pornographic movies, videos, or television programs.
- Read sexually explicit or pornographic books or magazines.
- Have sexual intercourse.
- Use cocaine ("crack," "coke").
- Skip school without a legitimate excuse.
- Run away from home.
- Sell marijuana, cocaine, or other drugs.

Peer Example of Delinquency

Offenses against Others

How many of your friends have done the following?

1. None   2. Some   3. Most   4. All

- Picked a fight with other kids.
- Taken money or other things from someone by using force or threats.
- Physically beat up other kids.
- Hurt someone badly enough that they had to go to a doctor.
- Openly defied a teacher or leader at school.
- Been in a gang fight.
- Threatened or attacked someone with a knife, gun, or other weapon.
- Purposely picked on other kids, made fun of them, or called them names.
- Cursed or sworn at one of their parents.
- Pushed, shoved, or hit one of their parents.
- Called someone on the telephone to threaten or bother them.
- Openly defied a teacher or leader at church.

Offenses against Property

How many of your friends have done the following?

1. None   *2. Some*   *3. Most*   *4. All*

- Stolen anything worth less than $5.
- Purposely ruined or damaged someone else's property or possessions.
- Stolen anything worth between $5 and $50.
- Taken something from the store without paying for it.
- Purposely damaged or destroyed things at school, the store, etc.
- Stolen something from someone's locker, desk, purse, etc.
- Thrown things (rocks, bottles, eggs, garbage, etc.) at cars, people, or buildings.
- Gone on someone else's property when they weren't supposed to be there.
- Stolen anything worth more than $50.
- Broken into a building, car, house, etc.
- Taken a car or other motor vehicle without the owner's permission.

Status Offenses

How many of your friends have done the following?

1. None   *2. Some*   *3. Most*   *4. All*

- Drunk alcoholic beverages (beer, wine, liquor).
- Been drunk or high on drugs.
- Smoked cigarettes.
- Used marijuana ("grass," "pot").
- Been involved in heavy petting.
- Engaged in sexual intercourse.
- Used "smokeless" or chewing tobacco.
- Watched sexually explicit or pornographic movies, videos, or television programs.
- Used other drugs (heroin, LSD, amphetamines, etc.).
- Been suspended or expelled from school.

- Used cocaine ("crack," "coke").
- Skipped school without a legitimate excuse.
- Created a disturbance by being loud, unruly, or disorderly at school or another public place.
- Cheated on a test.
- Run away from home.

Religiosity

Religious Beliefs
How do you feel about the following statements?
1. Strongly Agree   2. Agree   3. Mixed Feelings
4. Disagree   5. Strongly Disagree
- The Book of Mormon is the word of God.
- Joseph Smith actually saw God the Father and Jesus Christ.
- Jesus Christ is the divine Son of God.
- The Lord guides the Church today through revelations to Church leaders.
- There is life after death.
- The president of the LDS Church is a prophet of God.
- God lives and is real.
- Satan actually exists.
- The Bible is the word of God.
- God really does answer prayers.

Private Religious Behavior
How often do you do the following activities?
1. Very Often   2. Often   3. Sometimes
4. Rarely   5. Never
- I read the scriptures by myself.
- I pray privately.
- I pay tithing on the money I earn.
- I fast on fast Sunday.

Public Religious Behavior

How often do you do the following activities?

1. *Very Often*   2. *Often*   3. *Sometimes*
4. *Rarely*   5. *Never*

- I attend sacrament meeting.
- I attend priesthood meeting or young women's meeting on Sunday.
- I attend Sunday School.
- I participate in Church social activities.

Importance of Religion

How do you feel about the following statements?

1. *Strongly Agree*   2. *Agree*   3. *Mixed Feelings*
4. *Disagree*   5. *Strongly Disagree*

- I plan to be active in the Church.
- I plan to marry in the temple.
- I have a strong testimony of the truthfulness of the gospel.
- I am a good example of living the gospel to my friends.
- During the past year, I have really tried to live the standards of the Church.
- My relationship with God is an important part of my life.
- In my life there are more important things than religion.
- I very seldom think about religion.

Spiritual Experiences

How do you feel about the following statements?

1. *Strongly Agree*   2. *Agree*   3. *Mixed Feelings*
4. *Disagree*   5. *Strongly Disagree*

- I have been guided by the Spirit with some of the problems in my life.

- There have been times in my life when I felt the Holy Ghost.
- I know what it feels like to repent and to be forgiven.

Social Acceptance into Congregation
How do you feel about the following statements?
1. Strongly Agree   2. Agree   3. Mixed Feelings
4. Disagree   5. Strongly Disagree
- I am well liked by members of my ward.
- I seem to fit in very well with the people in my ward.
- I sometimes feel like an outsider in the Church.

Self-Esteem
How do you feel about the following statements?
1. Strongly Agree   2. Agree   3. Mixed Feelings
4. Disagree   5. Strongly Disagree
- I take a positive attitude about myself.
- All in all, I am inclined to feel like I am a failure.
- I feel like I have a number of good qualities.
- On the whole, I am satisfied with myself.
- At times, I think I am no good at all.
- I feel I do not have much to be proud of.
- I wish I could have more respect for myself.
- I feel that I'm a person of worth at least on an equal plane with others.
- I certainly feel useless at times.
- I am able to do things as well as most people.

Risk Taking
How do you feel about the following statements?
1. Strongly Agree   2. Agree   3. Mixed Feelings
4. Disagree   5. Strongly Disagree
- I like to take challenges or do things on a dare.
- I like to test myself every now and then by doing something a little risky.

- I get a real kick out of doing things that are a little dangerous.

Impulsiveness
How do you feel about the following statements?
1. Strongly Agree   2. Agree   3. Mixed Feelings
4. Disagree   5. Strongly Disagree

- I am one of those people who blurts out things without thinking.
- I often act on the spur of the moment without stopping to think.
- I am often said to be hotheaded or bad tempered.

Connection with Mother (or Father)
How do you feel about the following statements?
1. Strongly Agree   2. Agree   3. Mixed Feelings
4. Disagree   5. Strongly Disagree

- My mother (or father) is a person who . . .
  - Cheers me up when I am sad.
  - Gives me a lot of care and attention.
  - Is able to make me feel better when I am upset.
  - Makes me feel better after talking over my worries with her (or him).
  - Is easy to talk to.
  - Believes in showing her (or his) love for me.
  - Enjoys doing things with me.
  - Smiles at me often.
  - Makes me feel like the most important person in her (or his) life.
  - Often praises me.

Mother (or Father) Regulation

How do you feel about the following statements?
1. *Strongly Agree*   2. *Agree*   3. *Mixed Feelings*
4. *Disagree*   5. *Strongly Disagree*

- My mother (or father) is a person who . . .
    - Knows what I do with my free time.
    - Knows where I go at night.
    - Knows how I spend my money.
    - Knows where I am most afternoons after school.
    - Knows who my friends are.

Psychological Autonomy

How do you feel about the following statements?
1. *Strongly Agree*   2. *Agree*   3. *Mixed Feelings*
4. *Disagree*   5. *Strongly Disagree*

- My mother (or father) is a person who does not . . .
    - Stop talking to me until I please her (or him).
    - Avoid looking at me when I have disappointed her (or him).
    - Always try to change me.
    - Say if I really cared about her (or him) I would not do things that cause her (or him) to worry.
    - Only keep rules when it suits her (or him) best.
    - Want to control whatever I do.
    - Act less friendly to me if I do not see things her (or his) way.
    - Want to be able to tell me what to do all the time.
    - Always tell me how I should behave.
    - Tell me all the things she (or he) has done for me.

Family Conflict

How often do you see the following activities?
1. *Very Often*   2. *Often*   3. *Sometimes*
4. *Rarely*   5. *Never*

- My parents argue.

- My parents yell and scream at each other when I'm around.
- My parents nag and complain about each other around the house.

Depression

Below is a list of ways you might have felt or behaved during the past week. On how many days during the week did you

- Feel bothered by things that usually don't bother you?
- Feel that you could not shake off the blues, even with help from family and friends?
- Have trouble keeping your mind on what you were doing?
- Feel depressed?
- Feel that everything you did was an effort?
- Feel you could not get going?
- Feel fearful?
- Sleep restlessly?
- Feel lonely?
- Feel sad?
- Not feel like eating; your appetite was poor?
- Talk less than usual?

Appendix C

PUBLICATIONS BASED ON
THIS RESEARCH

BOOKS

2004. Top, B. L., & Chadwick, B. A. *Ten secrets wise parents know: Tried and true things you can do to raise faithful, confident, responsible children.* Salt Lake City: Deseret Book.

1998. Top, B. L., & Chadwick, B. A. *Rearing righteous youth of Zion: Great news, good news, not-so-good news.* Salt Lake City: Bookcraft.

CHAPTERS

2007. Chadwick, B. A., Top, B. L., McClendon, R. J., Judd, M., & Smith, L. Hanging out or hooking up: The culture of courtship at BYU. In M. J. Woodger, T. B. Holman, and K. A. Young (Eds.), *Latter-day Saint courtship patterns* (pp. 13–39). Lanham, MD: University Press of America, 13–39.

2005. McClendon, R. J., & Chadwick, B. A. Latter-day Saint families at the dawn of the twenty-first century. In C. Hart, L. D. Newell, E. Walton, and D. C. Dollahite (Eds.), *Helping and healing our families: Principles and practices inspired by "The family: A proclamation to the world"* (pp. 32–43). Salt Lake City: Deseret Book.

1999. Top, B. L., Chadwick, B. A., & Garrett, J. Family, religion, and delinquency among LDS youth. In D. K. Judd (Ed.), *Religion, mental health, and the Latter-day Saints* (pp. 129–168). Provo, UT: Religious Studies Center, Brigham Young University.

1998. Top, B. L., & Chadwick, B. A. Religiosity and delinquency among LDS adolescents. In J. T. Duke (Ed.), *Latter-day Saint social life: Social research on the LDS Church and its members* (pp. 499–523). Provo, UT: Religious Studies Center, Brigham Young University.

ARTICLES

2007. Chadwick, B. A., Top, B. L., McClendon, R. J., Smith L., & Judd, M. A survey of dating and marriage at BYU. *BYU Studies, 46*(3), 67–156.

2006. Top, B. L., & Chadwick, B. A. Helping children develop feelings of self-worth. *Ensign*, February 2006, 32–37.

2004. McClendon, R. J., & Chadwick, B. A. Latter-day Saint returned missionaries in the United States: A survey on religious activity and postmission adjustment. *BYU Studies, 43*(2), 131–157.

2003. Top, B. L., Chadwick, B. A., & McClendon, R. J. Spirituality and self-worth: The role of religion in shaping teens' self-image. *Religious Educator, 4*(2), 77–93.

2003. Top, B. L., Chadwick, B. A., & Evans, M. T. Protecting purity. *BYU Magazine*, Summer 2003, 46–54.

2001. Top, B. L., Chadwick, B. A., & McClendon, R. J. "Seek learning, even by study and also by faith": The relationship between personal religiosity and academic achievement among Latter-day Saint high-school students. *Religious Educator, 2*(2), 121–137.

1999. Top, B. L., & Chadwick, B. A. Helping teens stay strong. *Ensign*, March 1999, 27–34.

1998. Top, B. L., & Chadwick, B. A. Raising righteous children in a wicked world. *BYU Magazine*, Summer 1998, 41–51.

1995. Top, B. L., & Chadwick, B. A. Helping teens put on the whole armor of God. *This People*, Fall 1995, 18–26.

1993. Top, B. L., & Chadwick, B. A. The power of the word: Religion, family, friends, and delinquent behavior of LDS youth. *BYU Studies, 33*(2), 51–67.

1993. Chadwick, B. A., & Top, B. L. Religiosity and delinquency among LDS adolescents. *Journal for the Scientific Study of Religion, 32*(1), 51–67.

Theses/Dissertations

2003. Johnson, S. M. *Religiosity and life satisfaction of LDS women* (Doctoral dissertation). Department of Sociology, Brigham Young University.

2001. Harmon, C. *Religiosity and delinquency: A test of the religious ecology hypothesis* (Master's thesis). Department of Sociology, Brigham Young University.

2002. Janson, D. A. *Religious socialization and LDS young adults* (Doctoral dissertation). Department of Sociology, Brigham Young University.

2000. McClendon, R. J. *The LDS returned missionary: Religious activity and post-mission adjustment* (Doctoral dissertation). Department of Sociology, Brigham Young University.

1997. Garrett, J. *A model of delinquency among LDS adolescents: The effect of peer influences, religiosity, personality traits, school experiences and family characteristics* (Master's thesis). Department of Sociology, Brigham Young University.

INDEX

Italicized page numbers indicate a table or a figure.

Abma, J. C., 187, 190–91
academic achievement: religiosity and, 10–11; of LDS college students, 144–48; of young adults, 151–57; self-esteem and, 176, 180
acceptance: self-esteem and, 173, 179–80, 183; sexual activity and, 211–12; questions for measuring, 352. *See also* religious social acceptance
adjustment, of returned missionaries, 282–84, *283*, *286*, *287*, 292
Agnew, R., 67–68
Albrecht, S. L., 134, 257–59, 277
alcohol use: statistics on, 33–34, *35*; delinquency and, 97, 100; self-esteem and, 166; depression and, 313
American Psychiatric Association, 307

American Psychological Association, 164, 165–66
Assh, D., 299
Astin, A. W., 145, 147, 149
Astin, H. S., 145, 147, 149
authority figures, 83, 183–84
autonomy, psychological: delinquency and, 71, 78, *111*; sexual activity and, 198, 204; depression and, 300, 312; questions for measuring, 354

Bahr, H. M., 257–59, 260
Baumeister, R. F., 166
Beck, S. H., 192
Beeghley, L., 192
behavior. *See* private religious behavior; public religious behavior
Bible: study, 36–38; LDS young adult belief in, *45*

delinquency: religiosity and, 2,
4–5, 65–67, 103–5, *104*;
aspects of, 7–9; peer pressure
and, 9, 67–68, 176–77, 188,
189; family and, 68–72; personality and, 72–73; school
involvement and, 74; measuring, 74–79, 345–50; LDS youth
results for, 79–103; trend results
for, 79–103; testing, 105–12;
predicting, *108*; self-esteem and,
176–77; sexual activity and, 203
Denton, M. L., 194
depression: in Utah, 295–96;
among Latter-day Saints, *298*,
298–305, 307–12, *308*; statistics on, *304*; LDS and national
rates, 305–7; conclusions on,
312–15; questions for measuring, 355. *See also* mental health
discipline, for teens, 213–14
divorce: delinquency and, 69; sexual activity and, 195–96; statistics on, 248, 252, 257–61, *258*
drug use: parental regulation and,
72; delinquency and, 97, 100;
self-esteem and, 166; depression
and, 313
Duke, J. T., 267

education: importance of, 120–21;
religious affiliation and, 122–25;
LDS Church and, 125–32; religiosity and, 132–34; LDS youth
and, 134–35; enduring religiosity and, 148; secularization
hypothesis and, 151–57, 277;
Pygmalion effect and, 162–63,
165–66; of returned missionaries, 269–71, *270*; depression
and, 299, 312. *See also* academic
achievement

educational aspiration, religiosity
and, 135–44, *136*, *141*, *143*
Elder, G. H., 133
Ellis, Albert, 296–97
Ellison, C. G., 133–34
employment, 271

family: Boyd K. Packer on, iii;
influence of, 9–10; LDS youth
and, 39; religious behavior and,
40, 290; returned missionaries
and, *58*, 59, 271–74, *272*, *275*;
delinquency and, 68–72, 77–78,
103–5, 109–14, *111*; family
connection, 69–70; educational
aspirations and, 137, 138–40;
academic achievement and, *152*,
153; self-esteem and, 175–76;
sexual activity and, 188–89,
195–99, 203–4, *208*, 213–14;
overview of, 247–48; data collected on, 249–51; characteristics of LDS, 261–63; depression
and, 300–303, 309, 315
family home evening, 39, *40*, *58*
family size: of LDS families, 261–
63; mental health and, 300, 303
fasting: LDS youth and, *37*, 39;
BYU and, 49
fathers: education and, 126–28,
127; educational aspirations
and, 140–42; self-esteem and,
176, 180–82; questions on,
353–54
Feldman, S. S., 197
fighting, 80–82, *81*, 98–100
forced sexual activity, 190–91, 203
Forste, Renata, 330
Freud, Sigmund, 296
friends: religiosity and, 7; delinquency and, 67–68, 107–9;
educational aspirations and,

mothers: working, 69, 109, 196,
203–4; education and, 126–28,
127; self-esteem and, 176,
180–82, *182*; sexual activity
and, 205–6, 209–10; questions
on, 353–54
movies, R-rated, 287–88. *See also*
pornography
Muller, C., 133–34
My Fair Lady, 162

narcissism, 167, 183
National Institutes of Mental
Health, 307
National Mental Health Associa-
tion, 307
National Opinion Research Center
(NORC), 249
National Study of Families and
Households, 301
National Study of Youth and Reli-
gion (NSYR), 24–25, 194
Nelson, Russell M., 39, 274
non-LDS youth, religiosity and,
24–25
Norton, M. C., 190

Oaks, Dallin H., 24, 281–82

Packer, Boyd K., iii, 324
parents: religiosity and, 7; influence
of, 9–10, 71–72, 290; religious
behavior and, 39, *40*; parental
regulation, 70–71, 77–78, 176;
abuse of, 83; delinquency and,
103–5, 105–7, 109–14, *111*;
education and, 126–28, 138–
40; narcissism and, 167; self-
esteem and, 176, 180–84, *182*;
stepparents, 195–96; sexual
activity and, 196–98, 203–6,
209–10, 213–14; depression

and, 300–301, 303–5, 315;
questions on, 353–54. *See also*
psychological autonomy
Patterson, G. R., 70–71
peer pressure: overview of, 9; delinquency and, 67–68, 76–77,
107–9; educational aspirations
and, 138; academic achievement and, *152*, 153; self-esteem
and, 168, 176–77; sexual activity and, 188–92, 202–3, 204,
206–7, 213; mothers' regulation
and, 206; questions for measuring, 347–49
perfection, 169
Perkins, D. F., 189, 193
personality traits, 72–73, 78
Peterson, J. L., 197
physical intimacy, 230–31, *232*,
233–34. *See also* sexual activity
Pipher, Mary, 171
Pleck, J. H., 196
pornography, 203, 205, 206
prayer: LDS young adult belief in,
27; LDS youth and, 36, *37*, 38;
family prayer, 39, *40*, *58*, 59,
275; BYU and, 47–48, *49*, 146;
returned missionaries and, 56,
57, *276*, 277–78
premarital sexual activity. *See* sexual
activity
pride, 169
priesthood meeting attendance, *34*,
48, *279*
private religious behavior: of
LDS youth, 36–39, *37*; of
LDS young adults, 47–48; of
returned missionaries, 56–59,
57, 273–74, *275*, *276*, 277–78,
285–90, *288*, *289*; delinquency
and, 103; education and, 137–
40, 156; academic achievement

for dating surveys, 336–39; for
returned missionaries survey,
339–44
returned missionaries: religiosity
of, 51–61; conclusions on, 62,
290–92; education and, 125–
26, *126*; overview of, 265–69;
socioeconomic status of, 269–
71, *270*; family life of, 271–74,
272, *275*; comparing recent and
old, 274–81; private religious
behavior of, *276*, *288*, *289*;
maintaining activity among,
281–90; adjustment of, *286*,
287; depression and, 305–7,
308, *309*, 314–15; methodology
for surveys on, 339–44. *See also*
missionary service
risk taking, 73, 78, 133, 352–53
Rosenberg, M., 165
Rosenberg scale, 168
rules, for teens, 70, 107, 112,
181–82, 196–97, 213–14

Sacerdote, B., 123, 153
sacrament meeting attendance, 32,
34, *48*, 55
Salmivalli, C., 166
Schoenbach, C., 165
school, LDS youth feelings on,
130, 131–32. *See also* education
Schooler, C., 165
school involvement, delinquency
and, 74, 78–79
Schroeder, K., 193–94
scripture study: LDS youth and,
36–38, *37*; family scripture
study, 39, *40*, *58*, 59, *275*; BYU
and, 47–48, *49*; returned missionaries and, 56–59, *57*, *276*,
277–78

secularization hypothesis, 148–57,
268, 275–78, 321
self-esteem: overview of, 11–12,
161–67; delinquency and,
72–73, 78; in adolescents, 168;
among LDS youth, 168–72,
170; religiosity and, 172–74,
173; multivariate models of
predicting, 174–82, *178–79*;
conclusions on, 183–84; sexual
activity and, 211–12; questions
for measuring, 352
service, 284–85, 292
sexual activity: among LDS young
women, 8–9; among college
students, 13, 230–31; delinquency and, 97; self-esteem and,
166–67; overview of, 186–88;
peer pressure and, 188–92;
forced, 190–91, 203; religiosity and, 192–95; family and,
195–99; measuring, 200–202;
bivariate correlations with,
202–4; predicting, in young
men, 204–6, *205*; predicting,
in young women, 206–13, *207*;
reasons for, *210*; conclusions
on, 213–14; during dating and
hanging out, *232*
Shaw, George Bernard, 162
Sherkat, D. E., 122–23
shoplifting, 84, 100
Simons, R., 189
Simpson, D. D., 68
single-parent families: delinquency
and, 68–69; educational aspirations and, 139, 144; sexual
activity and, 195–96; statistics
on, 252
Small, S., 189, 197
Smith, C., 194